The Mindful Photographer

The Mindful Photographer

AWAKE IN THE WORLD WITH A CAMERA

DAVID ULRICH

rocky**nook**

The Mindful Photographer
David Ulrich

Project editor: Maggie Yates
Project manager: Lisa Brazieal
Marketing manager: Mercedes Murray
Copyeditor: Maggie Yates
Layout: Hespenheide Design
Cover design: Hespenheide Design

ISBN: 978-1-68198-841-2
1st Edition (1st printing, February 2022)
© 2022 David Ulrich
All images © David Ulrich unless otherwise noted
The essay "Pictures Are Not About Pictures" was originally published by *Breathing Color™, breathingcolor.com*
Excerpts of the essay, "Music of the Spheres," were originally published in Parabola, *To Honor the Sacred*, Vol 42. No.3, Fall 2017

Rocky Nook Inc.
1010 B Street, Suite 350
San Rafael, CA 94901
USA

www.rockynook.com

Distributed in the UK and Europe by Publishers Group UK
Distributed in the U.S. and all other territories by Ingram Publisher Services

Library of Congress Control Number: 2021944840

Printed in Korea

Contents

Introduction

I fell in love with photography as a child. After receiving a Kodak Brownie Starmatic camera for Christmas, I became fascinated with the visual world. Learning to see became my passion, then my lifelong quest, and I have never looked back.

For me, photography is many things: a means of interacting more deeply with the world, a path of personal growth and transformation, a challenge to strive toward becoming more whole and attentive, a catalyst for stimulating creative expression, and a vehicle for insight and understanding. Photography can be an inner practice that leads you more fully into a rich engagement with the world and a platform for sharing your questions, observations, and discoveries. It's a way of light and a way of life.

What could be more beautiful than a medium of light? And what could be more seductive and compelling—a device in our hands that is a metaphor for and an extension of our very brain and nervous system? If you add to this recipe our eyes, mind, and heart, you have a potent mixture called photography. It's no wonder it is so popular.

Most everyone has a camera and takes pictures—lots of them. And many people frequently—even incessantly—use visual communication: on social media, on websites, in printed material, and in personal messages. Now that the broad public has discovered photography and smartphone vendors update and promote their excellent cameras on a regular basis, where and how do people learn to make good pictures and communicate effectively with images? How can you learn, in a hands-on way, the resonant potentials of the photographic medium and to explore your own potential as an artist?

As a photography teacher, I must say, business is booming. I am teaching in a wider variety of venues than ever before: colleges, adult education workshops, museum schools, working with children and special interest groups, and in various online forms of interaction. It's hard to keep up with the demand. But it has been said that in the classroom the teacher is often the one who learns the most. I have learned much about photography and culture and people—more than I could have ever hoped for—through my frequent classroom interactions. I feel blessed and privileged.

One of the ways I organize my discoveries and express my insights is through writing. This forms my personal motivation for this book. My previous book, *Zen Camera:*

Creative Awakening with a Daily Practice in Photography, contains six lessons that help you engage the path of photography for creative expression, inner growth, and awakening of your natural wisdom. When I wrote *Zen Camera,* I found it challenging to fit the depth and breadth of my many observations and teaching tools within the structure of six lessons. I knew another book was on the horizon.

The Mindful Photographer furthers the material found in *Zen Camera* and provides a deeper look at my teaching methods and hard-earned advice that I offer my students in one way or another in most of the classes I teach.

In the late '60s, one of my principal teachers, photographer Minor White, was hired as a professor at MIT for an academic experiment, to see if an involvement in art and photography could help scientists, engineers, and other left-brained people become better workers, thinkers, and citizens. The experiment worked brilliantly but this initiative must be renewed, today, and needs to reach as many people as possible in these fractured, changing times.

Similarly, people come to my classes from all walks of life with diverse ages, cultural backgrounds, interests, and professions. Many are passionate about photography and most of them have no interest in becoming professional photographers. They want to unlock the richness of their creative spirit. They all have a camera; some own high-end SLRs and others use the optics in their cell phone. They are united in the fact that they are all searching for something that goes beyond simply taking "better" pictures.

On the first day, each student states their reasons for attending the class. I am consistently moved. Some of them recognize that the joy, fulfillment, and freedom found in an active engagement with creativity has eluded them or dried up in the face of their busy lives and multiple responsibilities. Others feel that something is missing in their lives, an essential sense of wonder and attentive respect for the world surrounding them. They have become jaded and cynical. And yet others feel internally fractured and believe that contact with the creative arts may stimulate their personal growth toward wholeness and awareness.

Self-knowledge is an oft-stated goal, as is a deeper engagement with the world itself through responsive seeing. Photography is unique in that it asks for both an inward look and outward gaze simultaneously. With its reliance on seeing and being in the moment, photography is a potent metaphor for how we might live our lives. With its necessity of a creative response to the moment in front of us, the medium offers an actual practice for living our lives with fullness, sanity, goodness, and responsibility.

This book is a meditation on the many benefits of an active engagement with photography. Divided into a series of short essays, you can dive into the book anywhere you like and follow your own meandering stream of interest and resonance. Or you can read it cover to cover. You will find an inherent structure in the essays, from the easy to the hard, from self to other, and from the inward look to outer engagement. Each essay is complete in itself yet relates to and builds upon others in the book as my thought and dialogue with you, the reader, deepens. Many of the essays contain exercises and a working practice to help you as photographers and creative individuals.

Each essay is accompanied with an image. Sometimes the image is a literal expression of the content found in the essay and sometimes it is a metaphor or an amplification of thought that cannot be well expressed in the linear rationality of words. The visual language often offers more nuance, more precision, and can stimulate parts of the brain, the feelings, and the body in a way that words cannot.

I believe strongly that any art form, indeed any activity approached with care and attention, can become an inner practice toward deeper awareness and fullness of being. The dual currents of photography, with one eye turned inward and other outward, offer an ideal platform to deepen your engagement with the world and others, enhance self-awareness, and find your unique mode of expression.

I ask you to think about photography as a way of knowing. Through the lens, you learn about your own vision, your own voice. Through your engagement with the subject, you learn to penetrate into the heart of a scene, a person, an event, or a condition of the world. Your attention has power and force, and can be used as a tool or a weapon in the service of others and to help heal the world, or as a form of protest to the outrage we feel in response to some aspects of what we observe.

I encourage you to keep a visual journal, and take photographs daily, or nearly so. Photograph what captures your heart and mind, or the impressions that resound from deep within the body. Practice. Find your voice, your vision. Those scenes and photographs that call you from a deeper place are your own, unique reflections of your being. Photographer Frederick Sommer remarks, "Consequently we would never become attentive to something unless we carry a great chunk of it within ourselves."

Seek your own private thoughts and moments—your unique identity. And seek those moments that reflect the intersectionality of life, the common threads of the human condition, and the social, political, and environmental forces that we all face in trying to live together on this objectively tiny planet.

Treat photography as an inner practice. Natalie Goldberg, in her excellent book on writing, *Writing Down the Bones* (from which this book is partially modeled), refers to "writing practice," where *we must continue to open and trust in our own voice and process.* She recounts studying Zen and sitting meditation with Dainin Katagiri Roshi in Minneapolis, who once said to her: *Why don't you make writing your practice? If you go deep enough in writing, it will take you everyplace.*

What I propose here is a form of "camera practice," learning to trust your own experience and the veracity of your own perceptions, making efforts toward expanding your awareness, and reading this book actively—verifying everything through your own process. Experiment; try to examine, explore, and test the capacity of vision. Camera practice is a way of learning about ourselves and the world through direct experience. It's a path of growth for your creative capacities and for the development of your attention.

Accordingly, I am using the word *mindful* in the title as an adjective which means, according to the Oxford Dictionary, "conscious or aware of something" and "focusing one's awareness on the present moment." The world needs our attention, now as never before. Others need our genuine care and insight. And we ourselves need our deep inward look—a look that sees, can accept, and can ultimately help heal and lead us toward wholeness. Photography and creativity can play a central role in this process.

* * *

For those readers who have not delved into *Zen Camera,* or those that want a summary of its insights, I will repeat the seven principles of camera practice that I offer students in all my classes. These principles have stood the test of time and have been distilled from more than 40 years of teaching photography. They relate to learning the photographic medium and to the growth of awareness of the human being behind the camera. I believe strongly that these principles can be adapted to other mediums, other pursuits. If you learn to do one thing well, you learn the fundaments of learning that can be applied to anything else: learning to cook, relating to others, all forms of creative expression, and innovation in business or other occupations. Becoming an artist of life is an aim worthy of our humanity.

1. Work every day. Photograph daily, or nearly so. Take photographs of everything that deeply strikes your fancy. Do not edit and do not judge your perceptions—not yet. Photograph freely out of a wide range of your responses to the world: love, beauty, outrage, indignity, affinity, resonance, agreement, criticism, and satire. Do not ignore humor or polemic insights.

   Keep a visual journal, a daily record of your thoughts, insights, and perceptions in the form of pictures. If you work in film, make contact sheets and keep them in a safe place. If you work with digital media, use file browsers where you can see all of your images in thumbnail form, and see the development of your ideas as they unfold over multiple images.

2. TMP. Take more pictures. Practice, practice. Work into the heat of the moment. Most photographers are not very good at foreplay or warming up. It's a form of arrogance to believe that arriving in a place, taking three or four pictures, and then moving on will yield strong or insightful results. Stay with a subject or a place. Warm up by taking photographs freely. Don't worry about the results. Dance with the scene and with the subject. You want to shake loose the reluctance to be wild and spontaneous and childlike. Be glue-like. Stick around long enough to synchronize with the subject.

   An athlete or a musician would never consider running the race or giving a performance before warming up—why should artists and photographers be different? My first photography teacher once said to me, "After you have taken the picture you set out to make, now is the time to really begin to explore the subject."

   Keep yourself moving. Take pictures as a form of foreplay until you can photograph freely, with measured abandon. Don't be afraid to lose control, mindfully. Lose yourself but stay centered.

   Look at your work carefully on a contact sheet or digital editor. Notice ongoing themes and recurring forms/shapes/color relationships. Which images feel like they are authentic, your own? Which images rise to the top and call your attention again and again? Look now and look later. Time is the best editor as you move beyond the subjective experience of taking the picture.

3. Be present. Quiet the mind. Don't overthink. Thinking is too slow to capture a moment. Use your mind to stay focused on the moment. Prepare and think about your intent in advance. Your entire history of thought and experience can be found in the present moment. Stay rigorously, but lightly, rooted in the body, connected to your feelings, and using the directed attention of the mind.

    Look beyond and beneath the noisy mind to the region where intuition resides, where your natural wisdom may bubble forth from the depth mind, the unconscious—and may find its reflection in outer circumstances. Above all, forget about yesterday and tomorrow.

4. Observe. Pay attention. The quiet of the mind leaves space for clear and present seeing. The meaning is often found in both the whole and the details of a scene. Look. Learn. Let the nuances speak. Find empathy. Leonardo da Vinci would use drawing in his sketchbooks as a means of studying both anatomy and the human condition, and, notably, as a way of establishing empathy with the subject. Empathy creates an invisible, indelible link between your mind's eye and the nature and character of the subject.

    All photographs are of time and light, and are about something, not just about taking a "good" photograph. To help focus your observations, consider how you use the five visual elements of photography in your image-making. Consider each of these and how they interact, in synergy, within an image.

    The frame
    The moment
    Light
    Use of color and tonality
    Treatment of subject

    For a description of these elements, please refer to Chapter One: Observation in *Zen Camera*.

5. Know your camera. Master your materials and tools. Ideally, your camera should become a seamless extension of your eye, hand, and brain. Learn to see how a camera sees. There is a sizable transformation between the three-dimensional world of

appearances in all the colors and the brightness range available to human vision and a lens-based, two-dimensional image with RGB color and a shortened dynamic range of tonal values. Photographer Garry Winogrand once said, "I photograph to find out what something will look like photographed." Good advice, and all the more reason to take many photographs on a regular basis.

You cannot be free with the medium and facile with your perceptions without knowing how your camera works, mastering the use of the exposure triad of f-stop, shutter speed, and ISO, and learning the expressive possibilities of either software or the darkroom. There are many excellent books and training videos on the technical aspects of photography. Don't shirk from learning the tools.

6. Work in projects, not only with single pictures. For a full engagement with the creative process, you need a direction and an expressive aim, something to get you out of the door. What moves you, interests you, draws you? Where do you find your passion and your commitment? Based on your particular background and life circumstances, what do you see and what can you speak about that no one else can?

    It is through sustained work on projects in which you interact with the subject over time, have an array of experiences and multiple observations, and get to know the subject intimately; these are where your strongest and most insightful images can be made. Create self-defined projects based on where you feel the most energy now, where you feel an urgency and necessity. Painter Wassily Kandinsky defines the most meaningful explorations as arising from "inner necessity."

7. Look and learn. Study photographs made by others. We are part of a young medium with a rich and glorious history formed by many accomplished practitioners. And due to revisionist efforts, we are discovering new voices from the past every day that were once marginalized, their efforts thankfully no longer unseen and unrecognized. Identify artists with whom you feel resonance with their work. Study them. Read about their lives and processes. There is a plethora of photography books: monographs, group collections, and biographies. Get to know and enjoy looking into the many works of others that can inspire you and teach you. I have referred to many well-known images, by title and artist, from the history of photography in

these essays. Look them up online as an adjunct to your reading experience. Every photographer builds upon past discoveries to find their own way of seeing.

Avoid clichés and tired tropes. Accept them as merely a first stage in the learning process. Don't be afraid of them; they are inevitable. But, learn to recognize over-used metaphors and conventions. Work through them to find something uniquely your own.

Everyone is creative. Everyone sees the world in a unique way. And anyone can learn to use a camera. I wish for you the fullness of creative expression and the potency of an in-depth interaction with the world. Creativity can help make us whole and camera practice can reflect the world back on itself and reveal the shape of your engagement—your passion, pleasures, and, at times, pained observations.

Ask questions. Explore freely. Embrace the questions and the state of not knowing. This provides nourishment for the fruits of discovery. Your search for images is nothing more than a search for self and a quest to understand life and to know others through direct perception in the here and now. The search itself enlivens our hearts and minds, and will, in time, bring clarity.

Have patience and learn to see how you see. For many photographers and those passionate about taking pictures, camera practice can become a way of life.

Seek Resonance

In 1975, I was one of photographer Minor White's chief assistants. He was in his late sixties and very busy: working actively as a photographer, traveling around the world to teach workshops, and writing a book summarizing his insights from 40 years of teaching ways of seeing through the lens. I was young and strong, and also a writer. I think he liked me because I could help him both with photography and the rigors of professional travel, and as an editor for his writing. During the summer, we made plans to travel to Puerto Rico in December, where Minor was working on a photographic project.

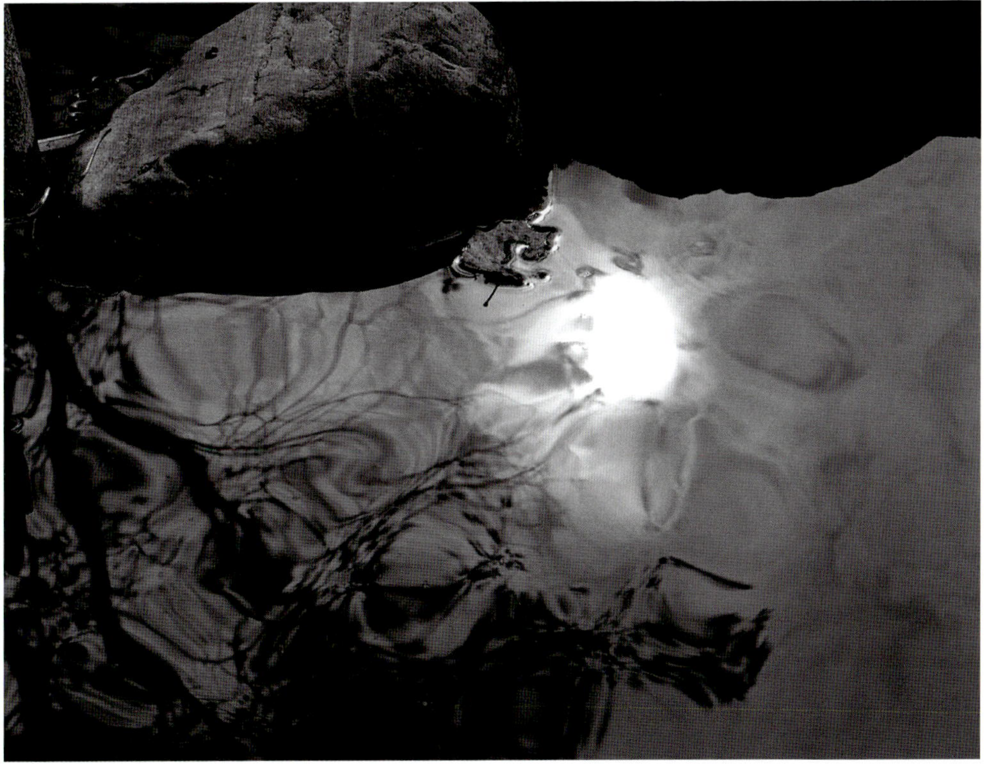

Untitled, Akron, Ohio, David Ulrich

In the early fall, Minor taught demanding workshops in London and Arizona. He decided to stop in Cleveland (my family home) to visit Nicholas Hlobeczy and me on his way home to Boston. Nick was one of Minor's very early students and one of my principal photography teachers. We were very close. Minor arrived on Friday evening and we were all staying in Nick's house for the weekend. It was a moving, powerful time.

On Friday night, we had a night of serious drinking—looking at photographs and engaging in life-altering conversation. Drinking, even heavily, was common in those days especially among artists and photographers. I was never good at it but I went along. Sometime during the evening, two significant events and insights occurred. First, as I sat there, the youngest member of this triad, I looked at Minor and at Nick. I felt deep love for them both, as friends and as paternal influences. It was the first time that the three of us were in the same room, privately, without many other workshop or class participants.

The insight struck with great force: *grandfather, father, and son.* We were part of an unbroken familial lineage dating back to photography's early days, including Alfred Stieglitz and Edward Weston (Minor's influences and teachers) and extending to the present moment in Nick's living room. I felt I was part of a spiritual and artistic family— with a legacy that someday would be my job to uphold. It was a humbling experience.

The second event that happened that evening bore equal significance. Minor had given Nick many photographs—maybe 20 or 30—over the years, most of them unsigned. For unknown reasons, Minor insisted that Nick retrieve and unframe *all* of these images so that he could sign them. It took a while to accomplish, but by that time Minor was a famous photographer and highly influential to the medium. Signing these prints increased their value and eventually Nick was able to retire partially with the proceeds from selling some of these photographs and others by Edward Weston and Ansel Adams. This thoughtfulness was a moment of prescient insight on Minor's part.

Saturday morning was an electric, busy time with friends and associates coming over to see Minor, say hello, and seek kernels of his wisdom. He was holding court, grace- fully. But it was easy to see he was exhausted. After lunch, he unexpectedly asked me to take a nap with him. As is well known, Minor loved men—yet I am heterosexual, and he knew that. He needed *something*, I didn't know what, and because of my love for him, I was happy to oblige. By his late sixties and due to a heart condition, as far as I knew, Minor was celibate. I did not worry about the possibility of sexual advances. I knew he cared for me and always showed respect. He would not have put me in an

     THE MINDFUL PHOTOGRAPHER

uncomfortable, compromising position. So, we took leave from the others and went to the bedroom.

At the moment, he was like a child and needed to be held. It felt urgent, even desperate. I took notice inwardly and tried to comfort him the best I could. He fell asleep for a short while. During his sleep, he let out the most unearthly cry, a shriek, almost a death gasp. I'll never forget the eerie, heart-rending sound. It shook me to my core.

After our nap, Nick's wife Jean prepared a coffee cake, one of the most sugary, rich pastries that ever crossed my palate. Minor had a sweet tooth and knew he shouldn't. But he did indulge, again almost like a child.

By mid-afternoon, he wanted to get away from the house and asked me to take him for a drive. We drove aimlessly around the Ohio countryside. He seemed to be looking for something. Finally, he saw a park with a circular fountain and beautiful, manicured vegetation. He asked me to stop. We walked toward the fountain, which felt like a focal center of this manicured landscape. We sat near the edge of the fountain on a white, stone bench.

He said one thing to me, and one thing only: "Seek resonance in your life and work. You will not be disappointed." I took it in but it felt scarily like last words. Everything about the weekend felt that way. We drove back to Nick's house and simply continued with the affairs of the weekend. There was no more deep conversation, not with me anyway.

On Monday morning, Minor flew back to Boston, arriving at the airport mid-day. Almost immediately upon arriving, he suffered a massive heart attack that nearly killed him. He was in a coma in Massachusetts General Hospital for weeks or months, I do not recall exactly how long. He did emerge from the coma and lived for another eight months—but was never the same again.

Seek Resonance. I've grappled with the meaning of this phrase for decades. I've come to understand it in the following way, and now see it as reliable advice in many areas of my life and work, including how I form friendships and relationships, how I spend my days in my professional life, and how I work as an artist. I see resonance as the foundation stone for our work as photographers.

I think about it this way. There are different forms of attraction: to people, to subject matter for our camera, to books and influences, and to the conditions of our lives, even the things we surround ourselves with. There is the attraction of *lust*, which is the lowest, most primitive form of linkage. There is the attraction of *like/dislike* and *friendship* or sympathy of life interests. And finally, there is the attraction of *resonance*, in which we seek people, things, influences, subject matter that are akin to our very being. When we are one with someone or something in our inmost hearts, a bond is created, a powerful form of connection that nourishes our essence and helps shape our paths in life. These kinds of connections catalyze us to growth, reveal the contour of our inner landscape through its outer reflection, and deeply stimulate our creativity. As photographers, we see what we are, looking beyond mild like and dislike to finding scenes and images that deeply correspond to our passions, commitments, and core interests.

In the series of books so popular in the '70s, the Yacqui shaman Don Juan advises Carlos Castaneda on making life choices. "Does this path have a heart? If it does, the path is good; if it doesn't, it is of no use…. One makes for a joyful journey; as long as you follow it, you are one with it. The other will make you curse your life. One makes you strong; the other weakens you….For me there is only the traveling on paths that have heart, on any path that may have heart, and the only worthwhile challenge is to traverse its full length—and there I travel looking, looking breathlessly."

When behind a camera, what subject matter makes your heart beat faster? When do people and scenes genuinely reveal themselves? Can you look beyond mild forms of attraction and wait and work? Wait until you find a scene or a moment in which you *must* press the shutter, that has resonance, that is a life-changing moment for you, when you feel an inner charge and you know that *this* is the moment that you were seeking.

Camera Practice

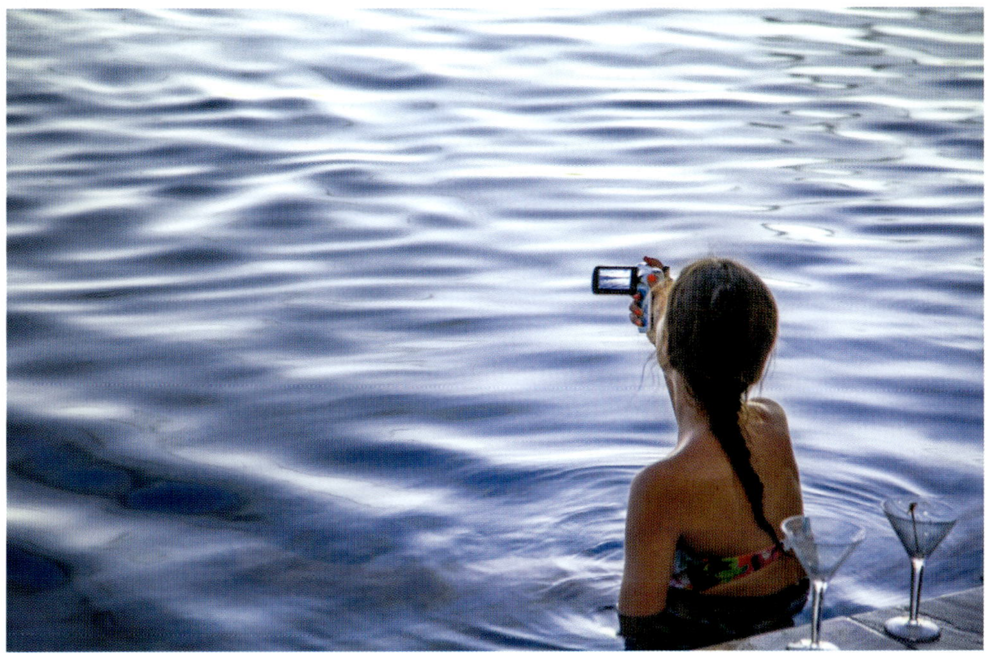

Waikiki Beach, Honolulu, Hawai'i, David Ulrich

In learning to write with clarity and force, "keep your hand moving" across the page, advises Natalie Goldberg in *Writing Down the Bones*. For photographers, it's important to stay active with seeing and sketching ideas. For most of my career, I used a large 5×7-inch view camera, which sits upon a tripod and uses individual sheets of film. At best, I could carry 10, two-sided film holders into the field; that's 20 exposures for a day's work. I needed to do the sketching of my ideas in my head, with my eyes and brain by cupping my hand around my eye to visualize an image. Working with a view camera often made me long for a handheld camera that I could use for playing and sketching, something that would help activate what Goldberg calls the "wild mind."

No matter what kind of camera you use, working with seeing on a daily basis forms the foundation, the practice of your craft. Musicians have their scales; athletes their routines. Visual artists often keep sketchbooks of their stray impressions, developing ideas, and random observations. Whether you use high-end digital SLRs, film cameras, plastic toy lenses, or medium format behemoths, you have a sketchbook constantly at your side. It's called a cell phone. Use it daily. When you see something that strikes you in any way, pull your ever-present camera out of your pocket—and take the picture. Don't stop at one. Explore the subject. We need to continually learn to see how a camera sees, and the constant activity of sketching with your cell phone will feed your brain and train your eye.

I fully appreciate the excellent camera embedded in my phone. It assists me in developing a creative momentum, it helps keep me attuned to my surroundings, to be more attentive to others, and to be sensitive to my own, often unconscious, responses to the things in the world around me. It lubricates my heart and my mind; it activates my creative spirit constantly and serves to steel (instead of steal) my attention.

Often, new ideas arise with force and directness through the flow of seeing with my iPhone. Unique ways of handling color and form are found through my constant experimentation and visual exploration. A looseness that often escapes my more "serious" work is evident in my digital sketching. I love the way it frees my eye; not to mention it is just plain fun.

Most of us think in words. I know I do. Students in my classes have a hard time not explaining everything about their photograph and how they made it while showing the image. Verbal thinking is linear thinking. Visual thinking takes place through form and image, not with words. Visual thinking is random, associative, archetypal, and yet more precise than the rationality of the verbal mind. Get to know the process of visual thinking through constant practice with a camera. It will assist you greatly by helping you be more in touch with the depths of the mind, the unconscious, which is often the seat of inspiration and intuition.

With any camera you use on a regular basis, get to know it as you know your own body. Hold it in your hand. Exercise the controls: the knobs, buttons, focus ring, and display menu. Learn how to use the basic settings to get what you want. Feel it in your hand and bring it up to your eye. Look through it. Focus it. Become one with it until it becomes second nature to leverage the controls you need. You don't want to fumble with your camera in the field while trying to attend to a rapidly changing situation.

The mechanical or electronic device does not have a life of its own. You lend it yours. You focus your being through its lens. It sparks your joy when you find just the right moment to release the shutter.

With today's technologies, photography is easy. Mastering it is hard. Using your cell phone camera or placing your SLR on Program or Automatic mode allows you to focus on seeing. Seeing itself is easy and automatic; mastering it, too, is hard. Camera practice places us on the path of learning: about your camera, yourself, and the multi-leveled richness of the world around us.

Even the human mind has a camera. It's called memory. The camera lens and your memory are equally unreliable as pointers to truth. They both depend on selection, viewpoint, emotion, and attitude. But that apparent unreliability is the camera's great power. You want to discover yourself as you discover the world. One eye turned inward and other outward is the camera's greatest strength.

Become the camera. Connect the camera to your hand and eye. Camera practice can help hone your instincts, maintain an alert eye, and tune your feelings.

Avoid the Merely Pictorial

Estimates suggest that over one trillion photographs were taken last year. And worldwide, people upload an average of 1.8 billion photographs *per day* on Facebook, Google, and Instagram. In a world in which so many photos are made and disseminated, how do you create meaning in photographs that will cause the viewer to linger and look? What makes some images memorable and others easily forgotten?

Beginning photographers often try to imitate images they see in print or on Instagram and other online sources. Imitation, of course, is considered a form of flattery and can be a valuable educational tool. But we need to discriminate. Many images today are

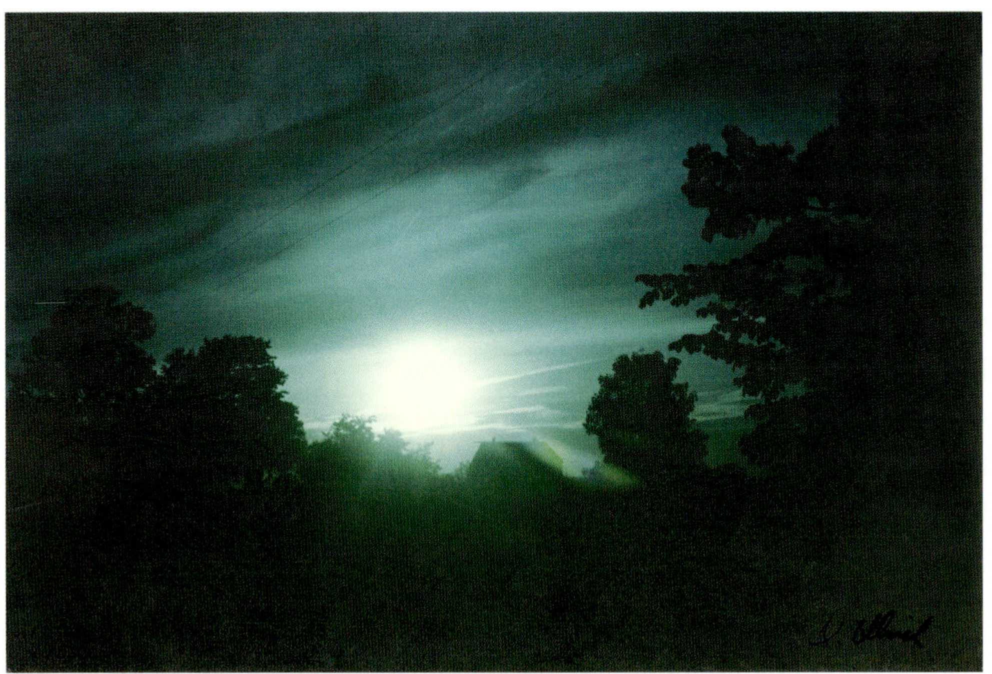

Untitled, 1968, David Ulrich,
As a young photographer, I sought clichéd subject matter such as sunsets and barns and even went so far as to put theatrical color gels over my lens to heighten the "effect" of the photograph.

merely pictorial, eschewing any depth of content. Photographers are concerned with making what are known as "high-impact" images or pictures that are merely pretty or visually pleasing. Giving primary attention to the pictorial elements of the frame over content is known as pictorialism. This is an educational step along the way, but one that can and should be transcended quickly. Photography is a highly potent form of communication and many people tire of the visual clichés prevalent in popular photography. What do you want to say? How do *you* see the world? What ideas and impressions touch your core?

Authenticity in image making is key to effective visual communication. I recently perused an online article by Hillary K. Grigonis on the website Digital Trends that analyzes data from numerous photo stock agencies and predicts photography's direction in the upcoming years based on what types of images are currently popular. The summary results are heartening and consistent with my thinking.

IMAGES THAT ARE HONEST

For me, one of the most touching genres of photography is the snapshot aesthetic—images taken within the flow of one's life that express daily moments of significance that have heart and are both real and raw. Stock agency CEO of Storyblocks, TJ Leonard, notes, "this trend is all about drawing inspiration from the unexpected images we capture every day on our smartphones but pairing the subject with the quality that comes with extensive professional experience." Brenda Mills from Adobe Stock writes, "The human need to share a full, honest range of raw emotions is now mainstream." Authentic images grow from our heart and mind out of the raw material of our daily lives.

IMAGES THAT END STIGMA

As visual communicators, I believe we all share in the responsibility to move beyond reinforcing common stereotypes and supporting the unconscious bias of outworn cultural attitudes. In the beauty industry for example, a healthy trend is slowly emerging known as body positivity that sees all body types and shapes as beautiful and worthy of attention. Further, many photographers are now rejecting extreme Photoshop techniques to retouch the marks and physical residues of experience and genetics that make us individually human. Systemic racism, prejudice in all of its forms, unconscious bias, and formerly taboo topics can be explored and challenged through sensitive use of images. Storyblocks agency noticed "a 40% increase in searches related to mental health, with topics like meditation up by 93% and addiction by 75%."

Photographers can help enormously in realizing the societal aims of diversity, equality, and fair treatment for all. Visual culture is a prime moving force that aids and abets prevailing cultural attitudes. Let's find a way to promote equal respect for all people and their circumstances.

IMAGES WITH A PURPOSE

Adobe Stock has observed a trend that they call "from me to we" and "looks at how individuals and brands come together to support major causes." Living in Hawai'i, I have always been struck by the sheer number of pictures that represent palm trees, sunsets, and all manner of images that perpetuate the "myth" of paradise. Many photographers here take clichéd images that ignore the realities of life in the islands: extreme climate change, rampant homelessness, the exorbitant cost of living, cultural displacement, gentrification of local neighborhoods, overdevelopment, environmental degradation, and the gradual erosion of cultural traditions that give these islands their richness and diversity. The good, the bad, and the ugly are equal in the eyes of the camera lens.

We can do better. The camera is a powerful tool to bear witness. Images can teach us, inform us, inspire us, and show us the shape of the real world. Mere pictorialism pales in light of the camera's power to show and tell the truth of what we see, feel, and observe in our rapidly changing world. Society needs those that speak truth to power, that are willing tell it like it is, and that direct an unblinking gaze onto the joy and tragedy of everyday moments in their own lives and communities.

Expand your range of expression beyond mere pictures into pictures with content that speak directly to the hearts and minds of viewers.

Pictures Are Not About Pictures

During a recent public photo critique, I made several interesting observations about the condition of contemporary, popular photography. All of the people participating in the critique had a serious interest in photography, followed recent trends in the medium, and seemed to have some awareness of equipment and technique. Without exception, these were serious folks that embodied the true meaning of the word *amateur*, which from the French means lover. They loved the medium and its expressive possibilities.

As people alternatively showed and talked about their work, one nagging observation came to the forefront of my mind: *pictures are not about pictures*. They are *about* something. They are not just about the skill of the photographer, or the camera and lens, and not about the mode of presentation. They reveal a point of view, highlight

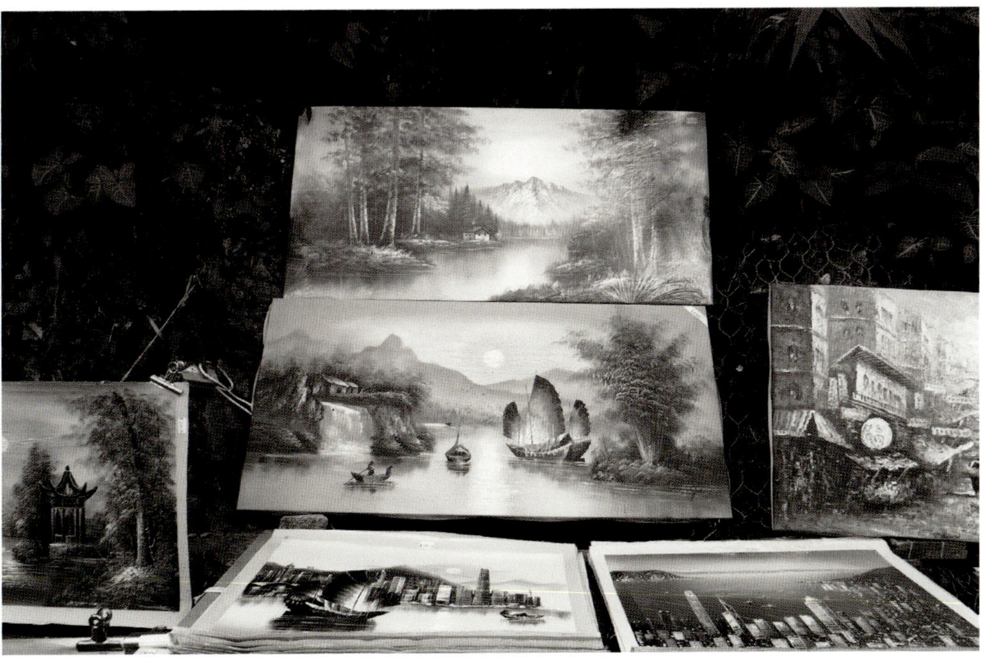

Picture Booth, Hong Kong Streetseller, David Ulrich

something about the world, or reflect our inner states of being or particular life conditions. They have meaning that can be decoded and can evoke something in the viewer.

I wondered, as people in the critique spoke of their images—how they were made, what they were striving for—whether they could read or even see the meanings embedded in their own images beyond the camera and lens choice, or the compositional decisions about making a "better" picture. Everyone seemed to have one goal: merely to make a "good" photograph.

Sometimes, in the hands of skilled practitioners, pictures *are* about pictures. Some contemporary artists are consciously using photography to subvert, highlight, deconstruct, or have dialogue about the way images reflect societal attitudes or outworn conventions. Media and marketing leave a legacy that can, and should be, scrutinized and deeply questioned by artists and photographers. If not us, who will reveal the systemic muck and humanistic exploitation?

Contemporary advertising—including that by photography vendors—appeals to the emotions, hungers, and desires of the viewer. We are told that the "right" camera, the perfect lens, the magic software, or the largest number of pixels can soothingly make everything alright, can transform a mundane vision into a masterpiece, and can somehow replace the need for an alert mind, an open heart, and quickness of perception. "Make your lens tell the truth." "Look what *you* can do." "It's time to look at the world from a unique perspective." These are all taglines from recent ad campaigns by photography vendors.

The best photographs have taught us that your own eyes and mind, not the camera, are what make an image unique and compelling. Many great pictures were made by run-of-the-mill, average, or even low-cost cameras. Many great pictures have broken the rules reflecting a genuinely unique perspective or a new, highly personal view of ordinary subject matter. And many great pictures say something, reflect meaning about the world and/or the unique truth of oneself to the viewer.

Rules of composition, like the rule of "thirds" or incorporating "leading lines," and aggressive post-processing are prevalent. The search for high-impact views of the world promoted by contemporary culture, and in turn the photo industry, do not make pictures that contribute anything meaningful to the world—or to oneself for that matter. Self-knowledge is one of the great ongoing human aims, and an active interest in the world and people is fundamental to a whole, meaningful life. *These* aims stand among the greatest subjects for pictures.

Attention to one's developing vision is paramount to becoming a successful, contributing artist. It is one's heart and mind, coupled with skill and solid technique, that can spring your vision to life. Several images in the critique moved me, astonished me, or brought me to a fresh, humorous, or deep understanding of something. Yes, pictures are about *something*. Can the camera, the software, the technique, the media, become transparent? Can they become vehicles for our developing vision? Can the growth of our craft become a flowing river through which the currents of our understanding and worldview can be expressed?

There are so many exciting possibilities today for genuinely expressing something of our growing way of seeing: Blurb books, great high-end cameras, plastic cameras, cell phone cameras, great print and canvas surfaces, and the kind of software with hugely expressive possibilities, where, if you can think it, you can do it. Let's put the emphasis on our vision first, and allow the rest, even the idea of a good picture, to flow from that one fundamental fact—the fact or the exploration of the question of how we see the world. The pictures that grow from this place—these are the pictures that matter.

Visual Learning

Photography is a language. Like any other form of communication, it has its own grammar, syntax, principles, and evolving history. Photography shares much with other forms of expression that revolve around the visual language. When I look at someone's images for the first time, I can tell immediately if they are conversant and educated in the visual language.

With the digital revolution, millions of people take photographs frequently without any visual training or knowledge of photography. There are multiple ways to look at this. On the one hand, the unselfconscious charm of snapshots and images that grow spontaneously and immediately from within a life seduce the viewer into an intimate glimpse of the photographer's affections and sympathies, like on an Instagram feed. Conversely, these types of images often contribute to what one designer calls "visual pollution." And finally, we have all manner of images that strive for effect, either with photographic tools and filters or with carefully considered postures and outfits designed to seek admiration from the viewer.

If you want to communicate effectively with images, I have one clear word of advice: learn the visual language. Read books or study websites that teach the principles of design. Learn about the expressive language of color, shape, form, line, volume, perspective, and composition. Savor light and learn to use it as a means of expression. Study the cultural and social representation found in image content and learn to decode meaning. Either do personal research or take a class. Make it fun, but go deep. Do not rely on popular formulaic tropes like the rule of thirds and the unnatural striving for "high impact" images.

The *very* first order of business in every photography class that I have ever taught is to help students break out of what I call the "popular photography aesthetic." Each of us carry in our minds the residual effects of thousands of images that we take in through the senses on a daily or weekly basis—that infect our mind in countless ways. These images reinforce stereotypes, rely on cliché, tend toward shallow and superficial meaning, and strive for blatant visual effect, like hitting the viewer over the head without consideration of nuance and subtlety. To think about content, rather than frivolous allure, is a new exercise for many beginning photographers.

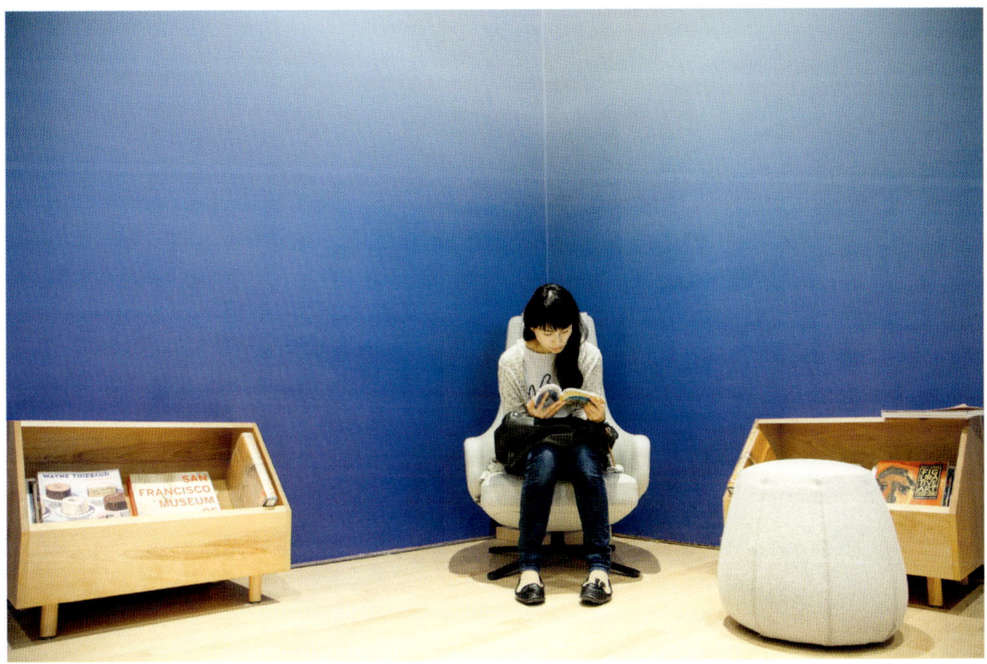

SF MOMA Reading Room, David Ulrich

A huge distinction can be made between images promoted in media and in many popular websites or magazines devoted to photography compared to images from the history of photography made by accomplished practitioners. Great photographs can be found in any of photography's thoroughfares or side streets: fine art, documentary, editorial, commercial, and even scientific (look at NASA's images from space exploration).

Your job, should you wish to learn photography well, is to learn to tell the difference between popular tripe and well-conceived, well-executed, in-depth explorations with the medium.

Don't rely solely on what you "like." The measure of a work of art goes beyond liking and disliking and is a product of the response of your whole being: mind, senses, feelings, and that intangible sense of quivering and intense absorption that a powerful artwork evokes. A great photograph sends out a call and elicits a response from the viewer. Good photography also relies on the artist's knowledge of sculpting an image with the visual language. Articulateness with the visual dialogue can be immediately recognized once you train your eye. Content is effectively conveyed. Great photographs have coherence of structure, form, and content.

When I was a young photographer, before I went to art school, I visited New York frequently to acquaint myself with photographs shown in galleries and museums. At first, I didn't understand or appreciate much of what I saw. I dismissed Diane Arbus as esoteric and uninteresting, with a vision of people on the fringes of society with whom I could not relate. On the other hand, Ansel Adams wasn't edgy enough and his work was not "beautiful" enough for me with my unsophisticated tastes. I had the opportunity to purchase a large Adams print of *Moonrise, Hernandez, New Mexico 1941* in a gallery for $250. I passed. Bad decision for me financially today. Very bad. Today these prints sell in the mid six figures.

Undertake your own education. Seek reliable sources. Museums and galleries often mount major historical and contemporary photography shows. Read reviews. Look at images in photographers' monographs and in respected periodicals, such as *Aperture* magazine, the *New York Times: The World Through a Lens,* and the *Guardian's* photography section. Study the *LensCulture* website, the Critical Mass competition from *Photolucida* in Portland, Oregon, and the Photo-Eye bookstore and online galleries originating from Santa Fe. Read the classic work found in many classrooms, *Criticizing Photographs,* by Terry Barrett.

Be patient and allow your sensibilities to evolve. Find the work that resonates for you and study what moves others. Over time, develop a sense of keen discrimination. For me, my mind and senses are continually being educated in a lifetime's pursuit of the visual feast of good photography.

First Sight, Beginner's Eye

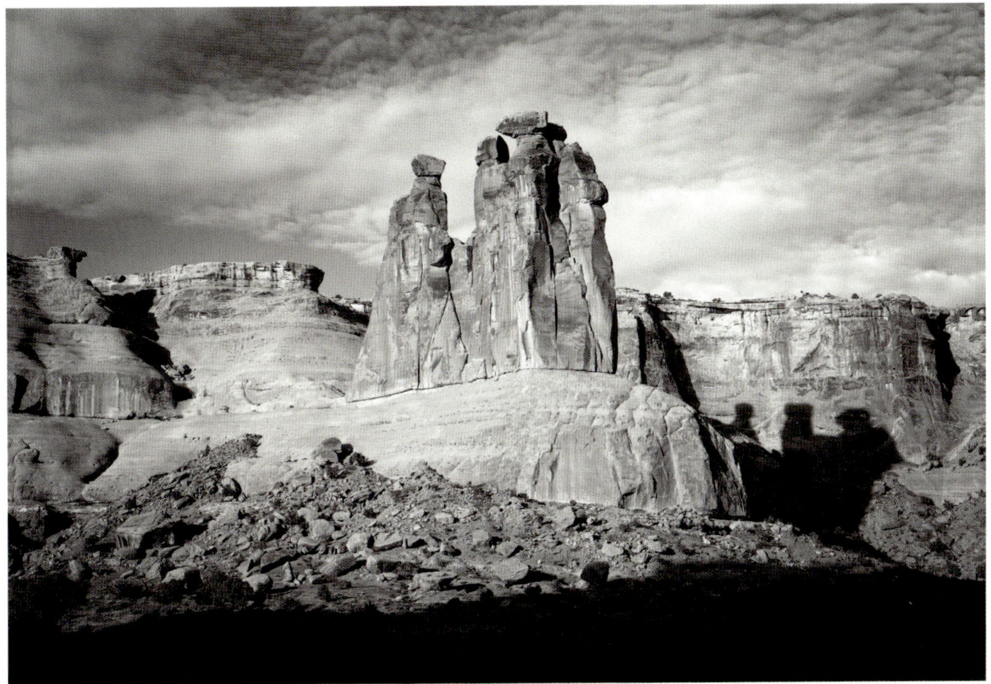

Arches National Park, Utah, David Ulrich

When I wrote *Zen Camera*, I was thinking about Shunru Suzuki's concept of "Beginner's Mind" and its role in our inner work, how it can help keep our mind fresh and alive, and not overly crowded and limited by our accomplishments and knowledge. What does it mean to see like a child, and how can this help photographers and creative individuals? A couple of summers ago, I spent weeks with my two brothers cleaning out over 50 years of accumulated stuff from our family home in Ohio. Hidden away in boxes and in the back of closets was a treasure trove of personal insight: my mother's manuscripts, boxes upon boxes of old photos and slides, school papers, yearbooks, and pictures I took with my first camera when I was only eleven years old.

My earliest memory, when I was between two and three years old, was of the summer light. It felt palpable, like I could touch it or taste it—and be home within its embrace. It permeated everything and seemed to arise from both within and without living objects. I fell in love with the light of the world: hungrily, ardently, eternally. I could not have identified this feeling as a child, but, looking back, my response to this light resonated as sublime awe. I felt a longing for the sun's inimitable gaze.

My adult mind tells me now we have definite limitations of what we can represent with a camera. Some things are better left unsaid. The recognition of transcendent awe does not comfortably fit within our range of experience in a society rooted in rational, enlightenment-era thinking. And even when we try to express the sublime, it often falls short into sentimentality and new-age fuzziness.

The beginner's eye is not beholden to these limitations. In shoe boxes and old carousel slide trays, I found images of my own making from half a century ago. My mind was stunned into a humble submission, recognizing the truth of what I had forgotten. The world is mysterious, beyond our rational knowing, and both wonder and awe are available to a child's perception. These were not good photographs in any sense of the word, but their reach was grand and their aspirations were profound. I remember clearly the wonder of making them and, even then as a child, the recognition that the world contained so much more than I could grasp with my young mind. I was willing to try to represent the unknowable—something I am too "mature" to attempt today. These photographs of yesteryear were Whitmanesque in their scope and depth, yet young and unfinished in their technical skill.

As a child, I made a photograph of a rock formation named "Three Sisters" near Arches National Park from a train window. The strong impression stayed with me for twenty-five years until I could return to the site with a view camera and try to capture what I saw and intended when I was twelve years old.

As a child photographer, I was not limited by convention or the mindset of *cannot*. I would climb trees and clamber onto roofs to see what things looked like from above. I would lie on the ground and photograph straight up. I regularly took photographs late at night, or under the light of a fire, or with makeshift studio lights and theatrically colored gels. I tried anything and everything. Once, I tied a string to the plastic shutter on my Brownie Starmatic and rigged a platform in the bird feeder with the camera and a trigger, so when a bird alit on the feeder, the shutter would be fired. That poor bird. I got the picture but the bird was traumatized by the camera flash, which I forgot to turn off.

By comparison, our vision often becomes boring as adults. I tire of seeing so many adult photographs from the same physical perspective, several feet off the ground or the height in which we hold a camera when it is glued to our eyes. Can we become free again to experiment wildly?

Beginner's eye bypasses the adult mind and goes straight for the jugular. Beginner's eye is not polite or bound by convention or shackled by past experience. It is fresh, spontaneous, alive, and untested, like the eye of a child. Children are marvelously creative. They draw and paint with abandon, and with sharp perception. They produce something amazing, and then they keep going. Their flaw is they don't know when to stop. They lack the rigor of accepting limits and of adult restraint.

The adult mind has power and force, but all too often it is governed by fixed attitudes and learned habits. We cannot let go of our opinions and preconceptions. But we can look beyond them, put them temporarily aside, and not give them our full attention. How can we learn anything new if we already think we know? Seeing can be fresh and in the moment. It can bypass our agendas and usual filters if we can learn to free the mind from its shackles. Krishnamurti asks, "Can you observe anything—a tree, your partner, a neighbor, a politician, a priest, a beautiful face—without any movement of the mind?"

The mind can be a blank slate, a silent receiver, much like our film or the camera sensor, taking in what it sees without rational interpretation. Try to photograph freely, spontaneously, from the intuitive mind. Your interactions with the world can be new and you can learn much through the richness of direct perception. Try to see and photograph through the state of "not-knowing." An exercise that can help in this quest is to stay rooted in the body; keep your hand and eye moving and become aware of the "nowness" of your feet on the ground, the wind on your face, the impressions being received within your corporeal being.

The question for artists is can we be instinctive and unrehearsed in our seeing and image-making, and yet apply the conceptual rigor and necessary knowledge of craft to our creations? Can we shake free the wild mind and intuitive sight by seeing spontaneously through a camera?

In *Journey to Ixtlan*, Don Juan admonishes Carlos Castaneda to look beyond his rigid, fixed perceptions:

For you the world is weird because if you're not bored with it you're at odds with it.

For me the world is weird because it is stupendous, awesome, mysterious, unfathomable; my interest has been to convince you that you must assume responsibility for being here, in this marvelous desert, in this marvelous time. I wanted to convince you that you must learn to make every act count, since you are going to be here for only a short while; in fact, too short for witnessing all the marvels of it.

The Camera in Your Hand

I read recently of a tech enthusiast who eagerly awaited the Tenth Anniversary iPhone from Apple. A busy professional, he used most of its features right away and was immediately and sorely disappointed. He tried hard to like his phone, given the hype around it, used it for several weeks and finally returned it to the Apple store. His problem: the phone was too large to wield in one hand. He couldn't live his life and use his phone without putting down what was already in his other hand.

Students ask me all the time: what kind of camera should I buy? I usually answer that I have no idea, but I can offer them the technical specs of many current cameras. There

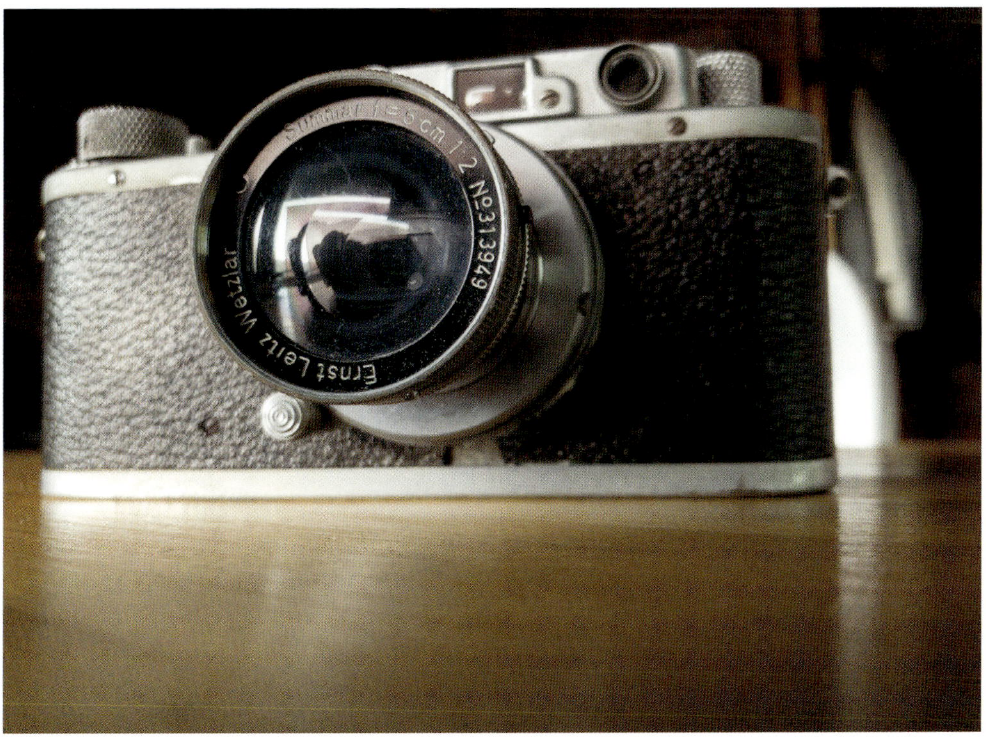

Leica Camera, Honolulu, Hawai'i, David Ulrich
Leica III, circa 1930. Same model as used by Henri Cartier-Bresson and Robert Frank.

are many camera types on the market for different purposes, different levels of quality, and different body types. Here in Honolulu, many people buy equipment online, which can be a big mistake. You should never buy a camera without holding it and playing with it for a little while. A camera needs to feel good in your hand, fit your unique size, work with your eyes, and be enjoyable to use. Writers frequent stationery stores to find just the right notebook for a writing project or seek the right software for their style of writing. Academics use software that fits their needs, while poets may use another. Carpenters spend time finding a hammer with the right weight or a saw with the right cut that allows them to effectively craft their creations.

We need all the help we can get in our quest for creativity and visual expression. You should like your camera, how it feels, and the knobs and buttons should align with your body in such a way you can use them without interference. I, for example, have less than perfect vision and have an exceedingly hard time reading 6-point type on low-contrast camera menus while I'm trying to pay attention to something in the field. One fellow photographer will not buy a camera without a tilting display on the back since he often photographs from very low or high camera angles.

For years, I owned a Leica rangefinder camera. It was a joy to hold and to use, not to mention the extraordinary German optics in its lenses. I will never forget the sound of its shutter, a quiet, sexy sound. It sparked joy every time I fired it.

Nothing is more frustrating than a tool that you wrestle with constantly. There should be a free flow from your mind to your eyes to your camera—an unbroken chain of command with no resistance. We have enough resistance in other ways; our camera should feel good. Look at cameras before you buy them. Go to a rental house and rent a camera for a few days that you are contemplating purchasing. A few days with the camera will teach you if this tool can become an extension of your hands and your eyes.

I often feel the need now to also consider what I call the moral factor in my purchasing decisions. Was this camera built with responsibility to the environment and to the workers who assembled it? For most of my career, I used a wooden 5×7-inch view camera called a Deardorff. Handmade in Chicago from sustainably sourced hard woods, Deardorff cameras were once praised by *Saturday Review* magazine as one of the best-made products of the twentieth century. The provenance of each camera was known and documented by the company. I bought mine in 1976 and knew who the previous owners were. It was a new camera, but owned by two trading companies before coming into my possession. I used this camera as my primary tool for nearly 35 years.

It bore its working scars well and, over time, the wood and the knobs adapted to my particular use. A piece of my soul is in the camera and the images I fed it over the years have become part of the machine.

Nowadays, cameras are disposable. We need to replace them every two to three years as new technologies evolve. My pocketbook and my conscience prickle with planned obsolescence of equipment. The camera chassis and lens can be built for a lifetime. Why not make a chassis and lens with a removable slot for new sensor technology—or some other sustainable solution? The cost to the environment for constantly changing new cameras and phones is excessive. The labor force that is employed to make some of these units are taken advantage of and exploited.

Modern materialism often demeans people and the planet for the sake of profits. We always have the choice of buying used equipment, which is a form of recycling. Many people retire cameras long before their useful life is over. Vendors should be encouraged by buyers to release products that are excellent, ergonomically friendly, and responsible to the environment. Consumers would likely flock to a camera company that stated those types of goals.

For me, I want to like, even love, the camera in my hand *and* have respect for the vendor's commitment to helping us all live together on this fragile planet without damaging it or harming the workers that they contract or employ.

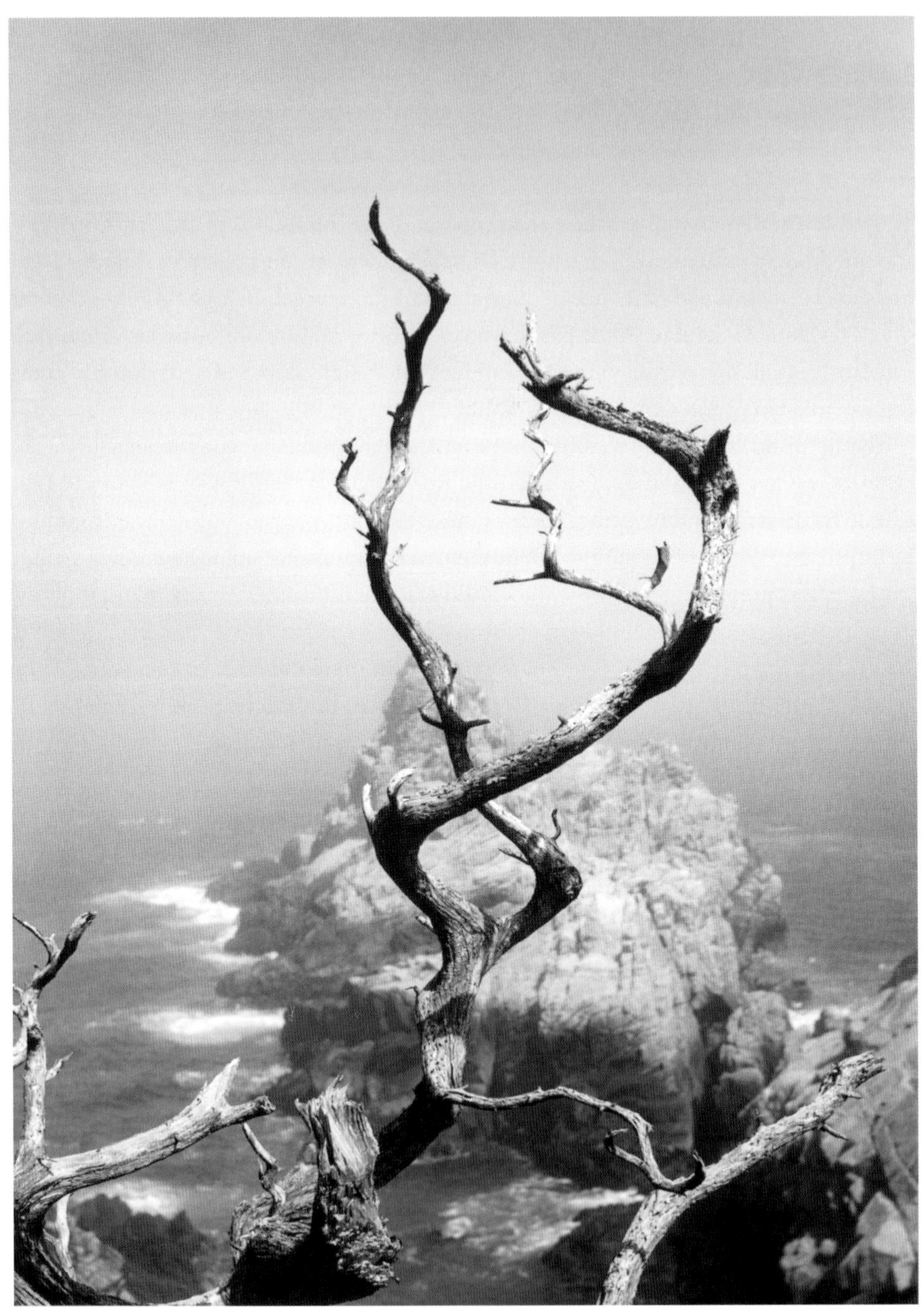

Seeing From the Body

All art is an expression of the ideas, perceptions, and explorations of the artist. We are embodied beings and live in a material culture. We exist within a complex, highly intricate system of organic matter and electrical impulses known as our bodies. Everything we see, do, and think requires the participation of the body. Our mind, senses, emotions, impulses, and all forms of action originate within our physical being. What role does the body play in seeing and making images?

Thought and feeling contribute to the meaning of an image in obvious ways. Sensation also plays a major role and is not as easily understood. The body contains the senses within its bounds. Seeing, hearing, smelling, tasting, touching all take place in the physicality of the here and now. And the body contains invisible channels of neural and electrical impulses that respond to impressions and are sensitive to the nature of thought and feeling. Physicist David Bohm, who has written about thought, dialogue, and creativity, refers to the term *proprioception* as the body's ability to sense itself. He believes that both thought and impressions leave their mark, have an observable influence within the body, and that this powerful proprioception represents a fundamental "sixth" sense.

It is easy to understand how music and chords resonate, or vibrate, within the body. A note is played on a piano and we sense the corresponding vibration. It resonates in a particular place, and in a particular way within oneself. It is the same with visual impressions and images.

Proprioception is a seminal way of knowing. Composition, color and form, and light all resonate within the body. By making the effort to be mindful, to be present to the body while working with a camera, you have a powerful instrument of discernment. Capturing a rapidly changing moment requires nimbleness of instinct and the sensitivity of the body. We can dance with the world. The inner sense of your body knows proportion and balance, the meaning of a line or a color, and even the different shades

Twisted Tree (Cypress Grove Trail,
Point Lobos State Park, California),
May 24, 1951, Minor White

of meaning and feeling embedded in a thought or a concept. David Bohm believes that individual thoughts and impressions can be measured by their influence on the inner body. We can sense a "rightness" or discordance or perhaps an imbalance as a reaction to this thought or that impression.

Visual harmony, dynamic tension within the frame, and representation of space, volume, and texture can be analyzed by the mind, but are felt within the body. Our eyes and mind are integrated with the whole of our physical constitution. Sometimes we may seek harmonic integration within the frame; at other times, our intent may be served through dissidence or artful discordance.

Experiment with this. While photographing, try moving the frame a little this way or that way and observe your sensations. In post processing, experiment with color, saturation, and cropping, and inwardly view their effects. While in the field, try to stay rooted in the body's sensation of the here and now, looking at how different scenes and moments resonate within yourself. All of our responses to the world take place within oneself and not in the great "out there" of the visible world. The body offers a powerful sense of discernment of everything that we see. Making images with the participation of all of our component parts—thought, feeling, sensation, and intuition—gives completeness and force to our expression.

We can see this by observing visual expression by others. There is always something one sided and awkward with images made without the subtle participation of the senses and the body. Read highly academic writing for an example of a tuned, developed mind divorced from the poetry of the body. We give a name for objects, artworks, photographs, and all forms of material culture that are holistic and satisfying to the senses. We call them *elegant*.

Mindfulness is the key. Half of our attention is turned outward to an exploration of the world and its circumstances. Half of our attention is turned inward to observe thought, feeling, and sensation, both those that originate from within and those that take place in response to what we see. We complete the circuit by remembering to include ourselves in our observations. We accompany ourselves in our paths through life. We become part of the world, not just observers of it. Attention given to the sensations of the body is an anchor that helps you stay present to the living moment.

It's All About Hormones

In a recent photography class, one of the members of the class questioned why she responded strongly to a particular moment while she felt indifferent to another scene, even though the latter, by all measures, was more enticing and visually appealing. She experienced a "charge" of energy when making certain photographs and not others. I responded, somewhat insensitively to this middle-aged woman, with the statement, "it's all about hormones." She was offended for a moment, and I shrank in my chair until I could fully explain myself.

The veritable cocktail of hormones and neurotransmitters produced by the body and brain and released into the bloodstream represents what I would call a science of

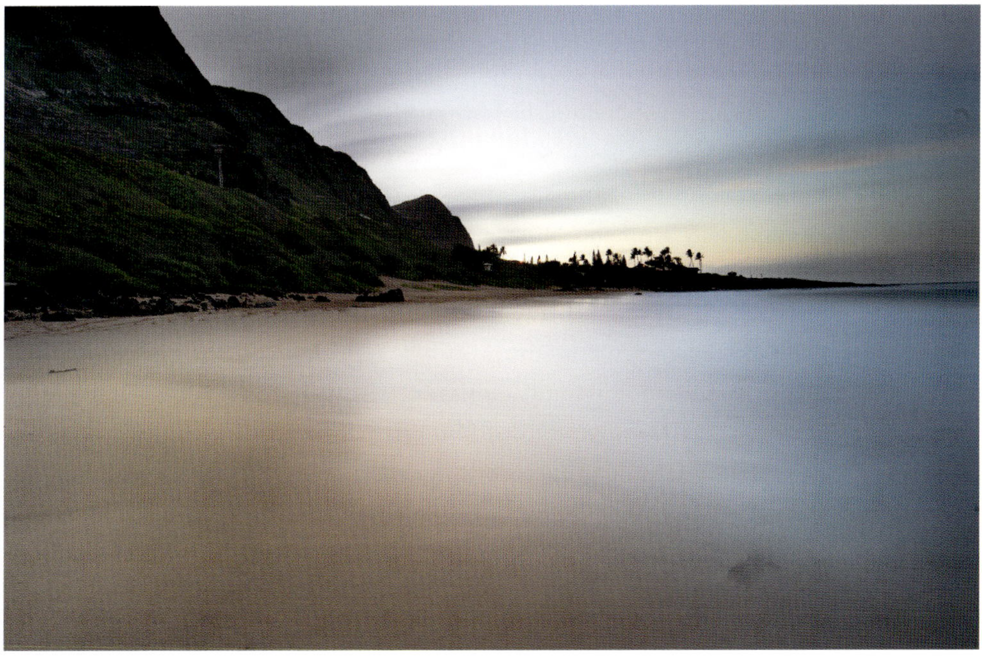

Makapu'u Beach, Hawai'i, David Ulrich
Researchers have found that viewing sunsets and other inspirational scenes increases serotonin, which regulates happiness, and decreases the stress hormone, cortisol.

response. New discoveries in neuroscience offers artists and photographers a way of thinking about what has often eluded our understanding of perception and response, especially while looking at art, photographs, and scenes in front of our camera. The hormones in play are testosterone, estrogen, and the endorphins—and the neurotransmitters are dopamine and serotonin. My intent is to begin to examine these from the standpoint of artistic process and not from a medical or psychological point of view for which I am unqualified.

I have noticed frequently that when I work in the field, or on the computer, or even when doing something physical like swimming, a consistent dynamic occurs. When I begin, the activity often feels flat and lifeless. I am just going through the motions—taking pictures or editing images in a mechanical fashion without knowing where I am going. But if I stay with it and bring fortitude and persistence to the moment, my connection to the activity springs to life. Sometimes it takes minutes, sometime hours, but after a while the endorphins are released into the bloodstream. Endorphins are the body's natural opiates that lead to relieving stress and increasing happiness. Chocolate, exercise, ginseng, sex, laughter, love, and creativity all have the capacity to release endorphins into the blood. In creative work, endorphins enhance the fluidity we bring to the task and dramatically increase mental clarity—we feel juicy and alive. We enter the flow of creativity where discoveries arise out of dialogue with ideas and materials, and a sharp attentiveness governs our hand and eye.

The key here is to stay with the activity and not be discouraged or give up in the heat of frustration. In my experience, when photography students don't take interesting pictures in the first 15 minutes, they often run away too soon. If you stay with a subject and work with it—diligently, attentively—your body and brain will not desert you. During the film era, when working on commission with paid models, unbeknownst to the model I often shot the first two rolls of film *without* film in the camera—to allow myself and the model time to develop a working relationship and to allow the endorphins to flow freely.

When in the field with a camera or in a gallery looking at works of art, why do some objects or scenes create an intense response? Yes, the eye becomes excited, but is that all? In visual dialogue with some objects, we feel a tingling or a noticeable charge of energy. These scenes or objects generate a response in the inner field of body that are unique, that actually alter our brain chemistry. For me, sometimes it even feels like a sexual charge of energy, with a response arising in my loins that brings a deep connection to the scene or object. Images made with this intensity of response tend to be the ones that stay in my portfolio, or the ones I return to again and again, that I can genuinely call my own, reflecting my deepest concerns. With these kind of responses, according to neuroscientists, we are experiencing a hit of dopamine.

The neurotransmitter dopamine that is released during many pleasurable activities has been identified as the nucleus of our response to "sex, drugs, and rock and roll." It's the sexy chemical in the brain, often called the "motivation molecule." Drug abuse is also related to dopamine. Caffeine, alcohol, sugar, sex, and for some, shopping or gambling increase the dopamine in your system. Nicotine, cocaine, heroin, and amphetamines are said to boost dopamine dramatically. Health researcher Deane Alban claims that dopamine is your pleasure/reward system that allows you to experience enjoyment and bliss. With too little of it, we are listless, fatigued, unfocused, and generally unmotivated. Dopamine enhances risk-taking and is associated with healthy decision-making and creativity.

It's an oversimplification, but accurate, to say that creativity is one of the healthy ways to enhance dopamine and that, conversely, the boost of dopamine we experience when looking at something that leaves us shaking in our boots is a way to more fully enter the resonant stream of the creative process.

Levels of dopamine relate to the boredom-versus-engagement axis of the brain, while the neurotransmitter serotonin relates to the pathways of the brain that govern calmness versus stress. The existence of serotonin counteracts the stress hormone cortisol that reduces our ability to think clearly and be creative. Baba Shiv, a professor at Stanford University, in a recent *Inc.* magazine article, has made an extensive study of the biological roots of creativity and believes that high levels of both dopamine and serotonin are ideal for creative work. "This will produce a condition in which you are both calm but energized," he states.

The visualization capacity of the brain is affected by serotonin. The right balance is needed for healthy creative work. LSD completely suppresses the serotonin system, resulting in vivid dream states and hallucinations while awake. By contrast, the drug ecstasy floods the brain with serotonin, influencing mood and causing induced emotional buoyancy. Yoga, meditation, exercise, and creative work can all help to naturally regulate proper levels of serotonin, allowing for a quiet, calm mind that can receive insight and inspiration from deeper levels of thought.

I find this fascinating material for creative individuals. It seems we need to find a balance between a quiet mind and an excited spirit as the optimum condition for creativity and image making. Apart from neuroscience, what remains as the lesson here is that by staying aware of one's own body while in the midst of seeing and working, we can observe and regulate oneself. Too much excited distraction or too much lethargy and calm are equally destructive to the heart of creativity. Balance and energy are needed—living on the razor's edge of the intensity of an inner fire tempered by the oceanic calm of a receptive mind.

Attention and Distraction

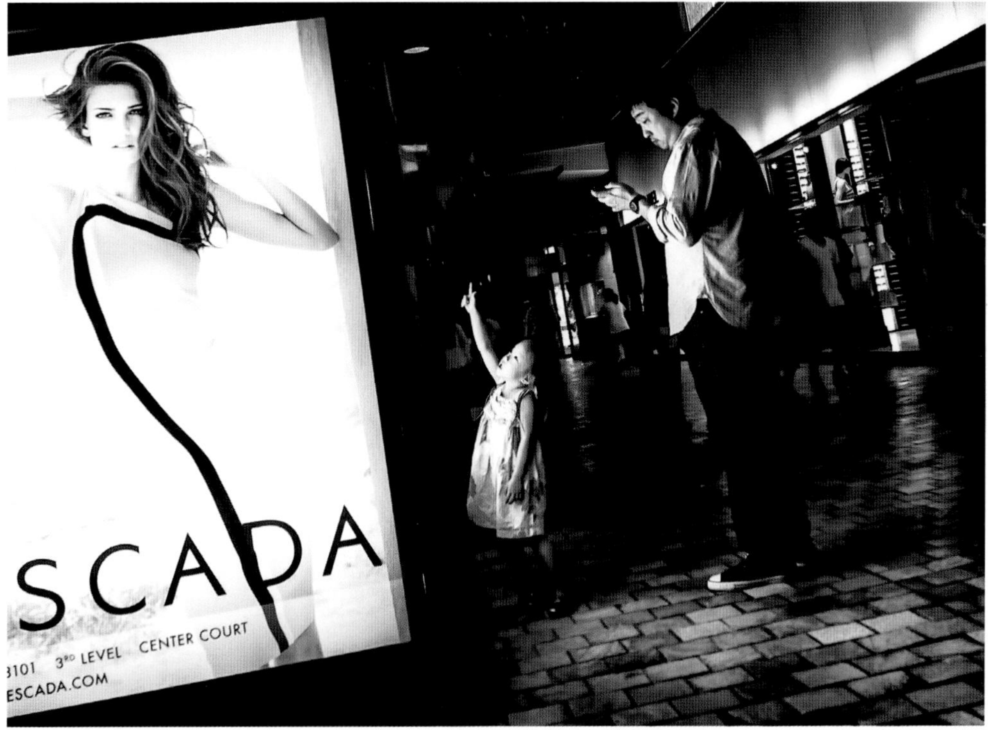

Time of Wonder, Honolulu, Hawai'i, Jon Shimizu

The greatest tool that a photographer has at their disposal is the quality of their attention. The ability to *attend*—to concentrate our energies in a desired direction—forms the foundation of our work with materials and our dialogue with the world. The capacity to *accompany* oneself, to become more aware of our interactions and experiences, to see one's own thinking and feeling, implies that attention is more related to the mind's witness than it is to thinking itself. Attention is a form of seeing and of caring. It is a force of union, that connects us first to ourselves, and then creates an invisible bond with others and the world itself.

Everything and everyone in the world have their own identity and character, their own life, just as you have your own integrity and identity. A camera can help you discover both at once: the nature of your own mind and the living quality of another. The thread that unites your camera to the world is found in your attention. "Pay attention" or "take care," we may say to others. Attention and caring are deeply related. Use the camera to look beyond the goal of taking "good" pictures and to enhance your experience of being in the world.

Photographer Alfred Stieglitz said, "When I photograph, I make love." You can also extend this idea to many other ways of interacting with the world: curiosity, questioning, savoring, protesting, celebrating, and seeking the truth about something or someone, even oneself. All of these modalities of seeing and image making have the need for attention at their core.

Attention leads to engagement. During a photography field trip with students from a class along with my co-faculty member Franco Salmoiraghi, we explored a rapidly developing industrial area of Honolulu, named Kaka'ako. The students scattered and explored mostly broken-down buildings, construction sites, and abstractions of rusted metal, broken glass, and graffiti. Many photographic possibilities to make "good" photographs were to be found.

Franco, on the other hand, wandered not far from the parking lot. He found a local small business, a fender shop, whose existence was threatened by the rising real estate values and gentrification. He put his camera aside for a while and went inside. It was late in the day and the five or six employees were finishing work. Franco hung with them for a while, talking, having a beer, and hearing about their lives: their struggles, joys, and the inevitable questions they had about the fate of their business. He then picked up his camera and made several portraits and documentary images of the long-standing business. He gave them his attention in an unqualified and non-judgmental manner. He dignified them by caring.

This was a powerful teaching moment for the students in the class. The experience was years ago, and Franco's images are the only ones I remember from that day. Franco created a sense of resonance by getting to know strangers without fear in an open, friendly approach.

Resonance is a function of attention. I believe that attention is visible in a photograph. It is a kind of force field of presence. The invisible link of our attentive connection to subject matter is made visible in an image. Photography is a test of our attention and a reflection of what we care about and pay attention to.

We can embrace one discipline that is arguably one of the most important for photography. When a camera is in your hand, even a cell phone camera, use it as a reminder to be attentive. The camera can enhance your experience of the world or it can be a substitute for experience. When you take photographs, try to interact deeply with the subject rather than simply taking the photo to show others you have really been to this or that place. Let go of the notion that photographs are primarily evidence of what you have done or where you have been: your meals, yourself standing in front of some tourist attraction. A camera in your hands can be about discovering the world with attentive, caring interaction.

On the other hand, the camera, and cell phones in particular, can be a source of endless distraction. We buy new cameras that we treat as bright and shiny toys that fascinate us, that feed our consumer lust, and take us far away from the essential activity of taking photographs invested with meaning. Cell phones and their apps—emails, text messages, games, incoming photo streams—capture our attention constantly. This represents a formidable test of our attention, but one that can have positive value and be used to our advantage.

What is the upside of this level of distraction? Recent studies confirm that the rise of frequent cell phone usage among young people is coincident with the rate of declining drug use in the same generation. While researchers have found no direct correlation, Matt Richtel asks the question in the *New York Times*: "But researchers are starting to ponder an intriguing question: Are teenagers using drugs less in part because they are constantly stimulated and entertained by their computers and phones?"

"People are carrying around a portable dopamine pump, and kids have basically been carrying it around for the last 10 years," said David Greenfield, assistant clinical professor of psychiatry at the University of Connecticut School of Medicine and founder of The Center for Internet and Technology Addiction.

Recall that dopamine is the "motivation molecule," the feedback loop for our pleasure/reward system in the brain. Yes, I certainly experience this with technology and I suspect that you do too. While writing this essay, I have stopped to look at my phone at least twice—and I know that feeling of a "charge" of dopamine. The positive value of this highly distracting activity is that dopamine gives us energy. It motivates and excites us. We can use the shot of energy that our phone offers for creative work, but we need to be disciplined and find balance. If we stay with the distraction of our phone for more than a moment, we lose the creative momentum and it can take many minutes to get back to work.

I don't want to minimize the extreme potential for distraction proffered by our phones and devices. But we can accept it, and, to some degree, resist it. In Buddhist practice and other forms of inner work, we are told that distractions are inevitable.

Have the courage and fortitude to witness your many distractions and strive to bring the wandering mind back to the present moment.

While sitting, for example, and watching our breath, we lose the thread of attention frequently. Our minds wander, our emotions intrude with the drama of the moment, and all kinds of itches and twitches assert themselves in the body.

We are told by the Zen masters to simply begin again… and again. This is the key to developing attention behind a camera or on the sitting cushion. When the phone or your shiny camera distracts you, accept freely the hit of dopamine, but do not get lost.

Come back. And come back again. Have the courage and fortitude to witness your many distractions and strive to bring the wandering mind back to the present moment.

Keep the French Fries

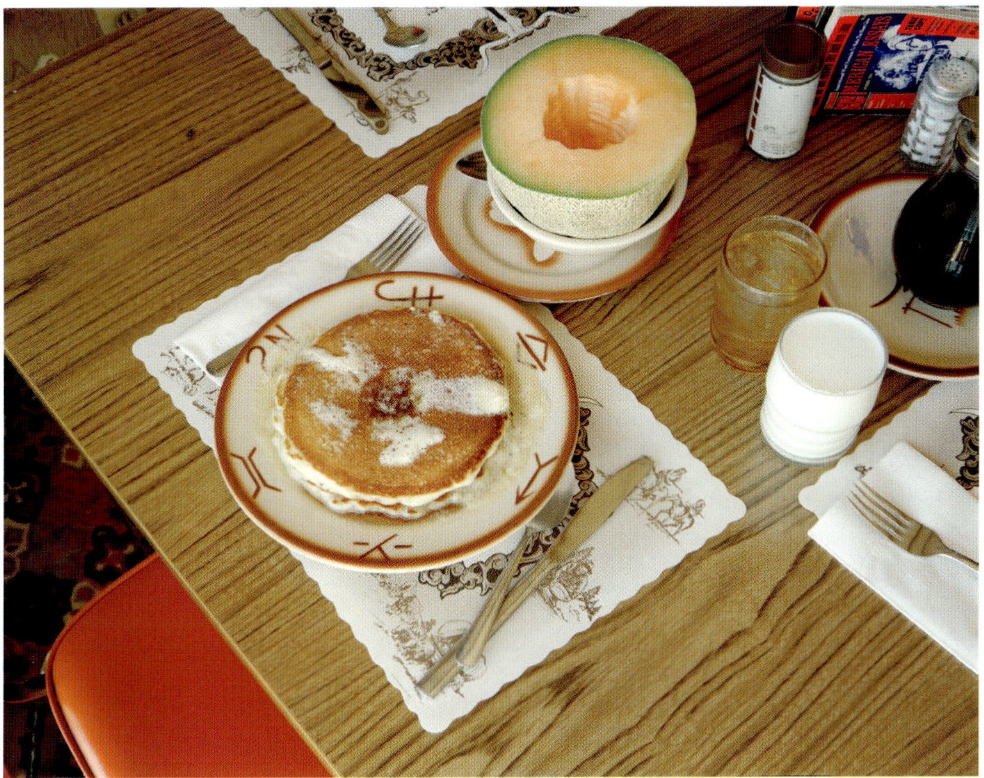

Breakfast, Trail's End Restaurant, Kanab, Utah, August 10, 1973
© Stephen Shore. Courtesy 303 Gallery, New York.

I am consistently inspired by photography's capacity to find order and meaning in the everyday details of life. I am reminded of Stephen Shore's photograph of his breakfast, *Trail's End Restaurant, Kanab, Utah, August 10, 1973*, from his iconic book *Uncommon Places*. A recipient of a recent retrospective at MoMA, Shore's photographs reveal the mystery and intense beauty of banality. Scenes and objects that are so common that we rarely pay attention to them take on an uncommon significance. His photographs contain a fresh look at ordinary reality, a lack of any kind of artificial striving for effect, and a way of democratizing images, where one scene is inherently no more interesting than another. He anticipated the Instagram generation and is currently an avid Instagram user.

The other day, I was watching tourists in Waikiki photograph each other. In one instance, a person was taking a photograph of a friend or family member at the table. He was eating a sinfully juicy hamburger, with lettuce, bacon, and grease sloppily spilling out the sides, and a plate of French fries slathered with ketchup and hot sauce. The photographer reached over and decisively slid the burger and fries out of view so they would not intrude on the aesthetics and purity of the moment.

I thought to myself, No! Stop! Reveal the carnal, messy details. They make the moment alive and real, and place objects and people in the sharp light of immediacy and truthfulness. Generic pictures can be found in abundance. Do a Google search for Waikiki and mostly what you will find is oversaturated sunsets and tourist tropes of the myth of paradise. These photos, in my opinion, contribute nothing to the world. Waikiki is a mecca of tacky shops, luxury stores, fast food franchises from everywhere, and middle-class tourists from mostly the U.S., Canada, and Asia; all set against the deep blue mystery of the Pacific. The details make it a fascinating and disturbing place in how it actually reflects our societal lives and values.

We are told by art and writing teachers: "Show, don't tell," or "Show and tell." Good storytelling comes with the responsibility of specificity. Be inclusive; show the particulars; revel in the details. Good photographs are shaped by culture and the state of the world, as much as they expose the individual expression of the artist. How you see the world, what you include in the frame and what you leave out, is part of your story. Details often bespeak the whole. Pay attention and be selective, but include the ordinary cues you need to make your intended point and to make the photograph interesting in a way that moves beyond the cliché and generic view.

The degree in which you include details speaks to specific identities. Clothing, bodily adornments, location, power dynamics of the frame (low, high, or straight-on camera angles), stray objects, environmental cues, and things of the everyday locate our subject in time and place, in a cultural context. Low camera angles give the subject a heroic, larger than life appearance. High camera angles looking down, as we might photograph children, can reflect an alpha position on the part of the photographer. And a straight-on view, eye to eye, can show respect and equality between photographer and subject.

Minimizing details can reflect the intersectionality of the human experience and give timeless views of the human condition. In art school, we often find life drawing and figure photography workshops that study anatomy, musculature, gesture, posture, and the particular balance of light from without and from within that the human form offers. In life drawing classes, I am impressed by the similarity of the human form the world over. Except for minor variations in body type, gender, skin color, and age, most people have a very similar structure. Universality in art or photographs can honorably reflect the conditions and traits we all share, including such things as our mortality, our need for human connection, our common life on the planet, and our desire to care for and create a better world for our children.

Reveal the carnal, messy details.

As soon as you put clothing and adornments on the figure, you are locating someone in time and place. You are pointing to race, economic status, life priorities and interests, and ethnicity. Photographs with wide collars or bellbottoms, inclusion of cell phones, designer labels, hats or scarves, etc., reflect the specificity of someone's condition and the era in which the photograph was taken. Have you thought about the fact that style choices we find attractive today will look dated and out of place, sometimes even ludicrous, ten years from now? Photographs made today will soon reflect our histories and not our present.

Likewise with landscape and urbanscapes. The existence of signage, commerce, buildings, types of cars, urban decay or pollution all point to timeliness, the conditions of an era and the vernacular of a particular place and time. Think about this when you make photographs. Consider how an image might look and feel ten years from now, or even twenty-five or a hundred years into the future. What details must you include to tell your story? Which are relevant and which are superfluous or even indulgent? Do you want to express the messy realities of a moment; or speak of political and social ideals; or show the kind of world you want to see? One is not better than another. They are different, and your selection of the details and specifics you place in the frame is a large part of the photographer's creative license and power of choice.

The camera is a witness but not an impartial one. It is a reflection of your discernment and intelligence.

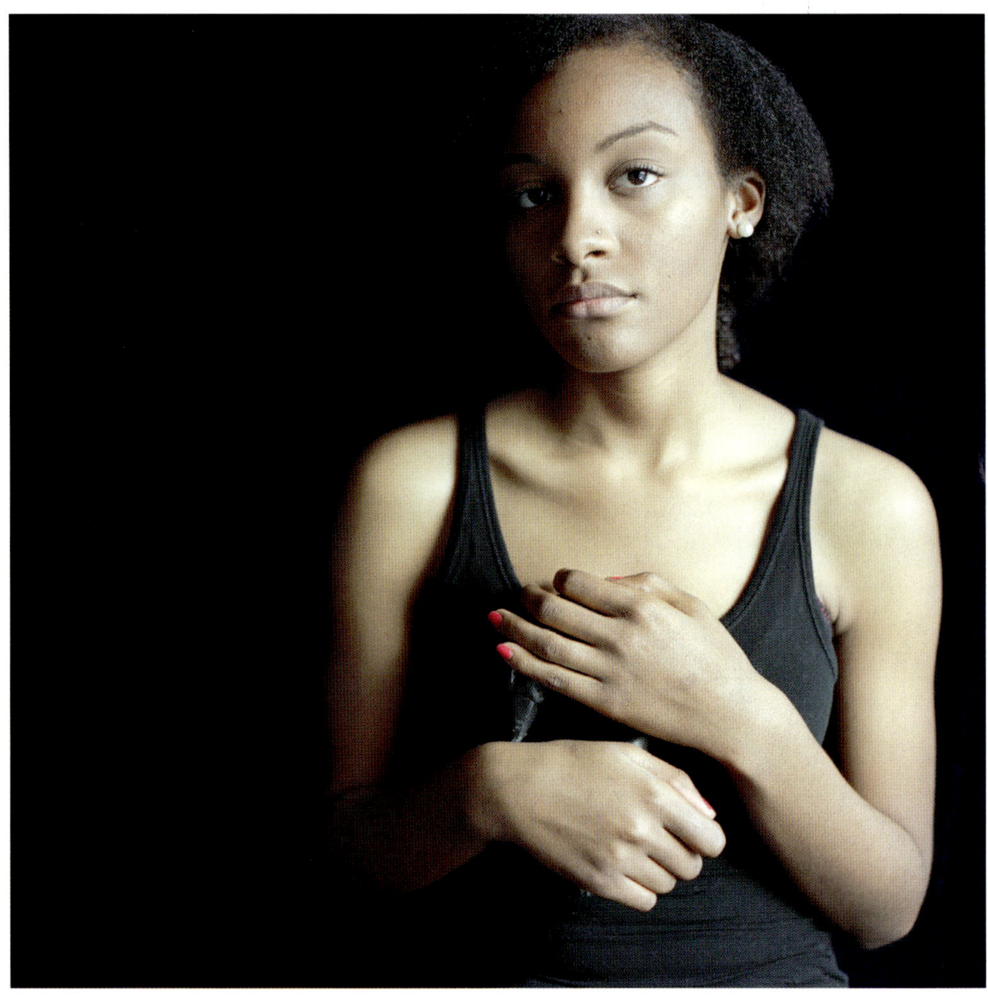

Elexia, from the series *Longing in Black,* Lydia Panas

Becoming Good; Becoming Whole

Why be good at something? How do we become good photographers and for what purpose? The search for excellence and mastery equates with the realization of our human potential and becoming whole. I have heard some art and photography teachers decry mastery as the vestiges of the patriarchy—a perpetuation of the mostly male desire for conquest and exploitation of people and resources. In my estimation, nothing could be further from the truth and, most importantly, this attitude denies a basic human need: to grow and evolve and make a contribution to life and others.

Going the distance with any art or craft will teach you many things. It puts you face to face with yourself—and your obstacles, resistances, and demons are thrown into sharp relief. Laziness, inattention, self-centeredness, doubt, cockiness, and insecurity all will undoubtedly alternate through your awareness and raise their unsightly, but quite typical, visages. This is normal and means, quite simply, that you are human. The desire to learn and the quest to be good at your craft will necessitate becoming aware of your own particular demons and shortcomings while learning to work with them and move beyond them. Often, we merely agree to continue to work in spite of them. From this effort, a new perspective may arise; one in which we find a way to navigate and push forward and to recognize that we are of two natures: one willing and capable and the other plagued by our inadequacies. It is a humbling experience that leads to self-knowledge, acceptance, and, eventually, an ability to resist those aspects of oneself that prevent learning and growth.

Traditional craftspeople believe that as you perfect your craft, you perfect yourself. The Zen arts, such as swordsmanship, archery, and calligraphy make demands on the practitioner to be fully in moment, with a coordinated mind, body, and heart, and a honed attention to the workings of their practice. Zen arts teach you to surrender to no-mind and instinct, to come into the body, and not rely solely on the thinking brain. Photography asks that we develop those same virtues. The end product, in both Zen practice and photography, reflects the development of our attention and expresses the truth of where we are, who we are. Learning a craft thus becomes a mean for seeking wholeness and growth of being—and for the ongoing evolution of self-knowledge.

You also learn what you are naturally good at and where you excel. Photography, or any art, places you squarely in front of your talents, skills, and predilections. You can see, almost immediately, where you shine. The process of finding your voice or your vision is equivalent to finding yourself. You can come into your own, become who you are.

It is very clear to me as a photography teacher that students have a natural capacity for certain things. Sometimes it's an affinity for color and form, for others it may be a quickness of perception in capturing a complex moment. For some, an openhearted, friendly manner that puts others at ease helps them shine at portraiture. I find often that the "darker" and more complex students have a strong awareness of psychological dynamics and a polemic disposition that helps them see and reflect aspects of society with clarity and force. Others are empaths or nature spirits and are deeply connected to other people or the environment. The shape and content of the photographs you make can be instructive, enlightening, and even shocking. You learn about who you already are.

Studying photography puts you in touch with the personal accomplishments of others and collective conditions. As we strive to see more clearly and be in touch with the realities of the world through a camera, we look at other pictures for research, study other photographer's working methods, and observe cultural attitudes and conventions that shape both our medium and our world. We become a part of the flow of history and participate in a dialogue with culture and society in a way that shapes our path toward the future. Excellence cannot be sought and found without seeing where you are within the scope of the photographic medium and its history. We reject some ideas and embrace others. We learn what we do not want to do and what we want to do. In our growth as photographers, we find a deep resonance with some artists, indifference to others, and clear opposition to other standpoints and perspectives.

You do not work in a vacuum. Get to know your medium and other photographers, and pay great attention to the culture of which you are a part. Art critic Arthur Danto once said something that has always stuck with me. At the beginning of a lecture, he expressed his gratitude to the audience by saying, "Thank you for allowing me to be part of the dialogue of our times."

Audience

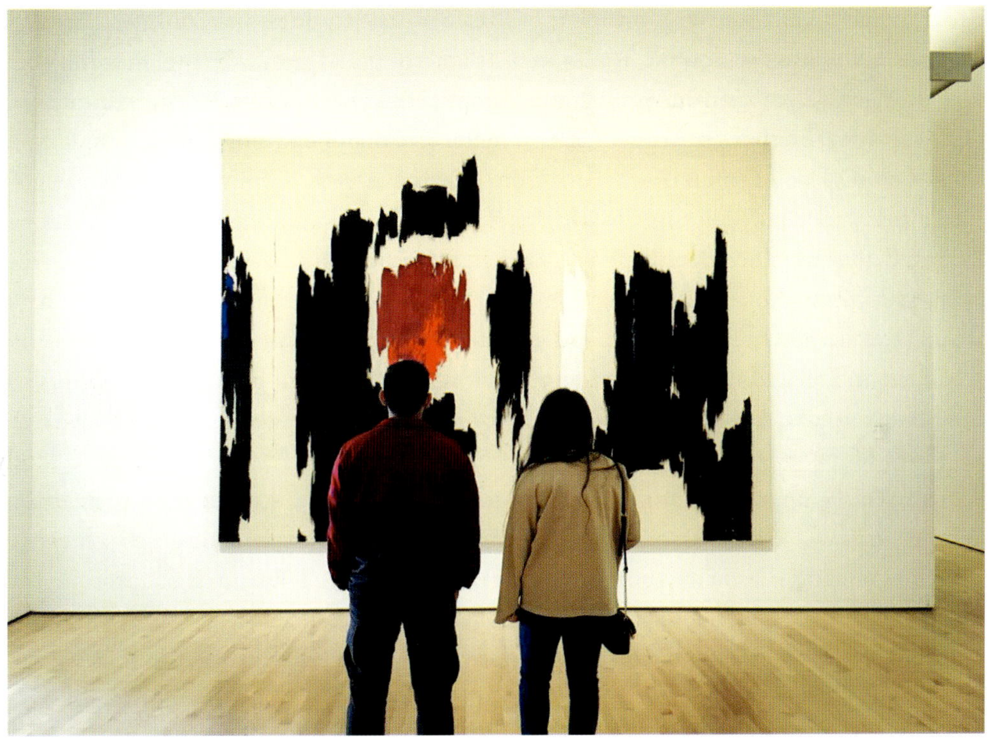

SF MOMA, Laura Dunn, Installation photograph: Painting by Clyfford Still, PH-261 (1962)

In responding to student work, I often feel compelled to ask my students, who is your audience? Certain kinds of work and cultural references are generational; others are specific to a certain culture or subculture; and yet others are more universal. In Hawai'i, where the mix of cultures and generations is wide and deep, students need to be aware of cultural standards and religious views so as to not offend or trample on long-standing beliefs and traditions. A native Hawaiian activist once asked those that have come to these islands to "do your homework" before making your mark in the community. In all cases, some homework is necessary to identify and understand your specific audience, those with whom you wish to communicate.

Many times, photographers make pictures without much consideration of their audience and mostly, often unconsciously, make images that speak primarily to their generational peers, those with similar lifestyles, cultural attitudes, and educational backgrounds as themselves. This is a common condition in photography, though it is limited. Not everyone is part of your peer group. Some people have very different educations, political views, lifestyles, and generational memories than you.

For example, academics often work from highly theoretical points of view, incorporating insights from philosophers and social scientists—and make images that can be mystifying to the general public. This group, in fact, often looks down upon the conventions and tropes of popular photography. Non-academics often find images made from within the academy to be esoteric and confusing, requiring elite knowledge to understand them. Try reading highly academic writing. The tortured prose and sentences so long that you cannot remember the subject by the time you get to the verb can be painful to read for the general public.

Conversely, popular photography and images made by the Instagram generation can be shallow and often assume that certain visual tropes, style choices, and lifestyle priorities are understood and shared by everyone. Not true. To many artists and highly educated people, these popular kinds of images seem superficial at best and sentimental with a head-in-the-sand-denial of modern reality at worst. The question arises, can we begin to find a balance between the esoteric and the popular, between depth and accessibility?

I think about this question frequently. In my writing and images, I seek to communicate with the widest possible audience. I am very careful to balance depth of insight with economy and accessibility of expression. An idea that has been highly useful to me in defining my audience is the concept of the "cultural creatives," a phrase coined by authors Paul Ray and Sherry Ruth Anderson in a book of the same name. Ray and Anderson assert that there are roughly 50 million American cultural creatives (over a quarter of the adult U.S. population) and approximately 80–90 million in Europe. Cultural creatives are distinguished by being highly educated, knowledgeable about art and music, cross-generational and multiethnic, progressive but not strictly liberal, have a strong moral compass, committed to social change with a certain idealism, and interested in self-expansion and improvement. For my work, this group constitutes my ideal audience. But I need to mindful of my own cognitive biases; many in this group hold somewhat different views and generational attitudes than myself, though we share many common characteristics.

For artists and photographers to effectively communicate, we must enter the mind of our intended audience. Empathy, then, forms an important element in our creative expression. What does our audience know and care about, and what attitudes do they resist or defend? Is our goal to disrupt the views of an audience, or to nourish, instruct, and speak clearly and compassionately of our hard-earned truth? The goal is up to you, but you should have one and be clear about what you are trying to say.

We can only hope to give voice to our concerns with integrity and coherence. We cannot control, or even know how an audience will respond. Indeed, the vibrating relationship between a work of art and the engagement of the viewer can be a creative act unto itself—and is not entirely subjective. Most sensitive viewers will strive to move beyond like and dislike as criteria for understanding photographs and art. Liking or disliking something is a very shallow form of response that takes our own cognitive and emotional biases as objective criteria. Most of us are aware of the danger of too much subjectivity. The visual language has its own grammar, syntax, and conventions that a skilled photographer will employ to their advantage, and a viewer will recognize when used effectively.

I recommend showing your photographs to as many different types of people as possible. Seek and gather responses as a form of research. This exercise can be enlightening and instructive. Remember that someone's response may say as much about them as it does your image. In my experience, most of my students and peers that respond to each other's work fit within the broad cohort of cultural creatives. A fascinating phenomenon emerges in responding to each other's photographs.

Everyone will respond in their own way, with a subjective bent or twist to their way of seeing. But, in an effective photograph or work of art, all responses often gather around a central point. While everyone brings their own story to the image, everyone is perceiving something, in their own way, of what I would call a collectively recognized meaning inherent in the image. For example, in Picasso's epic painting *Guernica*, made in response the Nazi bombing of a small town in Spain, critical responses include words like violence, disassociation, inhumanity, protest, pain, suffering, and chaos. Picasso himself said of the painting, "What ideas and conclusions you have got I obtained too, but instinctively, unconsciously."

In other words, one measure of the effectiveness of a photograph is how each viewer might come to a relatively similar meaning in their own way, in their own words.

We are all different, yet alike. Knowing this is the key to good visual communication.

Fitting into the Flow of Time

All activities and processes manifest in time. Every type of endeavor has its own rhythm, its own necessity. When you cook a meal for example, you must be sensitive to multiple dishes arriving at optimum completion in their own time, according to their own process. Photographers need to be hypersensitive to the moment, with an awareness of both the present and an anticipation of the future as to when the moment arrives that best suits our intentions and our expressive aims. Photographer Henri Cartier-Bresson calls this the "decisive moment," when the scene builds to a climactic crescendo of revelation within the frame.

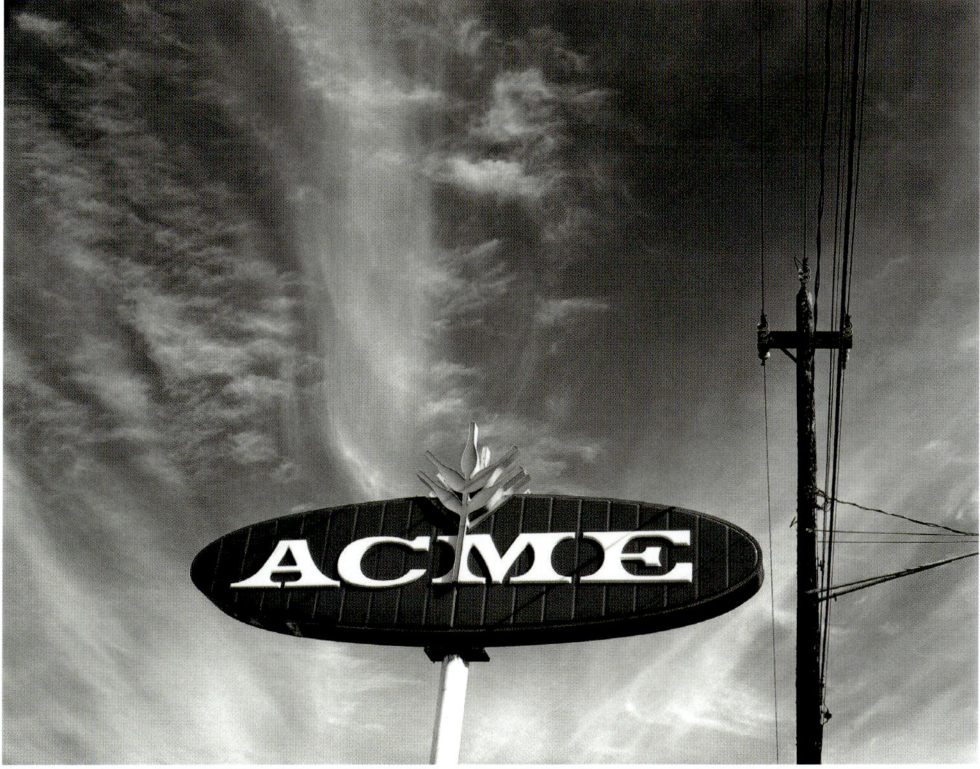

Acme Sign, Akron, Ohio, David Ulrich

Over the years, I have developed a remarkable and strange sense of timing, knowing how to "fit" into the flow of time to find the revealing moment in an activity—especially with a camera. My sense of timing is intuitive and uncanny—sometimes weird, even to me.

An example of my sense of timing can be found when I'm teaching a class. During critiques, students bring in examples of their work on thumb drives to be viewed and discussed by me and the other participants. I take note of how many portfolios are to be viewed within a class period, usually between a dozen and twenty. Once I determine how many there are, I find an intuitive flow and finish the review always within two minutes of the close of the class period. At first, I kept time. Nowadays, I have an inner sense of moving not too fast or not too slow that is extremely reliable. Keeping time with a watch is tight and rigid, and lacks flexibility when several people arrive late and throw off the schedule. My inner sense of timing is, however, able to easily accommodate these changes.

There is an art to synchronizing with the flow of time. Great athletes, musicians, dancers—and photographers—develop their instincts to such a degree that they can be fully present in a moment and anticipate future movements with split-second timing and great accuracy. Robert Grudin writes in *Time and the Art of Living*, "The striking awareness and control of time achieved by great athletes hold analogies of importance to all of us…. [They have] an unusual combination of talents in action: concentration, balance, speed, quickness, coordination, reflex, anticipation, providence and control of tempo." For those of us with a camera, all of these traits are necessary to develop, especially an awareness of tempo.

Each activity holds its own tempo that we can observe and fit into. Our camera choice and working method partly define the tempo with which we work, and the subject obviously has its own rhythm that we need to both recognize and anticipate. Photographer Joel Meyerowitz observes the difference between working with a handheld camera and one on a tripod. "[The small camera] taught me energy and decisiveness and immediacy…The large camera taught me reverence, patience, and meditation. I want to have an experience in the world that is a deepening experience, that makes me feel alive and awake and conscious." The lesson here is simple. We don't control time; we submit to it. In some arenas such as people and street photography, adrenaline and dopamine rule the day. We move through time, quickly and breathlessly, watching and working, synchronizing with the moment in a tango of quick sensitivity and bold action. We insert ourselves into the activity, become a part of it, and submit to its dynamic flow.

In still life and landscape photography, the needs are different. Stillness, an open, patient receptivity, and contemplative sight are employed to find the "right" moment, the "right" constellation of conditions. The word "right" means an inner precision, a seeking of a sense of resonance with the subject that emerges through patience—not right or wrong. Here serotonin rules. We often wait and watch, make minor adjustments to the frame or camera angle, and sensitively click the shutter when we feel an overwhelming resonance with the subject.

The rational mind functions too slowly for a responsive awareness of time. Intuition becomes the primary tool. Photographers can search to find an inner "sense" of when to approach a subject: early light, late light, midday activity, etc. The camera in your hand can help you remember to align your intuition with the prescient sight of anticipation, finding the right location and angle, and feeling the "right" moment to snap the shutter. Clicking the shutter can also align with our breath. An awareness of our breathing and being attuned to the timely flow of inbreath and outbreath, helps us immensely in coming into accord with time.

The following lessons represent a way of working that can be applicable to photographers and are a summation of the advice that Phil Jackson, former head coach of the LA Lakers and Chicago Bulls, gave his players before a game. They are adapted from his book, *Sacred Hoops: Spiritual Lessons of a Hardwood Warrior*. Jackson is an adept of Zen and attempts to help his players be in the moment, synchronize with each other and the game itself, and align with the overwhelmingly quick tempo of a basketball game.

Seek personal mastery
Do not hold the ball for longer than two counts
Awareness is everything
Great possibility comes with great danger
Practice the art of acceptance
Embody compassion
Have a love of the game, yet practice nonattachment
Strive to understand the soul of teamwork

Catch the Wave, Not the Ripple

To live your life through a camera was an ideal for many in my generation. With small cameras readily slung over our shoulders, we photographed many of the strong impressions that crossed our path. But we were limited, often to black-and-white film and by the expensive and time-consuming need to process and the print the photos. We often lamented that we wanted a receiving and saving device attached to our eye and brain, a way of photographing simply and directly with a camera always at the ready. Now that wish is a reality.

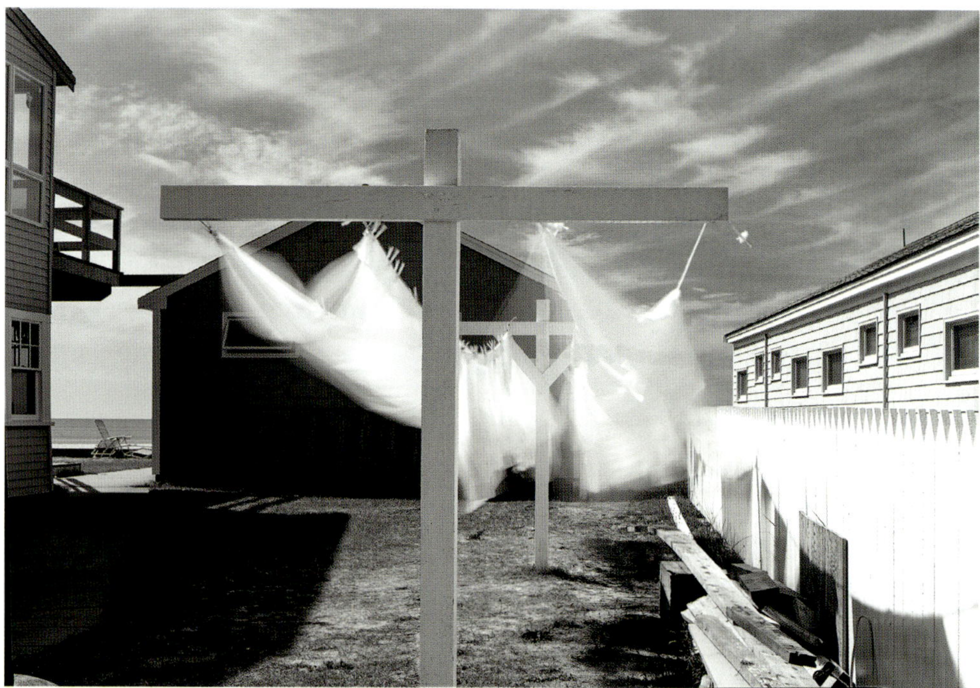

Clothesline, Provincetown, Cape Cod, Massachusetts, David Ulrich
I returned to this site several times before the laundry and clouds cooperated to reveal the coherent image I visualized in my mind's eye.

And what a reality it has become. We have come to take this power of seeing and recording for granted. An experience is not complete until we have photographed it. Cell phone cameras serve to validate our existence and prove to oneself and the world, *I was here.* Like a contemporary form of graffiti, we mark our lives, the places we've been, and the people we have met with pictorial tagging. Food porn, selfies in strange and exotic places, pet pictures, and family photos dominate our online universe. Today is Christmas and an Instagram friend, Stacy Platt, editor of the Society for Photographic Education's journal *Exposure*, has summed up well this condition by saying, "I have henceforth begun to hear the refrain of: 'No more pictures, Mama.'"

Minor White offered profound advice to those of us that are peripatetic picture-takers. He said, "Catch the wave, not the ripple." Discipline yourself to a form of abstinence. When you take in impressions through the eyes, they enter your mind and begin a process of digestion and transformation. You can externalize this event by taking the photo and releasing the energy—now. Or you can wait. You can allow this impression, and others like it, to gather inwardly, build force, blend with other growing thoughts in the depth of your mind, create an internal wave of realization and understanding, and finally, when ready, spout forth with power into one's creative expression. Know the difference between photographs that are sketches of a developing idea and ones that are more fully realized.

When impressions enter the contemplative factory of the mind and are not released immediately, a transformative process begins. Many times, I have sketched an idea with a camera, the results fell flat, and I admit to feeling disappointed. However, this process of sketching is informative and is a form of digesting and composting the material. An idea is building within the mind to completion. Each step of the creative process is no more important than any other step. Sometimes, we plant seeds; at other times, we harvest results. Don't attempt to undercut or speed up the process. Allow your impressions their journey through your mind and let them ripen to maturity. Don't grasp for immediate results. Sometimes waiting or sketching is the most creative action you can take.

In photography school, we would give a set of two assignments over several weeks. In the first week, we would have students expose 50-100 rolls of film over seven days. They would photograph every single impression that struck them in any way. Then, of course, they needed to process the film and view the results, not a trivial task. During the next week, they were only allowed to expose one roll of 36 exposure film. Each shot had to count. Whatever sketching was necessary to identify point of view or quality of light, they had to do in their brain without the camera. The results from both weeks were illuminating.

In the first week, there were many ripples and no strong waves. However, the value of taking so many pictures was revealed in the sheer number of developing themes and ideas that were in evidence. Sketching freely with a camera seemed to help unleash the wild mind and open it to new ways of seeing and representing the world. But it did not result in powerful, realized expressions. In the second week, there were large, breaking waves, evident in potent but incomplete image ideas. Without being able to sketch their ideas and build their connection with the subject through the action of taking a number of pictures, the images had powerful resonances but were not always elegantly expressed.

These results seem to suggest that free sketching and restraint both have their place in the creative process. We need to find a balance between freedom and discipline, fervent activity weighed against attentive looking and waiting. Sometimes we need to allow ideas to ferment in the mind, privately and sealed like in a wine cask, before opening them to the world. Not every stray image and impression should be fodder for Instagram and social media. Many times, I have seen images in student work that I knew were incomplete representations of process and not yet the crescendo of realization. But students often confuse creative processing with harvesting. They put the images out into the world on social media, thinking they had succeeded in representing their idea or perception, and felt the need to look no further, especially if they received a sufficient number of likes. In other words, they were finished and the image idea progressed no further.

Other students waited and held their process close to the breast. They did not release their unformed thoughts and impressions into the public arena—not yet. They kept alive their sense of wanting and longing for the fullness of completion. They kept working. They did not take "good enough" as the criteria and allowed the process to be realized over time. When ripening occurred, they reached up and found the fruit ready for picking, and then shared the generous bounty with others.

We need to discriminate between the private working out of an idea and its time of flowering into public view.

Learn to know the difference.

Of Time and Light

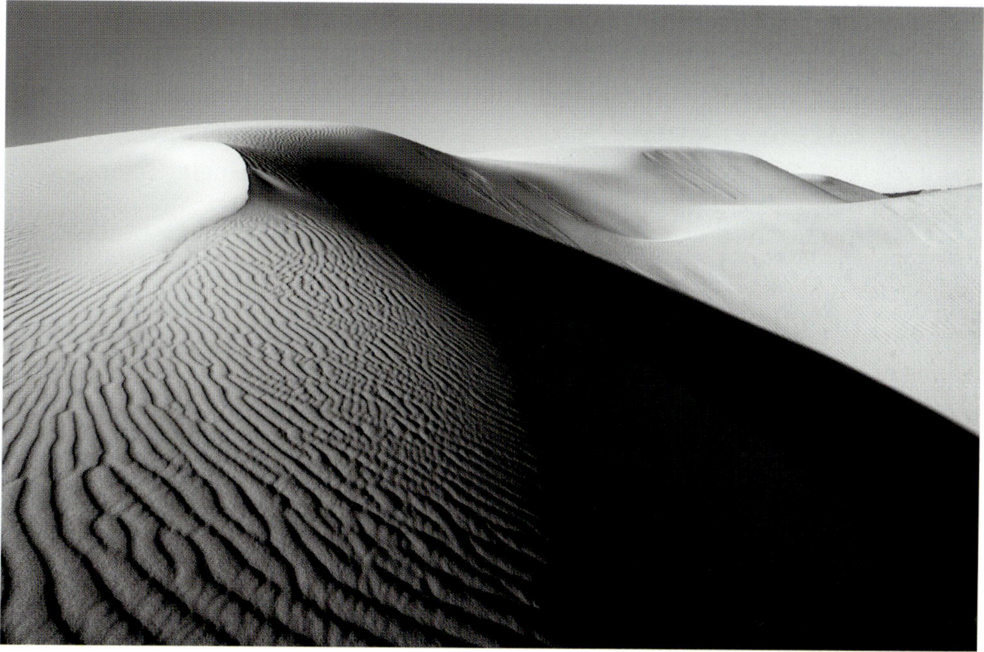

Oceano Dunes #82, California, 2019, David Ulrich

In winter, the light hibernates. In summer, it blazes forth with radiant intensity. In fall, the light clarifies the very atmosphere through which it passes. In spring, light births again and all creatures, big and small, rejoice. Light recounts the passing of time and narrates the dependable and steady movement of the sun and planets and moon. Day and night, clouds and sun, rain and wind, and now, sadly, pollution and purity give vastly different possibilities to the photographer's palate.

I often refer to midday sunlight in Hawai'i as the "noonday demon." Sharp light with the sun directly overhead flattens the volume of subjects, compresses space, reduces skin texture and organic surfaces to flat panes of bleached highlights and empty shadows, and makes colors look like they have come out of an icing tube for decorating birthday cakes. Do a Google image search for Hawai'i and look at the first page of your results to see what I mean. It's true of midday light in most places. Many photographers prefer softer light: cloudy, overcast, hazy, and enveloping.

This softer light reveals shape and volume, opens into depths of near and far, accentuates visible texture, and deepens color and color relationships. Early and late-day light are often ideal for landscape. Soft light highlights skin tones, and dusk or night photography broaches mystery and resounding depths.

Light is a language, and the alphabet of the language of natural light is time. Artists and poets have for centuries rejoiced in the many nuances of changing light. Shakespeare's Juliet moans, "Come, gently night; come loving, black-browed night, give me my Romeo." And in the same play, Romeo proclaims, "But soft! What light through yonder window breaks?" At the height of his career, photographer Minor White attempted to articulate the language of light for photographers. While his insights remain incomplete, and are even a bit awkwardly expressed, they begin to form a matrix of how we may view and use light in our image making. In White's view, there are seven qualities, or "levels," of light, which I will mostly paraphrase here. Quotations are in White's own words from his MIT exhibition catalog, *Light*[7].

LIGHT OF EMERGENCE

First light. Objects materialize and come into view from darkness. Often, the colors or tonal range are low-key and the subject begins to take shape in a recognizable fashion. Look at many of the photographs by *Life* magazine photojournalist W. Eugene Smith, especially the iconic image of mother and deformed son from his his book project *Minamata*. The "power of light to penetrate to the dark places." Carl Jung said, "One does not become enlightened by imagining figures of light, but by making the darkness conscious."

LET THE LIGHT MAKE LOVE

The type of light that savors, caresses, and absorbs—that interpenetrates as well as reflects. Look at Edward Weston's shells and vegetables and the exquisite color photographs from the book *Cape Light* by Joel Meyerowitz. In White's thought, this happens when the masks drop away to reveal the livingness of the subject. He once said, "With people I wait until the light of the person outshines the light falling on him."

The light of day where all things are sharply seen and revealed. "The surfaces by which the rock, tree, cloud, artifact, human being—realize their own I AM." The frequent aim of documentary photographers is to reveal and highlight aspects of the subject. Many images come to mind, but look especially at Dorothea Lange, Vivian Maier, Henri Cartier-Bresson, and Alex Soth. This can also include on-camera flash as in images by Diane Arbus and Larry Fink.

LET THE LIGHT KILL

"High contrast photographs [in which] the light seems to be as intense as a bomb blast." Over-contrast and oversaturation are immensely popular today amongst amateur photographers. White says of this, "Perhaps this unaccountable urge for high-contrast images is prophetic of searing light to come. Nature seems to have a way of making her image makers and artists point towards what is about to happen in the future." Robert Frank can do this well—and even subtly—with certain subjects. His gritty, grainy, and sometimes overblown images perceptively reflect the underbelly of America in the '50s. Also, look at the harshly rendered work of Japanese photographer, Moriyama Daido.

LET THE LIGHT REGENERATE

The healing power of light. Plants and people reach toward the light for survival and nourishment. Without light, some people experience SAD, seasonal affective disorder. "In this phase, light, and the subject it illuminates, are equal in their powers." Look at the desert landscapes by Richard Misrach and *Uncommon Places*, the seminal book by Stephen Shore. In Shore's work, the sheer banality of the subject matter is ameliorated by the enveloping radiance of the light that suffuses all things.

LIGHT FROM WITHIN

When the light from within the subject predominates. "Sometimes light is more a felt force than a seen subject." Look at Sally Mann's southern landscapes and the inner light found in the portraits by Lydia Panas. Also, Paul Caponigro's landscape work reflects the unique properties of silver-based, film photography in which prints on silver emulsions evoke a deep luminosity that eludes most digital photographers. Actually, I believe all three of these photographers still work with film.

The symbolic, spiritual light of the world, "when that which seems to be matter appears to be spirit. All of us walk in miracle constantly, but live isolated in apathy and unawareness." The contemporary photographer that, in my estimation, powerfully expresses the radiant realization of spiritual light is Indonesian photographer, Hengki Koentjoro. Also, of course, look at the majestic, mid-career landscapes of Ansel Adams, a master of sublime light in photography.

It often takes half of a lifetime's career to truly master light. You can start by experimenting with these various types of light in the field. Try to photograph in all kinds of light—to see what things look like throughout the day or evening, different times of year, and with very particular types of conditions. Learn to control exposure and post-processing options to evoke different qualities of light.

As an experiment, take one image into Photoshop, Lightroom, or the darkroom—or even into the software on your phone. Make it significantly lighter and darker, softer and more contrasty, as well monochromatic and vibrant with color. In a RAW processor such as Adobe Camera Raw or Lightroom, use the color sliders to control how each channel of color can be accentuated or diminished to radically transform a color image into black and white. Study your results carefully.

Experiment. Be bold and fearless in your explorations. Don't be timid. Over time, learn to use the expansive range of light and its myriad qualities for your expressive ends.

In Space

Space is an illusion in photography. The appearance of space in a two-dimensional image forms a part of the visual meaning in how a viewer reads an image.

The eye and brain have three ways of perceiving depth. The first is the binocularity of two-eyed vision. Each eye holds a slightly different perspective on a subject. The brain interprets these dual perspectives to allow us to recognize space between objects, between us and an object, and the relative location of objects in space. Binocularity operates only at distances approximately 15–20 feet away from your eyes, about the distance in basketball from the free throw line to the basket. All other forms of depth perception are monocular—one eyed—and similar to a camera lens.

The second form of depth perception is motion. If you are in a moving car, for example, the bushes in the foreground appear to be clipping past faster than the mountains in the background. If you are walking, relative motion appears to be more pronounced in subjects closer to you than far away. The third way of seeing and rendering space is perspective. The objects closest to us appear larger than the objects some distance away. If you are drawing a fence, for example, you can use standard three-point perspective, in which the closest fence post is rendered larger, and as the fence posts recede in space, they are rendered progressively smaller leading to the vanishing point.

Since camera vision is monocular, the principal means for alluding to space is through the rendering of perspective and lens choice. Anyone who has studied photography knows the basics. Long lenses (telephoto) compress and flatten space while short lenses (wide angle) serve to open space and render greater depth. What is called a normal lens, approximately 50 mm for a 35mm film camera or a full-frame sensor, offers a spatial perspective that approximates human vision.

Photographers might choose a long lens to zoom in on a subject, as in wildlife or sports, or step back from a subject for a wider view, as in landscapes and urban scenes. However, often photographers choose lenses based on their evocation of spatial relationships. The longer the lens, the more space is compressed; the wider the lens, the more space is opened and apparent depth is increased. This has far-reaching consequences in visual expression. Do we want to enhance or subvert the physical vision of the eye and brain?

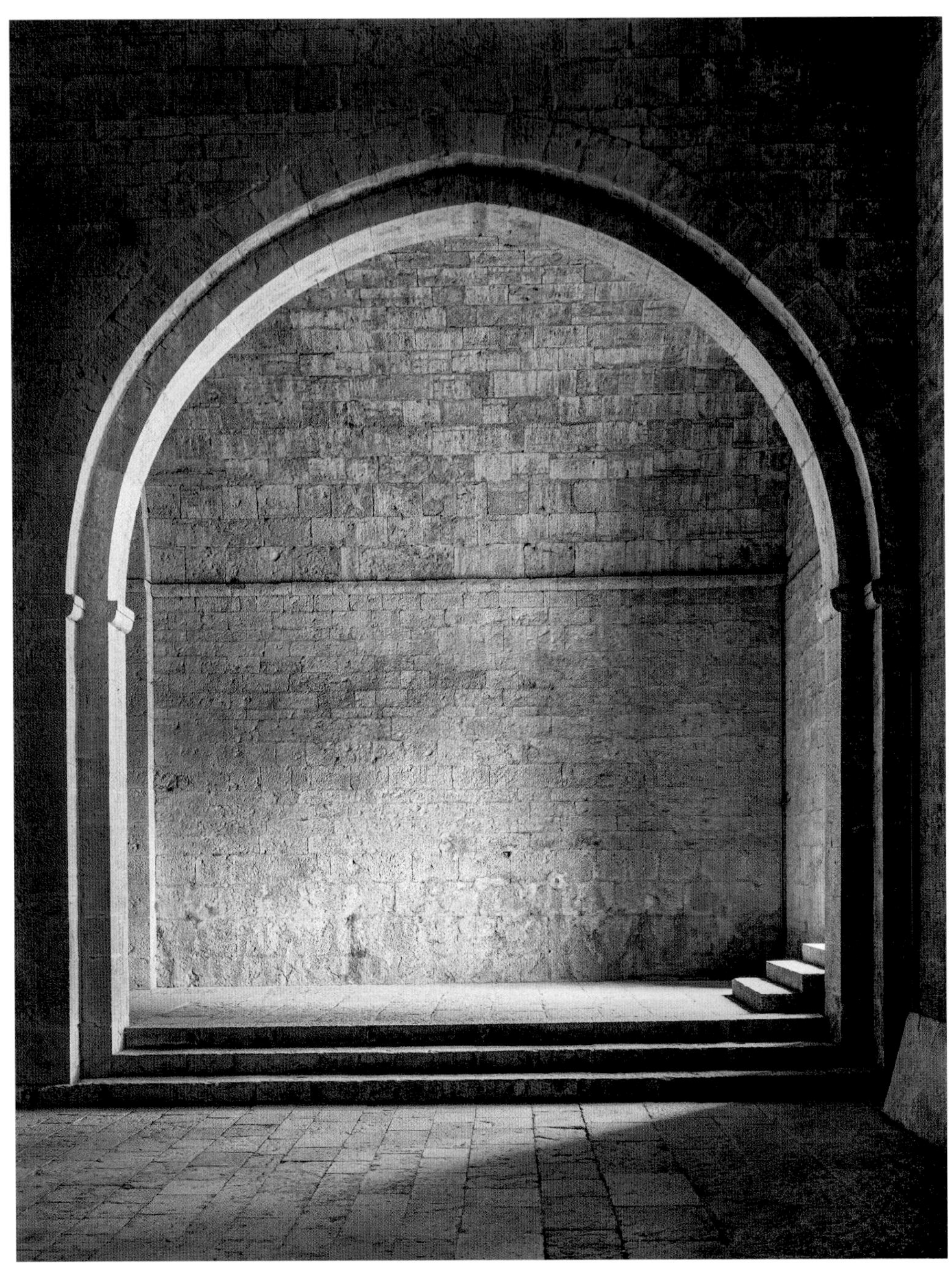

Compressing space flattens the subject. Cubist and abstract paintings, for example, show the planes of the subject concurrently and not extending into space. Medium-long lenses (70-85mm) flatter human subjects by offering a perspective of the human face without distortion of features. Wide-angle lenses, on the other hand, distort features. What is closer to a camera, like noses, appear larger, and what is farther from the camera, like ears, appear disproportionally smaller. Cell phone cameras have wider lenses, and photos at arm's length give a sense of comic relief due to distorted noses and lips and smaller heads than what we normally see. Thus, the popularity of selfie sticks, which keep you a greater distance from the camera lens and create less distortion.

Often, beginning photographers seem more comfortable with longer lenses while fine art or documentary photographers often lean toward slightly to moderately wide lenses. It's easier to organize space and form with longer lenses. You can highlight a single subject with less stray material in the frame to integrate. It's harder to photograph with wide lenses; more material is contained within the fabric of the frame that needs to be integrated into your visual document.

What meaning are you trying to convey in your photographs? Are you looking *at* something, as you might do with a long lens, or *into* something, as you might do with a wide lens? Do you want to evoke depth and space, or work with flat planes of color and form?

Many cameras, including cell phones, have limited lens choices. In these instances, photographers need to employ other tactics beyond the lens to represent space. For instance, try to experiment with near/far relationships, or what we call figure/ground. Place or find an object in the near foreground, closer to your camera, and observe how space opens up as the object interacts with the background. Then, try photographing a scene with nothing in the foreground and observe how the space seems condensed.

Also, when seeing the world through a camera, become aware of negative space, or the space that surrounds and defines objects. The atmosphere itself can evoke spaciousness or constriction, lightness or heaviness. We breathe freely in viewing certain scenes or images, and breath becomes tight and constricted when viewing others. As a photographer, concentrated emotional states or even the expression of anger and fear can often be evoked through the flatness of space, where objects collide and ricochet off each other within the frame.

A friend and fellow photographer, Franco Salmoiraghi, has defined the term, "photographs of nothing," which refer to images made without any definable focal point in which the space and light and the atmosphere of negative space become the central subject. In these images, the space and the air itself richly vibrate with substance and livingness. As an exercise, try to make images in which the negative space becomes dominant or equal to the definition of the subject, or when the atmosphere itself is rendered with living light.

Can you photograph the air we breathe? For example, writer Barry Lopez believes that, in many photographs by Robert Adams, he displays "An obvious passion for light in his prints, the light streaming down at times like a shower, an effulgence in the air." He is able to evoke in a photograph the light and atmosphere itself, "making it visible like a plein-air painter."

And finally, what about the poetics of inner space? Images and art made with capacious perception—mindful seeing—can evoke a broad inner spaciousness, such as the flat canvases of resonating, resounding color by Mark Rothko or the evocative photographs of David Heald of Cistercian Abbeys in France from his book, *The Architecture of Silence*. In mindful seeing, we strive to locate part of our attention in our body, to become aware of the spaces within and seek to find correspondence in the things we photograph. Images made with sensitive awareness can bring that focused attention invisibly forward into the image. We feel a sense of resounding presence and spaciousness in the neural pathways within the body.

Finding Your Mojo

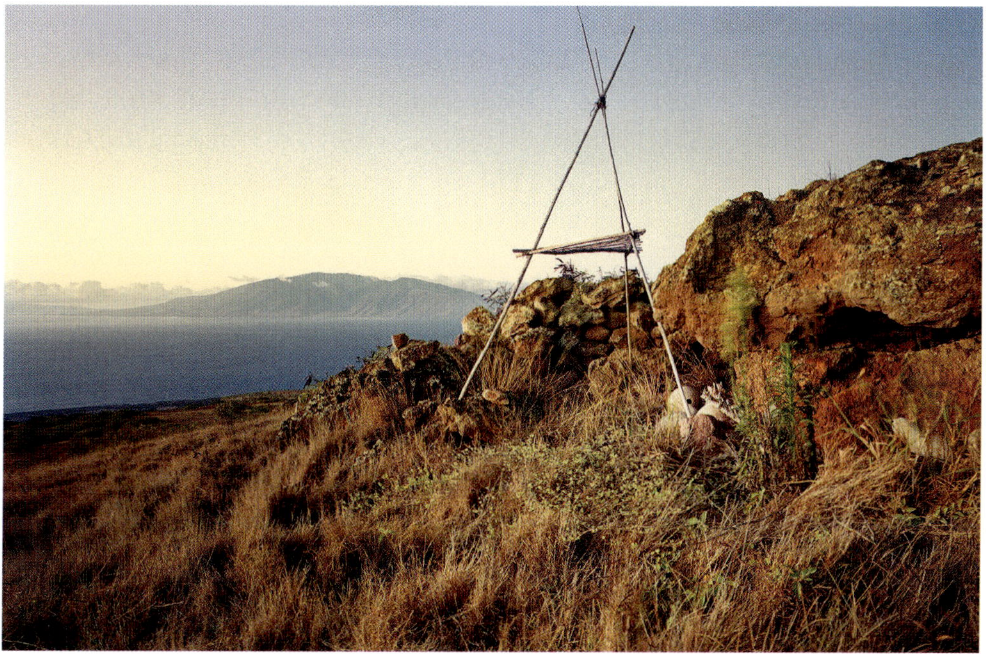

Crest of Moaʻulaiki, Kahoʻolawe, Hawaiʻi, David Ulrich
I have been deeply inspired by spending time on the island of Kahoʻolawe, historically sacred to the Hawaiian people and used for ordnance training by the U.S. Military for fifty years.

Creativity flourishes in a full, active mind. Discovery inevitably comes to the inquisitive disposition and eludes the bored and disinterested. The power of an artist can be directly measured by the quality and depth of the questions they ask, the influences they follow, and the impressions they seek. An active engagement with thought and ideas through reading, looking, listening, and the particular nature—and subsequent enjoyment—of what we take in through the senses can enliven creativity and get our juices flowing. It's a form of psychic nourishment.

Literature professor Ngũgĩ wa Thiong'o at UC Irvine, in writing about the novels of Joseph Conrad, reflects admirably on his sentences: "The majesty and musicality of his well-structured sentences had so thrilled me as a young writer that I could cure a bout of writer's block simply by listening to the opening bars of Beethoven's Fifth Symphony or reading the opening pages of Conrad's *Nostromo*. It instantly brought my mojo back."

What can help us find or renew our mojo? For me, several bodies of work in art and literature can reliably and immediately stimulate the flow of my pen or activate my camera eye: the poetry of Rilke, the late paintings of Mark Rothko, the musical lyrics of Bob Dylan, and the mystery found in the southern, large format landscapes of Sally Mann. When I am involved in a writing project, I keep most books and influences aside and limit my reading, except for those that can directly catalyze my thoughts on my current project. To assist in this book, for example, I am currently reading the perceptive observations on photography found in Robert Adam's book, *Art Can Help*, and the profound insights on art and creativity expressed in Rachel Corbett's book, *You Must Change Your Life: The Story of Rainer Maria Rilke and Auguste Rodin*.

I can ignore neither the soulful depth of the world or its depravity.

All art and photography form an interaction, a dialogue with culture, society, nature, other artists and photographers, and the conditions of the surrounding world. Art is born of its time—and place. What influences do you choose to receive? What sparks your passion, kindles your joy, and conflagrates your outrage? As a photographer, I work from both bliss and anger. They are equally and powerfully stimulating. I find bliss in moments of unity discovered through the camera lens with people, the environment, and with the exquisite splendor of the everyday. And I experience much dismay and anger toward the collective conditions that are destroying the environment, creating vast injustices and inequalities, and leaving behind a broken world for our children. I can ignore neither the soulful depth of the world or its depravity.

We are what we eat. Or, perhaps better stated, what we eat, we become. My advice to artists and photographers is simple: become a person of *interest*. Look into and learn about the things you like, and find a respectful interaction with the things you do not like. Follow the threads of your questions and passionate concerns, look at and listen deeply to the works of artists, photographers, writers, musicians, and filmmakers. Stay tuned to contemporary culture and recent events. Enter a dialogue with the thoughts and works of others, both from centuries past and today. Above all, be democratic. Do not live in the echo chamber of your own mind. It will not serve your growth and the cultivation of in-seeing, the ability to know the conditions of others and to feel how they think and think about how they feel. Be tolerant and consciously take in ideas and impressions that run counter to your own way of seeing and thinking. All aspects of your education, knowledge, influences, background, and interactions with the world and people are focused into view whenever you snap the shutter. Much great art and writing comes through friction and harmony at the same time. Look at photographs you vehemently do not like as much as you look at pictures you love and enjoy. Both can be powerful learning experiences.

Beatles members John Lennon and Paul McCartney both vexed each other and loved each other. Through their profound differences *and* their similarities, they challenged each other, grinded against each other, and alternately inspired each other. Their friction created sparks that turned to flames that grew to bonfire proportions. Paul admitted recently to one astounding fact about his collaboration with John. "The most amazing fact about it is that every time we went to sit down—and it was normally about a three-hour writing session—we never came out without a finished song. So that was like 200 days that we sat down to do that. And never had a dry moment."

Who among us can say that every time we go into the world to take pictures or sit down at the keyboard to write, that we create an enduring work of creative expression?

Your mind can think fast and slow. The mind can be energized to quickly make connections and find synergy between disparate ideas and exciting impressions—and the mind can slow down and listen to the silence, in the unconscious where creative ideas gestate and bloom. Sculptor Auguste Rodin worked quickly, constantly, and incessantly—scrutinizing, revising, looking and weighing, and widely experimenting. The poet Rilke, who for a while was Rodin's student and studio companion, was the opposite. He sought solitude and silence, and wrote, "I must wait for the ringing in the silence," out of which his poems were born.

There is an art to knowing what can feed you and what conditions can deeply catalyze your creative flow. One simple mark of creative maturity is to find *your* muse.

River of Consciousness, Stream of Images

It's an exhilarating time to be a photographer. Opportunities abound to communicate using images of our own making within a global arena. We are, or can be, active producers of live content filtered through and expressing our observations, attitudes, intelligence, commitments—and conscience. While websites and all forms of social media rely on images, in my estimation one of the most important development for photographers in the 21st century is the swift adoption of Instagram by hundreds of millions of people in less than a decade.

I suppose all artists can say this, but I feel very lucky to have a medium that can both encourage the growth of my awareness and reflect my consciousness, reveal my internal terrain, and witness my interactions with the world and others. It is my personal stream of life. During the film era, I made an inviolable distinction between my use of the camera as a tool for making art and my "snapshots" of events, family, and friends. After childhood, I never mixed the two aims and purposes of the camera: to reflect my "serious" dialogue with the world, and to witness and document the everyday events of my life. This very mixture is the strength of Instagram and what makes it so appealing, seductive, and instructive.

I first became interested in Instagram several years ago in witnessing the image feed of photojournalist Lynsey Addario. Acclaimed for her photographs of displacement, genocide, armed conflict, and violations of human rights in war-torn regions, she is best known for her commitment to the plight of women in traditional societies, including her project on the suffering and human dignity of rape victims in the Congo. Her Instagram feed is a study in contrasts. She has photographs of conflict-ridden zones and portraits of victims of sexual violence all mixed together with her grandmother's birthday party, her children's daily joys, and promotional images of her book and public events. Her feed truly represents the multiple streams of her life, her engagements, and the many dimensions of her thought.

As a child, I was obsessed with reading biographies. I loved the behind-the-scenes look at how great men and women were shaped into becoming who they are. I

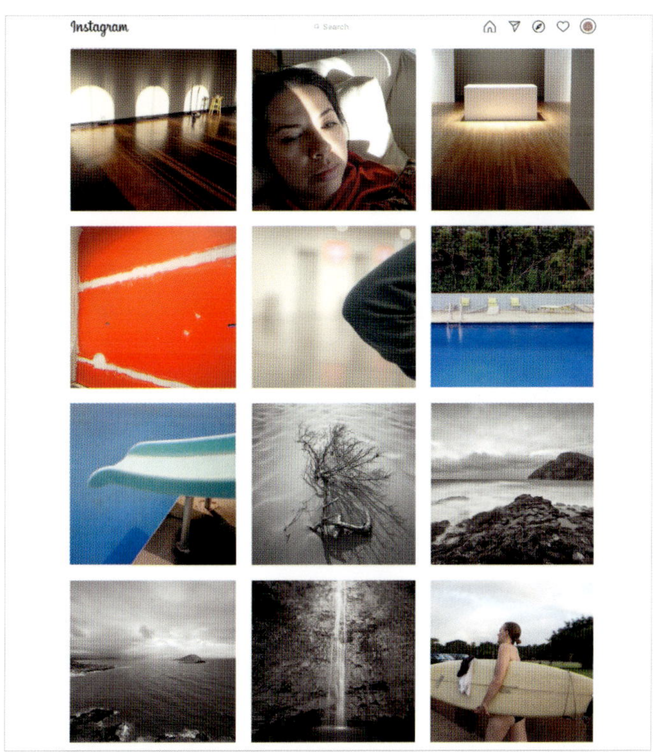

Instagram Feed, David Ulrich

appreciated the opportunity to see their flaws and struggles in light of their achievements. And, I believe, this is what Instagram offers: an inside view of a life, from the mundane to the profound, and from the spontaneous, unrehearsed private moments to the thoughtful and considered expression of our deepest commitments. It can reflect the true range of our humanity, like a diary or journal. Let's allow it to do so. Our histories and present perceptions can be integrated, shaped into a river of consciousness, and become instructive and inspiring for oneself and others. Instagram contains a great potential for both self-knowledge and self-expression, equally at once, and all rolled into an easy, elegant platform.

You do not need to be good or skilled at photography to use Instagram. It is highly democratic. You might use Instagram as a visual journal of all the impressions that cross your path that move you in any way. As artists, we need to shake loose the creative mind, access the reservoir of the unconscious, and help release its insight—making its contents conscious. Nightly dreams often reflect aspects of our character and being that are hidden from view and often in opposition to how our conscious mind sees the world. Instagram can be used in the same way, as "dreams with a memory," as Minor White often called photographs.

By photographing frequently, daily, and all the moments that you find interesting, you are uncovering the many dimensions of your being. And you are exposing yourself to being seen, a powerful and necessary step in creative and psychological development. You are offering others a glimpse of truth of the shape of your terrain and the forces that sculpted it.

And what about ego—the false construction of self that inflicts us all with its insistent, distorting influence? Do we use image making for self-display or self-knowledge? Do we employ Instagram to speak the truth of our self and our genuine perceptions of the world, or to create a facade, the brand called me? Many communities and sub-communities exist within Instagram's broad reach: celebrity culture, fashionistas, food aficionados, business promotion, and travel junkies as well as serious practitioners of the medium and everyday people showing everyday moments. I think we all need to ask: Is my stream of images opening dialogue, supporting the development of human potential—individually and collectively—healing this broken world, and nourishing the hearts and minds of others? Or, is my feed merely designed to seek admiration and the shallow satisfaction of an ego boost? Our conscience can know the difference if we look hard and reflect. We all have an ego and, at some point or another, when we are ready, need to form a wave of resistance to its dehumanizing voices. One important aspect of the search for enlivened creativity is the cultivation of an attentive curiosity of the world we live in. Instagram teaches us to look up and look around, all the while staying in contact with and using the shamanistic power of our captivating devices. Taking pictures in this way can help us be more fully in the moment, present to ourselves and the world in equal measure.

Many serious photographers have turned to Instagram as a form of communication and exhibition. Instagram is a publishing platform and offers a way of having an immediate visual dialogue with those that are already familiar with you and your work, and with those that are discovering your insights for the first time. It is a form of creative practice.

Rodin's advice to Rilke was *travaille, toujours travaille* (work, always work). By working daily behind the lens, you are tuning yourself to the world and to your own process.

In my experience, the strongest work arises when we come to a state of creative momentum, a synchronizing of ourselves with our tools, our thought and perception, and with the world itself. This momentum does not take place immediately. We must work for it, by working regularly with a camera. The use of Instagram as a daily journal of our thoughts, impressions, and the moments that make our heart beat faster can actuate our creative forces and entrust us with a stage to responsibly share with and reach out to diverse others. It constructs visual histories that chronicle the many streams of our lives.

Why Selfies?

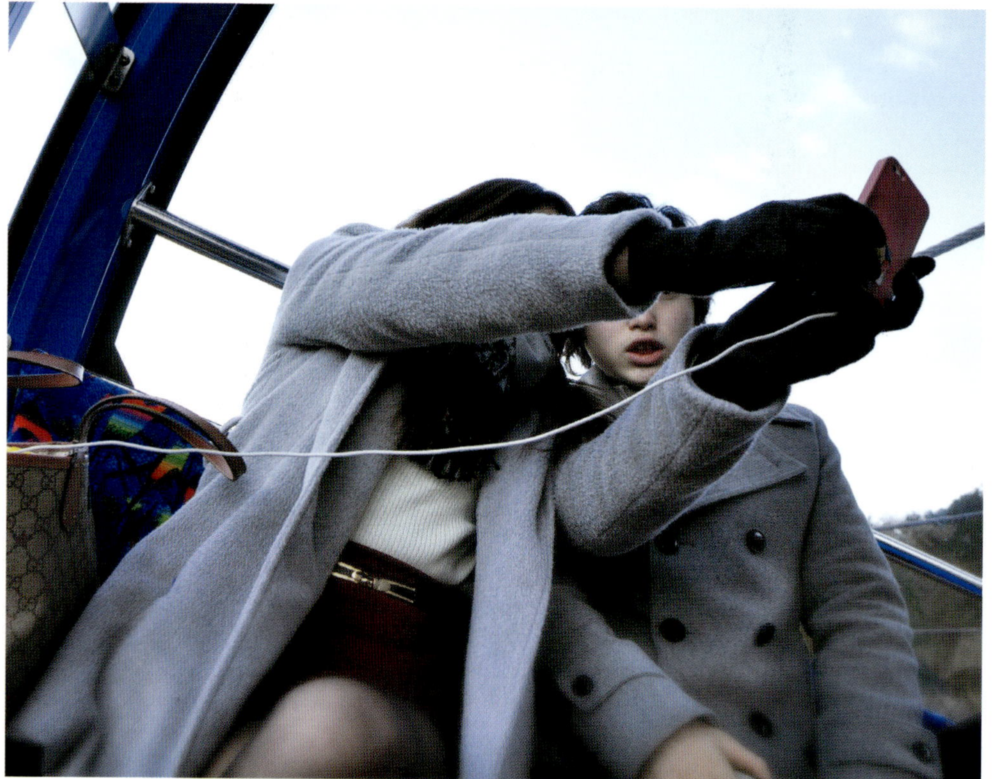

Selfie, Steven Lum

I get it—to some degree. The camera proves I was *here,* in this place, in this time, and with this other. It's reassuring to have a memory prompt. Further, we all have our insecurities and need to feel loved and acknowledged. It's a normal, healthy, human need. Posting photos of oneself and counting likes provides a powerful boost of dopamine. But it does not and cannot give real love. Counting likes is not equivalent to the earned satisfaction of accomplishment and personal triumph.

Incessant selfie takers need to ask: is the act of posting photos of your carefully considered face, your body on an exotic beach, cool and jaded eyes, and exuberant smiles a substitute for something else? In the same way the Beatle's once sang, "can't buy me love," our perfectly posed selfies cannot fill the empty places within—no matter how hard we try.

Natalie Goldberg has a chapter in *Writing Down the Bones* called "Don't Use Writing to Get Love." In it, she writes (please substitute the word writing with photography): "Writers get confused. We think writing gives us an excuse for being alive. We forget that being alive is unconditional and that life and writing are two separate entities. Often we use writing as a way to receive notice, attention, love. 'See what I wrote. I must be a good person.' We *are* good people before we even write a word."

We need to know that we are good and beautiful or handsome, and that we fit in. The social pressures today among young people to conform to a standard of beauty promulgated by images and the media are enormous. Even if we know that these standards are impossibly unrealistic, our unconscious has been seeded since birth with these de-humanizing images of Barbie and Ken dolls. It can be very difficult to feel good about yourself in the face of media distortions, especially if you are of another skin color or body type than most models. Thus, young people flock to selfies. It's a way of recognizing one's personal power.

But is there another way? Something happens on the path toward maturity for healthy people. We stop giving our primary attention to the ego self and begin to focus on the reality and needs of others, and of society itself. Do we want to perpetuate negative stereotypes in our own images and on our own social feed? What we pay attention to, where our enthusiasms are found, can inform the content of strong, meaningful images. The camera provides a path back into the world and it offers a means for genuine self-exploration.

Here, we begin to focus on the deeper aspects of self and our connections with the world and others. Seeing the self and witnessing the other simultaneously form the dialectical power of photography. Every photograph is of something in the world and every photograph is a self-portrait—mirrors and windows, both at the same time. With a camera, we can grapple with the more complex aspects of our identity beyond surface appearance: race, ethnicity, psychological dynamics, heredity and conditioning, sexuality, gender, economic status, personal evolution, and many other factors that contribute to our unique individuality. As a powerful alternative to selfies, try making images that show who you are *without* using yourself as the subject. Use allusion, metaphor, concept, mirroring—and find resonance. Seek your inner reflection in the outer world. Self-portrayal through images that reveal your unique background, character, and circumstances—not just your appearance—is one of the great aims of art. Here we use the camera as a mirror.

Then turn the tables and use the camera in another way, one that supports its power to pay dispassionate attention. Make an image of a person, place, or thing that reveals its essence and character beyond your opinions and preconceptions. Use your senses, mind, and heart—your deepest attention—to understand and convey something about the inherent truth of something or someone else. Here we use the camera as a window.

Robert Adams writes succinctly about landscape photographs, but his powerful statement reflects the potential of all forms of photography. Geography here is taken to mean an attention to the realities of the subject itself, the photograph as document. "Landscape pictures can offer us, I think, three verities—geography, autobiography, and metaphor. Geography is, if taken alone, sometimes boring, autobiography is frequently trivial, and metaphor can be dubious. But taken together… the three kinds of information strengthen each other and reinforce what we all work to keep intact—and affection for life."

Selfies are often merely the path of least resistance. I think the selfie impulse springs from a healthy need—to understand yourself and make your mark upon the world. With selfies, we observe and interact with what is closest-at-hand, our appearance and ego self. The essential key for all forms of photography is observation. Direct perception in the present moment—of self and other—is a form of knowing that cannot be substituted by mediated perceptions found in entertainment, books, websites, blogs, and other people's images. Mindful looking implies self-observation and looking outward simultaneously to awaken to our own genuine points of connection with the world. A moment of seeing with a camera connects our inner states directly with the realities of life beyond our eyes. We are led inward and outward simultaneously.

Self-discovery through a camera? I am scared to look for fear of discovering how shallow my Self is! I will persist however… Camera will lead my constant introspection back into the world.
—Minor White from *Mirrors, Messages, Manifestations*

When to Put the Camera Down

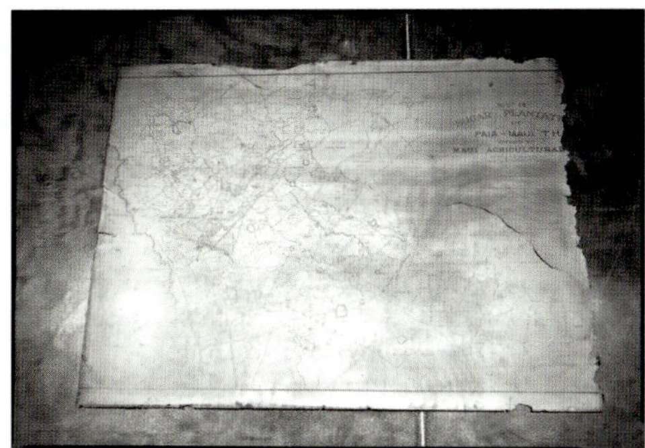

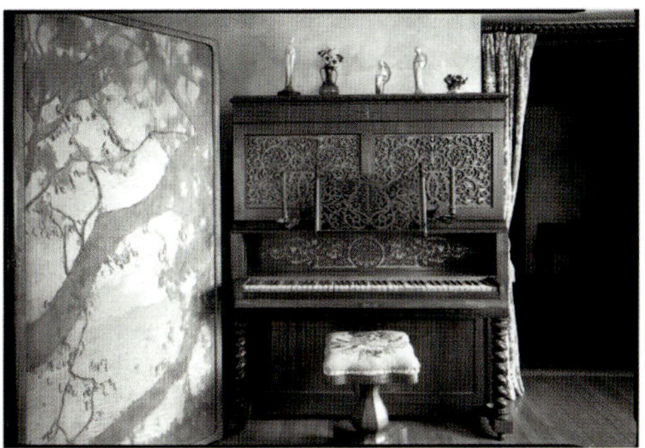

1917 Map of Sugar Production and Imported Piano, Maui, Hawai'i, from the project, *Dreams of Hope. Legacies of Power,* David Ulrich

With permission, I photographed within a home of the missionary descendants in Hawai'i. Since my approach was critical of sugar production, I waited until after the death of their matriarch, who graciously offered me access, to publish or exhibit these images.

Constraints are essential in any art form. Without limits, both life and art would be diffuse and undifferentiated. Poetry and prose have their own conventions of language, grammar, and structure. So too does painting and photography—and all the visual arts. Creativity can soar by freely accepting and even pushing against the limits inherent in your medium—and by acceding to the boundaries set by your conscience and ethical beliefs.

Digital photography opens the entire world to a camera. Respect for private spaces and moments has gone out of fashion with cell phone pictures. Digital camera usage is ubiquitous and often seems immune to polite restraints. I once had to ask an acquaintance taking photographs indiscriminately in my home without asking permission to not point his camera in certain directions. He was offended and couldn't understand how or why I might limit his cell phone creativity, especially since I am a photographer. My rationale had to do with privacy and vulnerability. I didn't want certain items of high value to be plastered over social media, potentially with location services activated on his phone. Surprisingly, he never considered this in whipping out his camera. He also did not know that it is illegal to photograph in private spaces without the owner's explicit permission.

This is the age of consent. We have a legal and ethical responsibility to ask permission when photographing in privately-owned spaces, except large stadiums and malls, which for purposes of law are considered public. The owners of these large spaces, however, may restrict photographers and that is within their clear prerogative. We have a moral responsibility to ask permission in certain situations or cultures. For instance, from a cultural perspective, it is not okay to photograph someone's children in Hawai'i without seeking permission from a parent.

Common sense should prevail. Do you trust everyone online? Do you want to be responsible because a child or teenager was harmed due to your photograph and location spread over social media? You can legally photograph people in public spaces freely. Free expression is one of our most fundamental rights. The vigorous flow and exchange of ideas and opinions expands our minds, can help create tolerance and respect, and supports both innovation and broad, diverse creative expression.

What are our attitudes toward people that *are* in public spaces? If someone is suffering or grieving, or in a compromising situation, what is our ethical stance with a camera? Do we respect their desire for privacy? Someone may choose not to be photographed for very good reasons. They may be hiding from an abusive spouse and not want to be found. Or, in an instance I encountered, their life and family could be endangered if their location was made public in countries where they fear kidnapping for ransom. They may have a justifiable need for privacy. Photojournalists often make the argument that the value of reporting the news trumps the wishes of private individuals. Most photographers need to grapple with the question, at some point, of whether to take the picture or back off and allow someone their privacy.

A documentary photography teacher once perceptively remarked that we are often most comfortable photographing people at a lower station in life than our own. Young middle-class photographers seem inexorably attracted to photographing the down-and-out, the homeless, and the rural poor. Photographing people in such a way that you see them as merely a visually interesting "basket of deplorables," seems to me mostly a function of ego and asserting one's moral superiority—all the while showing a profound lack of respect and understanding toward others.

I have seen many photo projects of the down-and-out that were made for very good reasons: to stimulate social change, to reflect and reveal the inherent humanity of others, to foster support for suffering people in various kinds of plights, and to engender deep empathy and compassion.

Does the legal right to free expression outweigh our ethical obligations of consideration and empathy toward others? Sometimes photographers can have blinders on by holding the attitude that "getting" the photo is of prime importance regardless of the cost to the subject. At mid-century, there was a common phrase known as the "ugly American," that referred to entitled westerners traveling to other countries for mere enrichment and enjoyment and not leaving their cultural baggage at home, expecting other people to conform with their attitudes, food choices, and social conventions. *Saturday Review* magazine once featured this form of privilege with an article titled, "The Third World as Tourist Theme Park."

Resourceful individuals are lucky to be able to deeply enrich their lives by trekking in Nepal, hiking the Inca trail, investigating the sacred sites of India, Polynesia, and the Southwest, experiencing the historical treasures of Europe, and many other powerful cultural explorations. But I think we always need to ask some questions before boldly gesturing indiscriminately with our camera lens or cell phone. Have we done our homework? Do we know the cultural conventions and protocols of where we are, in this place and in this time?

Do our activities enrich or exploit the lives of others? Are we perpetuating negative stereotypes, depersonalizing someone by making them exotic, or showing disrespect and violating deeply held cultural standards?

Do we really need the image of the toothless, elderly woman with a lined face and dressed in highly colorful garb? Why are we taking the picture—to impress others or to honor and dignify the human being in front of the camera? Often, the relevance and meaning of an image depends on the photographer's approach and intent. Documenting the world can be instructive to your audience. It can help engender empathy for others and give awareness of their conditions. Or it can be a selfish and narrow-minded act.

As a photography teacher for over forty years, I have seen it all: both insensitive exploitation and touching respect. Once, I had a flight attendant as a student. She returned from a trip to Kobe, Japan, days after the major earthquake. In class, she was chattering excitedly about her images of visually haunting forms of twisted metal, charred remains of neighborhoods, and gaping cracks in the earth. I admit, the photographs were visually powerful—but it was just plain wrong. She showed a selfie with her outfit of pristine white shorts, Colgate-white sneakers, and a cute designer handbag, while complaining about how the residents of the city treated her poorly and impeded her visual investigation. I don't think it occurred to her that they were probably urgently searching for survivors.

Some things are best left alone. Put your camera down.

Mindful Sight

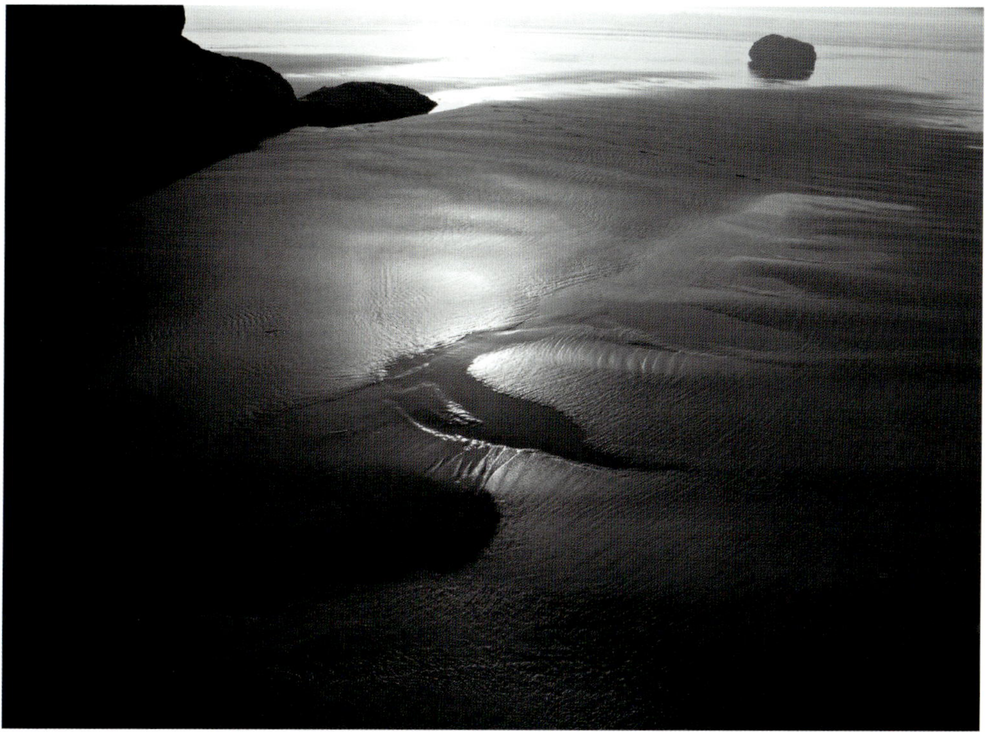

Zig Zag Rocks, Oregon Coast, Nicholas Hlobeczy

Awakened perceptions have power and force. They are a natural high. Sometimes in acute moments such as in great love, sexual contact, trauma, and childbirth, or in making a great discovery, we feel unmistakably *here*, wholly occupied in the present moment. Our senses are tuned and alive, our minds clear, and our heart is wide open. There is nothing else but the eternal now. Our entire being is focused on the head of the pin of *this* moment.

Do you know this experience? Sometimes presence comes through fortuitous circumstances or in contact with nature such as the dome of the sky and stars on a moonless night, or in the shock of new encounters. Moments of presence can also be engendered by our own volition, through our own efforts toward mindful perception with a camera. We use the camera in our hand as a reminder to try to awaken to the present moment and all that it contains.

How do we approach this essential task? The key is given in all the world's great teachings and is, perhaps, best known to us in the Buddhist approach to mindfulness. In mindful attention, we simply strive to become aware of our facts in the moment. We look within, impartially and without judgment, at the movement of breath, the various stirrings within the body, areas of tension and relaxation, and the rhythm of our bodily movements. We observe the mind, the coming and going of thought—without fixating or attaching our attention on the stray thought forms that arise naturally. Thoughts pass the screen of our awareness like clouds moving across the sky. And we merely take note of our emotions, be they agitated or peaceful or anywhere in between, again without judgment and without fixation. We look at them but allow them their space and strive to be aware of their influence on our inner state. We attempt the nearly impossible—the approach is what is important—to simply be, not grasping or seeking any result from our efforts.

The body and mind begin to relax and become more awake, fluid, and present.

We become conscious of our body moving through space and have a global awareness of the self from the mind's witness. The mind quiets. When the body and mind come together; when the mind's attention is brought into the body, a new quality of feeling can emerge—one that is responsive and becomes a way of knowing that can feel into the subject. Sight becomes acute; the senses enliven. From this more centered state, we can look outward and make photographs.

In this striving toward mindfulness as photographers, we locate some of our attention toward our mind and inner conditions, observing them as impartially as possible, without judgment. The rest of our attention is directed toward the subject of our interest. As we look outward, we observe that the objects of our attention stimulate widely varying responses in the body, mind, and emotions. We strive to stay present, focused on the moment of interaction. Metaphorically, we can say that one eye is turned inward; the other outward. The dynamic between the inner view and outer view is what shapes our camera vision.

Photographer Cartier-Bresson writes, "I believe that, through the act of living, the discovery of oneself is made concurrently with the discovery of the world around us, which can mold us, but which can also be affected by us. A balance must be established between these two worlds—the one inside us and the one outside us. As the result of a constant reciprocal process, both these worlds come to form a single one. And it is this world that we must communicate."

The eye of the mind, the eye of the heart, the eye of the body; these are limited forms of perception—partial, incomplete. Mindful seeing integrates the vision of the eyes, mind, and heart—and intuition—into a broad and embracing field of awareness that can resonate with the outer world. Think of yourself like a tuning fork. The impressions you receive of the world resound within your body, mind, and emotions—like a musical instrument—playing on the strings of your open and receptive sensitivity. Different sounds emerge from various outer and inner impressions. You watch and wait, carefully and sensitively, with your hand on the shutter. When an impression is received that touches you deeply; when you see something that corresponds to the movements of your own mind; when your heart is touched or your senses rocked, you snap the shutter. Without question and without thinking; the time for thought is before you take the exposure.

The life of the subject penetrates your life. An uncommon clarity infuses your vision of the world. You are awake and alive and no longer fragmented into parts. You recognize many aspects of the subject that hitherto went unseen and unacknowledged. Your attention is both sharp and broad, and you see into things in a way that the camera cannot help but capture. Your photographs made with mindful seeing are infused with your present attention and expanded awareness.

Attention begets attention. Images made in this way touch and awaken presence in the viewer. It is a sharing of consciousness, brought to life by your mindful seeing and your devotion to the craft of picture making. This state of awareness is not easy. It is hard-earned and easily broken by the noisy mind, intrusive emotions, and ordinary distractions such as thinking about dinner, hearing the shrill sound of multiple cell phone notifications, and a wandering attention attracted by all kinds of inner and outer stimulation. Several exercises can help.

Try sitting quietly in state of mindful awareness every day, perhaps for fifteen or twenty minutes. Sitting on a regular basis serves to water the seeds of awareness that can extend into the day and into your life. Try to return to that state of quiet awareness periodically throughout the day, by coming in touch with your breathing, or settling into the body and bringing attention inward, allowing muscles to relax and the mind to quiet. An exercise that has served me well over the years, and can contribute to mindful seeing, is to become aware of my feet on the ground and the actual sensation of my body moving through space, such as when I'm walking up and down and around the subject. I have also found it highly useful to remember physicist David Bohm's reminder to be aware of the "proprioception" of thought, and to scrutinize how my thoughts, perceptions, and impressions of the outer world awaken certain inner sensations and feelings. An inner measure of authenticity for your own images can be discovered.

In my own experience, images made through mindful sight, when I am able to be more awake and alive in the world, are the ones that stay in my portfolio, that generate the most intense response from others, and hold content that nourishes and instructs for months and years. These are the photographs that I can call my own, their authenticity and presence ring out like bells in the night that reverberate outward to those in synch and in sympathy with the search for an awakening mind.

Creative Time

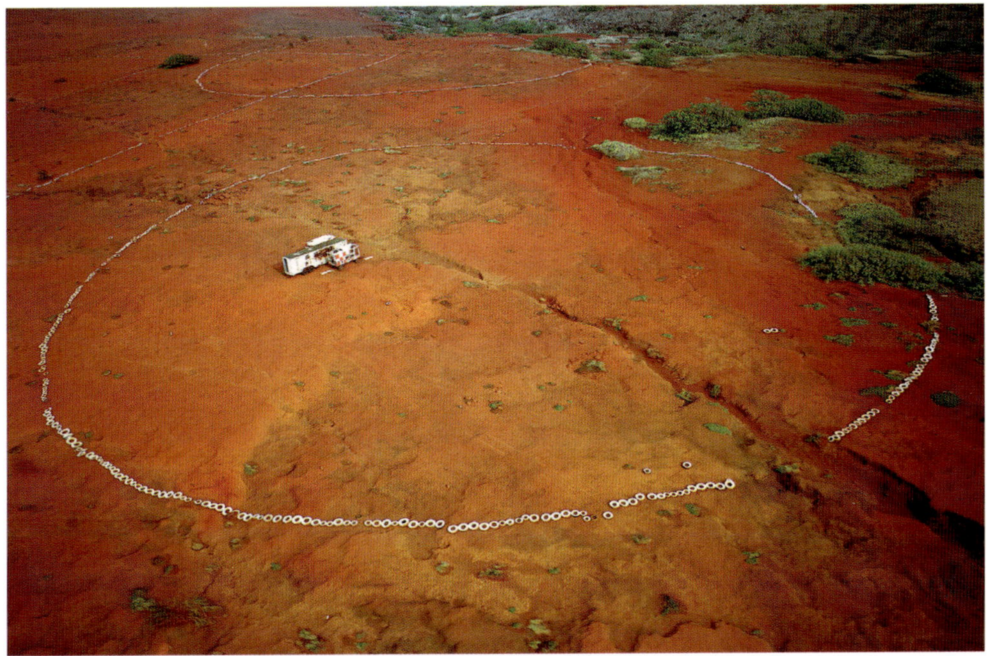

Military Bombing Target, Kaho'olawe, Hawai'i, David Ulrich

As a photographer and writer, I work quickly. I like to do my research on a topic for an upcoming project, contemplate the potential story, and live my inquiry over a long period of advance time. Then when it comes time to write or make images, I swoop vigorously into the project and work intensely in a focused manner to the exclusion of other tasks and responsibilities. I can write the first draft of a book, or see the initial shape of a photographic project, in a matter of weeks or months. The first draft of *Zen Camera* appeared in five concentrated weeks of writing.

But there is a clear paradox here. I measure the progression of most of my creative projects in years and decades. It can take me nearly a decade or more to fully unfold and complete a photographic project. When curators ask to see recent work, I often wonder what do they mean by *recent*? Usually, current work means from the past year or two. For me, recent work can extend backward in time over a number of years.

In one major project, two other photographers and I, along with an archaeologist/ guide, were commissioned to document the Hawaiian island of Kahoʻolawe for a book and traveling exhibition. Smallest of the eight principal Hawaiian islands, Kahoʻolawe is sacred to the Hawaiian people with nearly 3,000 archeological sites and features.

On December 8, 1941, the day after Pearl Harbor, the entire island was commandeered by the U.S. military to use as a target range for ordnance training in the form of jet strafing and bombing and artillery practice from ships. Never before had I encountered land with such powerful *mana* (spiritual power), nor a landscape so thoroughly devastated by colonial power and military might. Thousands of bombs, some weighing up to 500 pounds each, were detonated on the island and in the surrounding waters. It was, and is, a tragic study in contrasts.

The actual photography was accomplished in less than two years with fourteen to sixteen trips to the island. We were paid for four. It became a labor of love to interpret and express our observations of this fragile, wounded land. Then I spent a year in the darkroom poring over and editing contact sheets, making selections, and making proof and reproduction prints for the book. The following year was also devoted to the darkroom, crafting high-quality, large prints for the exhibition venues. Following that, we traveled to many of the exhibition locations and interacted with viewers. The project finally closed over nine years after it began with an exhibition in Washington D.C. at the Smithsonian. To this day, I am still editing and tinkering with the photographs, finding evocative negatives I did not recognize at the time of their making. I was, and am, passionate about the cause of the island and its meaning for the people of Hawaiʻi.

One measure of meaning in a photographic image is the degree of the artist's engagement with the subject or idea. Indifference and half-heartedness are antithetical to the creative process. The unfoldment of your creativity is better served by a short or long-term engagement with a subject or theme that rocks your world rather than with stray, single images; "monumental tombstones," as Minor White calls them. A project that takes place over time can encourage many things. It can be an enriching learning experience that kindles an ardent engagement with the subject through an in-depth exploration. Working on projects builds a momentum and lights a creative fire that awakens your mind and informs your vision. Further, projects provide a useful structure for your work and get you out the door, as well as create opportunities for growth-producing challenges that put your back against the wall, and once met, can bring about the triumph of personal accomplishment. For me, most of my strongest, enduring images have grown directly out of long-term projects.

How do you identify a project? Start modestly with something that can be realistically accomplished. Photography is a form of storytelling. What story are you moved to tell? What do you know and care about, and what interests and enthusiasms do you have outside of photography? Choose a project that is invested with meaning, in which you feel a passionate engagement that energizes you and keeps alive a sense of abiding curiosity. Over time, the work should possess you. Find your areas of deep kinship with the world that you can reasonably bite into with a camera in months or a year's time. What kind of inquiry will enrich your life and become a deep learning experience?

Maybe it's something about your life or identity. Or, it could grow from your observations and passions about social conditions, politics, or the environment. It could be a visual diary of some form of self-exploration. Or, maybe it's an investigation of color, form, or a certain type of technique. One definite word of advice: do not define your project too tightly. Leave room for serendipity and in-process discovery of unexpected themes or emerging ideas. Keep some space in your mind and working practice for unconscious insights to appear that may move and shift your direction. Allow your project to evolve naturally in creative time, not linear time.

Identify what works for you, where you can have a resonant, fluid exchange between the world and the human being behind the lens.

In this there is no measuring with time, a year doesn't matter, and ten years are nothing. Being an artist means: not numbering and counting, but ripening like a tree, which doesn't force its sap, and stands confidently in the storms of spring, not afraid that afterward summer may come. It does come. But it comes only to those who are patient…
—*Rainer Maria Rilke*, from *Letters to a Young Poet*

Minding the Darkness

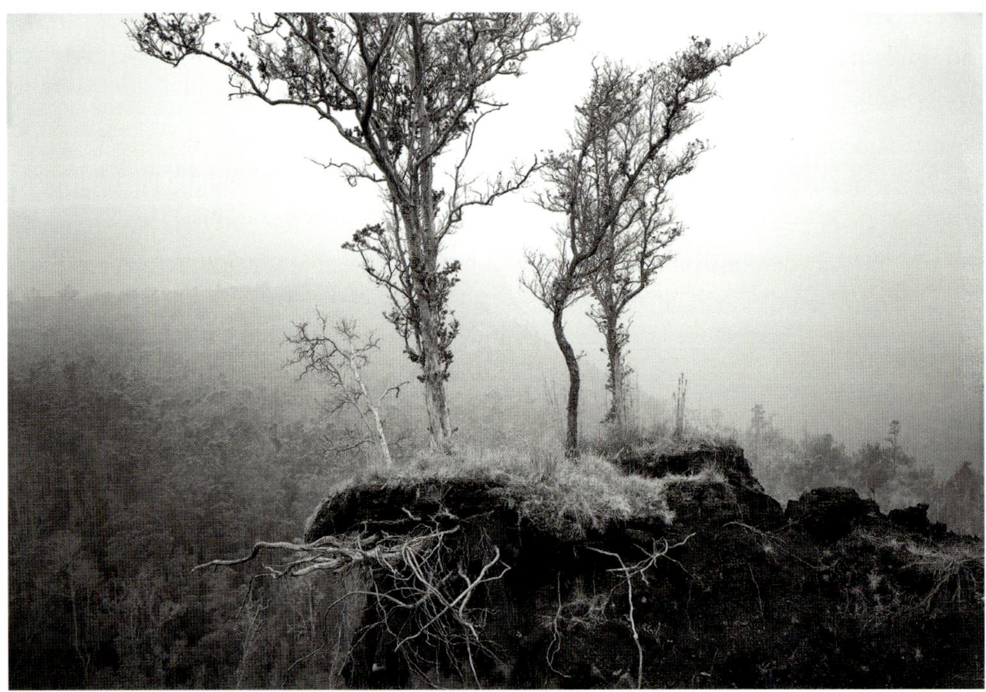

Crater Rim, Kilaeau Volcano, Hawai'i, from the series, *Hawai'i: Landscape of Transformation,*
David Ulrich

None of us are immune from suffering. Darkness and light are both inherent in the human condition. Whether suffering stems from the inner world (pain, depression, illness) or from the outer world (injustice, inequality, forms of violence), the complicated emotions and experiences that arise can deeply serve our creative process with photography or any art medium.

As a young man of 33, I enjoyed a reputation as a successful photographer and was at the height of my physical prowess. That year, I bought a house and reveled in the challenge of home renovation. I muscled through a good deal of the work without assistance, on my own steam. On a fateful Sunday morning in August, while cutting and stacking wood, a large stick was dislodged and flew out from the woodpile striking my face directly under my right, dominant eye. I was rushed to the emergency room and discovered I had suffered a massive retinal tear. After eight hours in surgery, I was told that I would never see out of my right eye again for the rest of my life, and that it should be removed. The weeks surrounding the second surgery, in which they removed my eye and implanted a prosthetic, were scary and debilitating. I did not know if I could ever be a whole and happy human being again.

Several years after the injury, I wrote a passage for my first book. "Fearing the loss of my capacity to see and photograph, and with all hope to the contrary, this blow helped to awaken my own awareness. Losing an eye and facing the resulting need to learn to see again, this time as an adult, assisted the growth and development of my perceptual capacities—and helped me better understand the function and process of sight. Above all, I learned to not take vision for granted. It was a profound learning experience, one that continues to this day. The experience was traumatic and painful—like nothing else I have ever experienced—and a great privilege."

By honoring the difficult, we give voice to central aspects of the human condition.

I embarked on several photographic projects that reflected the death and transformative rebirth found in the volcanic landscape of Hawai'i. These images documented the powerful landscape but were also potent metaphors of my own experience of loss and fragile healing. I soon learned that the images I made, as well as my writing about creativity and perception that grew directly from my injury, served to nourish, instruct, and mirror the experiences of others who suffered painful experiences.

Entering your personal domain of darkness can be enlightening and can help make you whole. There can be no completeness, no living on the light, without first encountering and eventually integrating our shadow. Likewise, pain, injury, and illness—if approached with awareness—can be deeply transformative. These kinds of experiences can help weed out some of the pettiness and ego concerns that govern part of our lives. All forms of suffering can be worked with through a camera in ways that help you and others simultaneously.

After losing friends in Vietnam and witnessing the Kent State shootings, I felt raw and disturbed by the violence that was closing in around me. I began to make metaphoric images of dead animals, burning baby dolls, and the advent of light within darkness. One image of a burst of light interacting with shadowy blacks in a reflecting pool helped me realize that deep within me there was hope—the hope of consciousness.

Seeing this overspreading light within the dark field mirrored my belief that consciousness alone was the force that could bring positive change into our lives as individuals and in societies.

Other photographers work in similar metaphoric ways. Richard Misrach's project, *On the Beach*, consists of large format photographs looking down from a hotel window in Honolulu on people in an uncertain relationship with the water at the edge of the vast, mysterious ocean. The motivation for these photographs came, in part, from the events of 9/11. He writes: "I was drawn to the fragility and grace of the human figure in the landscape. My thinking about this work was influenced by the events of 9/11, particularly by the images of individuals and couples falling from the World Trade Towers, as well as by the 1950s Cold War novel and film, *On the Beach*. Paradise has become an uneasy dwelling place; the sublime sea frames our vulnerability, the precious nature of life itself."

Many strategies can be employed to explore complicated emotions. You can approach it directly through forms of self-portrayal. Or, you can employ metaphor and allusion or symbolism. Or, you might use a conceptual approach and stage images that use yourself or others to express aspects of your private reality. The work of Cindy Sherman comes to mind. In another instance, African-American artist Carrie Mae Weems photographs herself, clad in black, standing with her back to the camera as a looming, shadowy figure outside the gates of prominent art museums in which her work has been excluded. In *The Museum Series*, she is exploring the legacy of race and gender inequality, and whose histories are given access and featured within the museums.

Artists can "universalize" aspects of their very private experiences to make them accessible and meaningful to others.

Documentary photographers often confront pain and suffering on a daily basis. The images they record can touch us in ways that engender empathy—and possibly spring forth direct support—for individuals in trying circumstances. By shedding light, we are bringing awareness and attention to their plight. If we approach making images for the right reasons, and not to exploit or condemn, we are offering a service of expanding knowledge and expanding awareness in viewers.

People can be released from their suffering—for a moment or a while—through your affirmation and the mirror of your understanding. They can traverse your journey with you, as you can with them, through the simple act of attending to the painful and shadow parts of your being with a camera. By honoring the difficult, we give voice to central aspects of the human condition.

The Potency of Metaphor

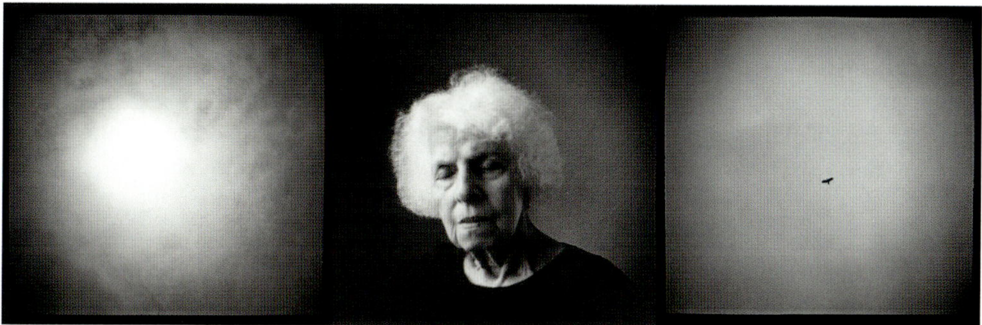

Dementia and Transience #3, My Mother Annie, St. Paul Minnesota, 2002, © Franco Salmoiraghi

On his use of a plastic, toy Diana camera to photograph his mother's dementia, Salmoiraghi reflects, "In the Diana camera photographs, I was able to feel her experiences of fuzziness of thought, a sense of timelessness and an alteration of space perception which caused a distancing from her previous reality."

Ralph Waldo Emerson observes in his essay, *Nature*: "Every appearance in nature corresponds to some state of the mind, and that state of the mind can only be described by presenting that natural appearance as its picture.… A lamb is innocence; a snake is subtle spite; flowers express to us the delicate affections. Light and darkness are our familiar expression for knowledge and ignorance; and heat for love."

I would venture to say that most photographs contain some form of metaphor. When you represent a thing, what the viewer sees is not the thing itself, but a metaphoric allusion by the artist that points to the subject portrayed. Many images contain metaphors of the state of mind of the artist who created them or the society to which a person belongs—or often a measure of both. Metaphor is a powerful way of signifying your own unique way of seeing. Photographer Robert Adams claims, "Both poetry and photography tend toward metaphor."

How do we understand metaphor? The Big Apple of course is not a giant apple; it's a metaphor for New York and its centrality in world culture. Or the City of Light hasn't any more light than other places at the same latitude. It's a metaphor for the luminous nature of Paris in history and romantic legend. Both of these are effective metaphors because they are unique and memorable, symbolic and highly descriptive.

Artists and writers develop their own unique metaphors that serve to effectively capture their experience. Poet W.B. Yeats had his tower; Maya Angelou her caged bird. Photographer Alfred Stieglitz employed clouds as metaphors and Georgia O'Keeffe used flowers. To observe a brilliant use of visual thinking and metaphor in photography, study Teju Cole's book, *Blind Spot*, consisting of personal essays and images. Each short essay relates to observations of a location to which he has traveled accompanied by an image. Most of the images are metaphoric and not literal companions of the subject featured in the written text. They are often unexpected and fresh and capture highly original visual thinking. Cole is the former *New York Times* photography reviewer and is conversant with metaphor in both photography and writing.

Even documentary photographers use metaphor in a way that can amplify content. For example, I am deeply impressed by how Robert Frank employs metaphor in his seminal book, *The Americans*. In one photograph, *Charleston, South Carolina, 1955*, an African American nanny holds a well-appointed white baby in her arms. The tonal rendition of the photograph portrays an overwhelming "whiteness," interrupted only by the black skin tones of the nanny. The metaphoric use of tonality amplifies the indictment of racial inequality presented in the photograph. In another powerful image, three rotund men sit in a train club car, two with their backs to the camera. Their checkered sport coats refer to a kind of nouveau riche and are mirrored by a row of circular lights on top that are rounded much like the corpulence of the men's bodies. I can almost imagine the flashy rings on their pudgy fingers that are suggested by the shape and diamond-like style of the lights above.

Metaphors in photography rely on juxtaposition and connotation. Visual metaphors arise through connotative content in which one thing suggests or symbolizes something else. Metaphor can also take place with subjects that are related to another in the frame in a way that creates new meaning that goes beyond the literal content.

Study many photographs. Try to identify where and how metaphoric content is expressed. Metaphor is everpresent in photography. I have a photograph of burning sugar cane on Maui photographed in pre-dawn light. Burning sugar cane stalks is how they harvest the sugar. The entire image has a fiery red color with sugar cane and flame in the foreground. The background is an apocalyptic orange color with haunting light.

While the photograph documents the harvesting of cane, for me, it also a metaphor of the burning earth and how we treat the environment worldwide.

Be very careful in your work to avoid tired tropes and overused metaphors. Seek and find your own particular metaphors that are spontaneous and fresh yet fall within the parameters of a commonly used and intelligible visual vernacular. Look carefully at your own photographs made over long periods of time and examine consistent uses of light, the frame, color, form, and content. Are there recurring elements in your work? Can you observe metaphors that you return to frequently, naturally, and even unconsciously? Your unconscious responds to the world in ways that extend well beyond your conscious, rational perception. Gaining access to the deep reserves of the unconscious can help you discover your own unique symbolic and metaphoric language. It's a necessary step on the way to self-knowledge and a powerful means of personal expression.

The key is merely to be natural. See how you see. Don't edit or judge your photographic seeing. Allow it to unfold instinctively and effortlessly, but not without attention. Where do you find resonance with the world? Where are your points of connection, and how are they expressed? The depth of the unconscious will emerge whether you want it to or not. Our experience of the world speaks equally in literal, denotive content and metaphoric, connotative content. Explicit and implicit content balance and integrate together into a fullness of expression. Effective and unique, personal use of metaphor adds potency and dimension to your photographs—and provides levels of meaning that make an image a world unto itself and not merely a representation of the visible one.

Mapping the Internal Terrain

What is the shape of your inner landscape? Where lie your peaks and valleys, strengths and weaknesses, flowing streams of energy and blocked passages? Who am I? The eternal question is renewed in each individual and calls for not a fixed answer but a vigorous approach to uncovering the truths of your existence.

There cannot be a definitive answer; it shifts and changes throughout one's life. Your personality adjusts to changing conditions and your true nature hopefully grows and evolves from birth.

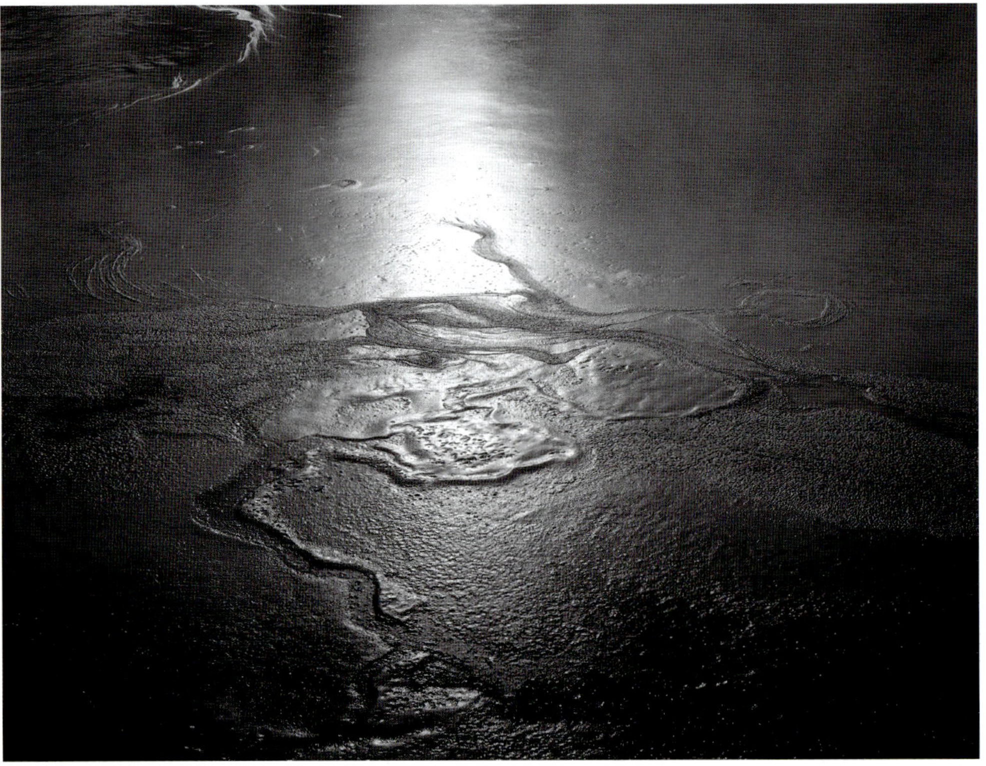

Ice & Light #2, Kent, Ohio, David Ulrich

There is an art to turning inward, and, in my experience, many art and photography students today don't feel the need for sustained, deep inner exploration. I don't want to generalize because some students emphatically embrace the discovery of their inner worlds. Often though, the inner search has been replaced with examinations of identity, the relativity of experience due to such factors as race, ethnicity, gender, socioeconomic status, sexual preference, and political views. Certainly, these factors are worthy of, and demand exploration. But all of these can be seen as the outer edge of our deepest nature. They do not constitute the whole of a human being and our complex dynamics.

Maybe it's an age-old theme. Some are hungry for inner wisdom and some locate meaning in the circumstances of external existence; and these are not mutually exclusive interests. I have been gifted through education and perhaps through my intrinsic nature with an understanding of symbol and metaphor—and know that photographs reflect the inner world of their maker in very precise and comprehensive ways.

Many of the ideas in this book can help one forge a dialogue with the world and culture through a camera. Here, I am espousing the foundational need to know oneself—as fully possible and in an ongoing manner. The search for one's true nature forms the heart of many of the world's wisdom traditions. In the best of worlds, art and photography can be allied with the means and tools of these traditions to offer deep insight into the nature of self and one's personal angels, demons, obstacles, and gifts. Many photographs can be explored and read as direct reflections of your inner world in light of both their literal and metaphoric content.

With the aim of self-knowledge, get to know your own personal metaphors and symbols, and observe how they recur in your work and, over time, grow and change. The things you most resonate with in the world represent pieces of yourself. After observing these recurring symbols, metaphors, and visual gestalts in your work, begin the process of interpretation and untangling their complicated meaning.

Whether you intend it or not, the photographs you take say as much or more about you than they do the subject. Study them with a critical eye. Let no detail be considered unimportant especially if you find yourself attracted to similar things again and again. Our attractions reflect our being. Images can show the outline of a current map of your internal terrain and they can also be prescient. I have seen, time and again, symbols appearing in my work that were confusing as to their source, only to discover, over time, that they were harbingers of a future condition in my life. In my photographic projects, I have noticed that certain images, often made toward the end of an exploration, seemed new and different and clearly did not fit within my current project. They raised new questions and generated new insights. I have come to deeply respect the revelations from the depths of the mind that often exceed my rational understanding.

In one instance, I was intuitively led to a place where I made a photograph of forms in ice that transfixed my attention in a kind of aesthetic arrest. I observed that these twisting, metaphoric shapes and forms were precise, *exact* transcriptions of my inner world. I could observe where in myself energy moved freely and where there were blockages and limitations.

Sometimes the metaphors found in nature or urbanity that are reflected in your photographs can be read freely as messages or manifestations from within. Learn to read your symbols and metaphors with a free imagination and without reservation. Simple word associations can help understand your own symbolic language. For example, when you see the shape of an outstretched tree appearing frequently in images, ask yourself what the *very* first word or concept is that comes to mind in response to its shape or form. Be free and do not edit or judge your associations. Just observe what comes to mind and see if you can relate your associations with the metaphor found in the photograph.

Looking at your own images in silence with a still mind can help. What rhythms and movements are felt in your body? What emotions arise? What do the metaphors and symbols evoke in your mind?

The characteristics and shape of your inner world—its harmonies, gifts, strengths, conflicts, complexes, and obstacles—are made visible if you can learn to read their mysterious language. The brain thinks in words and concepts, the unconscious speaks in metaphor, symbol, and allegory, often wordlessly with form. Thinking in form and color is part of the deeper language of the mind that we can learn to read. Look at works of art, beyond just photography. Study symbols themselves but remember that your symbolic language is personal and cannot be fully explicated through universal descriptions. Learn to use symbols and metaphors consciously, intentionally, and not only as features that bubble up spontaneously from the subconscious.

Treat this exploration as a question that doesn't have a fixed or definitive answer, but as a process in which the material unfolds organically through your study and your lived experience.

What Helps?

Photographer Harry Callahan, who taught at Rhode Island School Design in the '60s and '70s, was rumored to begin a class by deliberately tearing up a twenty-dollar bill (a good sum in those days) and send it sailing in pieces out the window, while saying, "*This* is photography."

The lesson is clear: photography asks for resources, time, and supportive conditions. Fortunately, the cost of entry for digital photography is affordable. Today's cell phone

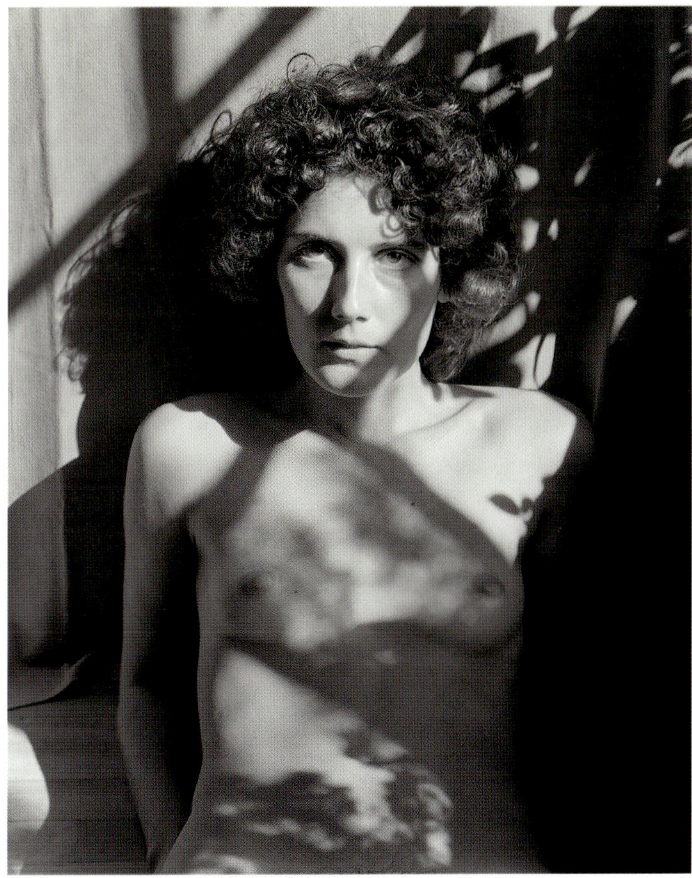

Mary Ann, David Ulrich
The year that I began my full-time teaching job, I had little time for creative work. To keep my creativity alive, I did portraits of the friends and partners nearest to me.

cameras have evolved to be of very high-quality and entry level prosumer cameras can be purchased for several hundred dollars. Tablet or cell phone apps that allow you to edit photos can be purchased for a nominal fee. Even the high-end Adobe programs for the desktop, Lightroom and Photoshop, are bought on a subscription plan for a reasonable monthly amount.

The challenge for many people is finding time for the creative focus needed for an active involvement with photography. The great modernist photographer, Edward Weston, writes in his *Daybooks*: "Peace and an hour's time—given these, one creates. Emotional heights are easily attained; peace and time are not." Most people have busy lives, with jobs, families, and multiple commitments. In the midst of this tyranny of urgent concerns, if we want to fulfill our creative lives, we need to create the right conditions.

Several strategies can help. First, discover a passionate interest. Maybe you are drawn to learn more about photography and engage it seriously. Or, certain subjects can capture your deepest attention. In other instances, you might love nature, and hiking and exploring with a camera brings you joy. You could feel strongly about something in the world, social realities or political conditions, that demand your attention. Whatever you feel strongly about is a call that should be followed. In my experience, when I have an intense absorption with a subject or topic, and I follow it with a camera or a pen, the strength of that interest inserts itself naturally into the rhythm of my daily schedule. I am surprised by how much time I can find to engage my passion. Other commitments seem to make way for my inner necessity. Once committed, I find an hour here, an afternoon there for the necessary engagement with my topic. And don't ignore the powerful tool of your cell phone. Whatever you might be doing, wherever you are, the cell phone camera can be used to sketch images and ideas, and keep your creative momentum flowing.

Second, learn what commitments are necessary to meet immediately, and which ones can wait and become secondary to your creative life. When in the midst of a compelling project, I easily turn a blind eye to mundane tasks that really do not need my attention in this moment. Laundry, house cleaning, paying bills, and cleaning out my email inbox can often wait several days or even a week. If your creative life is important, place it high on your list of priorities.

Third, see if you can enlist the aid of other people. Having a supportive community helps greatly in stimulating your creative flow. Talk to those closest to you about giving support and leaving room for your creative aspirations. Find other people with similar interests and view each other's photographs, go on field trips, and have dialogue about your aims and goals. Share your struggles and triumphs. Take a class, find a teacher, or join a camera club. Groups of people coming together with common interests and sympathy for each other's challenges on the path of learning can help give you energy and direction. Find trusted eyes that can look at your work and offer honest response.

Use online resources. Join the Instagram community or other forms of social media in which sharing images are the currency. Many groups devoted to photography or some particular aspect of the medium can be found online. Many learning resources are available on the internet.

Finally, and most difficult, look yourself squarely in the eye and take note of your own brands of neuroses. We all have them. Are you a perfectionist and impede your own progress through fear and a sense of inadequacy? Are you a people pleaser and spend your time being a "good" girl or boy to others while ignoring your own needs? Many of us are often lazy and do not like fighting against the resistance to move forward with something that is essential for our souls. If you find inner voices that say, "I am not good enough," or "I don't deserve this," or "what if I fail?" simply take note of those voices and continue anyway. Discipline doesn't arise all by itself. You need to get out the door in spite of your personal obstacles and demons.

The words, *in spite of* represent one of the greatest wisdoms we can incorporate in our creative lives. We work *in spite of* self-limiting inner dialogue. We proceed *in spite of* challenging outer conditions. We move forward *in spite of* lack of resources or time. We take pictures regularly *in spite of* not having the perfect camera or ideal lens. We simply find a way.

Analyzing Your Images

Photographers find it difficult to evaluate their own pictures. We're too close to them. The experience of making the photograph, while not often visible to the viewer, colors the way we see an image. And our own subjective likes and dislikes may not be obvious or even relevant to our audience, those with whom we want to communicate.

I propose ten tips to help analyze and evaluate your own photographs. Some of the advice in this section has been covered elsewhere in the book but is collected here as a summation of tools and questions to help you better discern and discriminate between images of your own making. Try to become intuitive in your response and analysis.

A photograph lives in the space between it and a viewer where a response takes place. You cannot know how viewers might respond and what they bring to an image, but you can examine and scrutinize your own responses and adjust the image accordingly.

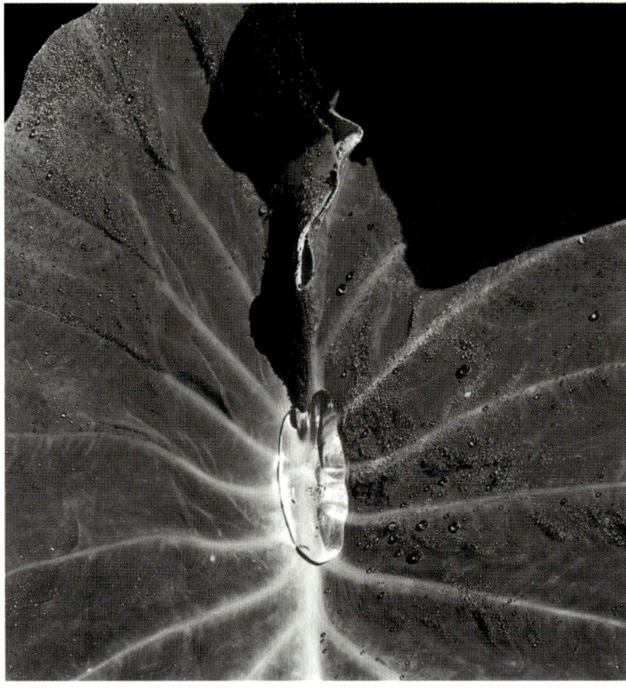

Wai'apo, Waipi'o Valley, Hawai'i, 1978
© Franco Salmoiraghi

1. Employ the whole person. The response of the body and the feelings are of equal weight to thought. The senses know proportion and balance, the meaning of a line or shape. The emotions offer a way of knowing that relates to what is evoked in oneself and in a potential viewer. And the mind, of course, is given the task of grappling with meaning and content, both on conscious and unconscious levels.

2. Does the composition support what you are intending to say? Are you striving for equilibrium, vital tension, dissidence, calm, vigorous activity, or contemplation? Would cropping help? Is there dead space? Does everything in the frame contribute to the meaning you intend? Try different versions. A photographer should be able to take responsibility for everything in the frame. Sometimes a fraction of an inch change to the edges of the frame can make an essential difference to the image. Minor White once said, "Composition is the strongest way of seeing."

3. Is the image a cliché; does it contain overused tropes or metaphors? One of the key criteria for art and photography is originality. I would change the word originality to authenticity. Is it authentic? Does it grow from your own unique perceptions? Your own heart and mind? Is it merely an imitation of other images you have seen? We all need to work through these images we carry in our mind to find something of our own.

4. How do you respond to the formal elements of the image: tonalities, color, lines, shapes, forms, and space, both positive and negative. Are they heavy or light? Elegant or earthy? Take note of positive and negative space. Are there recurring forms and shapes that you find often in your work? Recurring color relationships? Are these recurring relationships part of your style or part of your visual solution for a particular project?

5. What is the emotional content of the photograph found in color, light, and the treatment of the subject? Do they evoke particular feelings? Does the color and light soothe or abrade? Are the color relationships and saturation consistent with what you are trying to say? Does the image need color, or would black and white be effective? Images can often spring to life when the right color or tonal relationships are established.

6. What concepts are being expressed to the mind? Can you read and determine the explicit and implicit message that the image is conveying? How does your subconscious read the image? What are you communicating to others on a conscious and unconscious level? What symbols, metaphors, or allegorical relationships are present in the image, and how can your further them? Since all art is a metaphor, the photographer's role is to bring awareness and intentionality to this powerful form of language.

    Sometimes the cultural references are pivotal to the meaning of an image. Photographer Franco Salmoiraghi writes about the image featured in this essay, "I have lived in Hawai'i for over fifty years and my photography has been influenced by the language and culture of the Hawaiians, which is deeply poetical and varied. This photograph is of the dew which collects in the curve of the leaf of the *kalo* (taro) plant. *Wai 'Apo* refers to the water caught in the *kalo* leaf. It is sacred, pure, and used for ceremonial purposes."

7. Identify and consider your audience. With whom are you intending to communicate? Is the image inclusive? Does it speak to all people or are there cultural, racist, or sexist overtones? Does it exploit or diminish others? Are you perpetuating stereotypes? What are the cultural signs and symbols, the semiotics of the work? What meaning can be decoded by studying the cultural signs and symbols? Many of these can be subtle but very real components in how an audience views your work.

8. Bring immersive attention to the work. Look at it carefully and quietly for a period of time with no distractions. Study your own responses, determine if you have met your expressive intent, and ask if software or darkroom tools can improve the work, and how? Or, perhaps, do you need to reshoot? Many images are the result of multiple sessions behind the camera, in the darkroom, or in the digital studio.

9. Remember the basics. Examine your use of:

    The frame
    Light
    The moment
    Use of color and tonality
    Treatment of subject

Ideally, all of these elements converge into a seamless, effective expression, with each element serving the common whole.

10. Presence. Is the photograph a living document? Does it have presence? I make a large distinction between eye candy, high-impact images, and various forms of spectacle with the more expressive aim of presence. Does the image reach out and touch you on an emotional, intellectual, sensual, and intuitive level? Will you remember the image? Can it offer more and deeper impressions over time? Does the image have dimension?

Cultivate a group of friends, associates, or teachers who you trust to be both perceptive and honest. Being able to rely on others with trusted eyes can be invaluable in helping you bridge the gap between your intent and your expression.

Sift, Edit, and Refine

Photographers are often the worst editors of their own work. Editing in the form of selecting images is an art that can make or break your portfolio, website, book, or image feed. A sequence of images is only as strong as its weakest link. Learn to cull the coherent images from the stray sketches and random observations. Stay focused on the theme you are striving to express and ruthlessly remove those images that do not fit. When editing, I always keep in mind writer William Faulkner's advice to "kill your darlings," referring to those elements of the story that you love but do not contribute to the whole.

Learn the art of editing by constantly moving, adding, subtracting, and changing sequential relationships between images until you feel fully satisfied. I offer some suggestions based on my experience in the classroom and with my own photographs.

1. Use a file browser that allows you to see thumbnails on a page or make a contact sheet from negatives that allows you to see the entire roll of film. Look at the images globally rather than focusing on individual images.

2. Review the images as a whole to identify developing themes or subthemes, recurring forms, shapes, or certain kinds of light or color relationships, and particular ways of handling a subject. Use the review process for self-knowledge and to learn about your own (often unconscious) use of the visual language.

3. Again, look at images from within your body. The body and senses—not the rational brain—are what know proportion and balance and evocation through color and light. Be mindful, look within, seek which images have coherence, and closely observe your responses. Which images give you a jolt of dopamine, or release serotonin, or cause your heart to "beat faster?"

4. Seek coherence. Which images feel complete and "jump" off the page when are reviewing the entire set? Do certain images glow more brightly than others? You are seeking to see through the intuitive mind, the seat of wisdom and creativity. Sometimes even an eighth of an inch difference in framing or a split-second difference in the light or the moment will give an image coherence, grace, and elegance—that others lack. Which images spring to life?

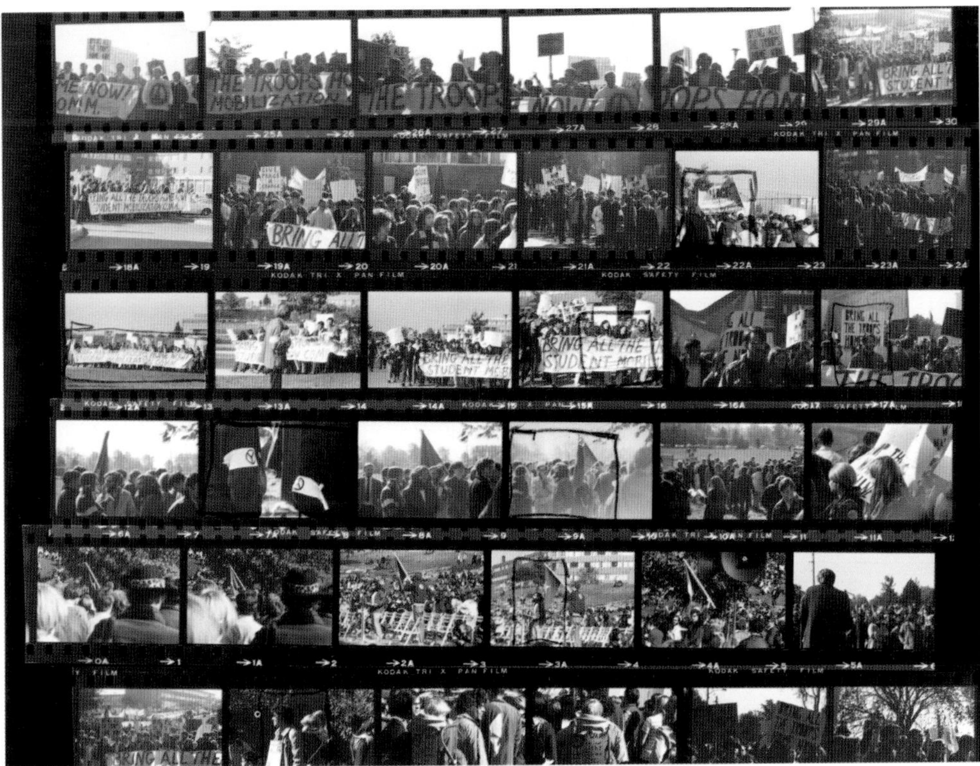

Student Demonstration, Kent State University, Ohio.
May 1970, David Ulrich

5. Use the ranking system (stars) in file browsing programs such as Adobe Bridge, Lightroom, and others, or use a grease pencil with printed contact sheets to mark and separate images in your initial viewing that reflect coherence and presence. Look at these images separately from the entire group. Maybe place them at the top of the page in digital browsers.

6. Wash, rinse, repeat. Look, study, look again. Time is the best editor. Put your browser or contact sheets aside for a day or two, or even a month of two, and come back with fresh eyes. The ego and rational brain are remarkably resistant to allowing the truths of the unconscious and intuition to appear. Find other strategies to see with fresh eyes. During the film era, photographers would mount "work" prints or contact

sheets on a wall that they see daily and view the images out of the corner of their eyes while taking care of their daily tasks.

7. Study the cultural "codes" and symbols. How do you treat content? What social codes, conventions, or biases appear in your work? How does confirmation bias (we see what we know or what we believe) impact your image making? How does your cultural background or identity and education influence your sight and inform your images? When editing, make absolutely certain that the political and social views you espouse through your work are the viewpoints you can stand behind.

8. Identify metaphors and symbols and allegories in your work, especially recurring ones. Learn to understand your own unique use of metaphor and symbol. Use images as a means to slowly unravel the language of your unconscious. Find the strongest of images that use a particular metaphor or symbol and put the rest aside. Make a distinction between images that are sketches of developing ideas and the ones that are complete with coherence and strength.

9. Can you see the influence of other photographers and artists in your work? That is normal and not to be resisted. Yet, how does your work differ from theirs? Where does your uniqueness lie? Seek to discover the seeds of your own authentic vision by looking at your work globally through contact sheets. What factors continue to be present in your work? Edit out of your portfolio those that are overtly imitative and edit into group the ones that are the most authentic and reflective of deep observation. Look for images that have an element of originality and surprise, that both delight and inform. Can you truly call your own each image in the group?

10. Strive to embody simultaneity, objectivity, and impartiality in your review of images. Simultaneity means being present, attentive, in the moment with your whole being—body, mind, and feelings, moving toward intuition. Objectivity means seeing things as they are, not how you want them to be, and not shirking from any enlightening or difficult truths that may appear. Impartiality means freedom from judgment. Analysis is worthwhile; constantly judging your own work is not productive and self-defeating. "Am I good enough?" is not the question, but rather "what *am* I good at?" and "what is natural for me?" are the important questions.

   THE MINDFUL PHOTOGRAPHER

Sequencing

Photographers carefully place images in a particular order for many reasons: narrative, the development of an idea, and to contextualize meaning between one image to another. The careful and sensitive sequencing of images underscores our intended message and creates a rhythm, a flow between images, and helps meaning evolve. The impression of an entire page of photographs on Instagram or a website is a potent form

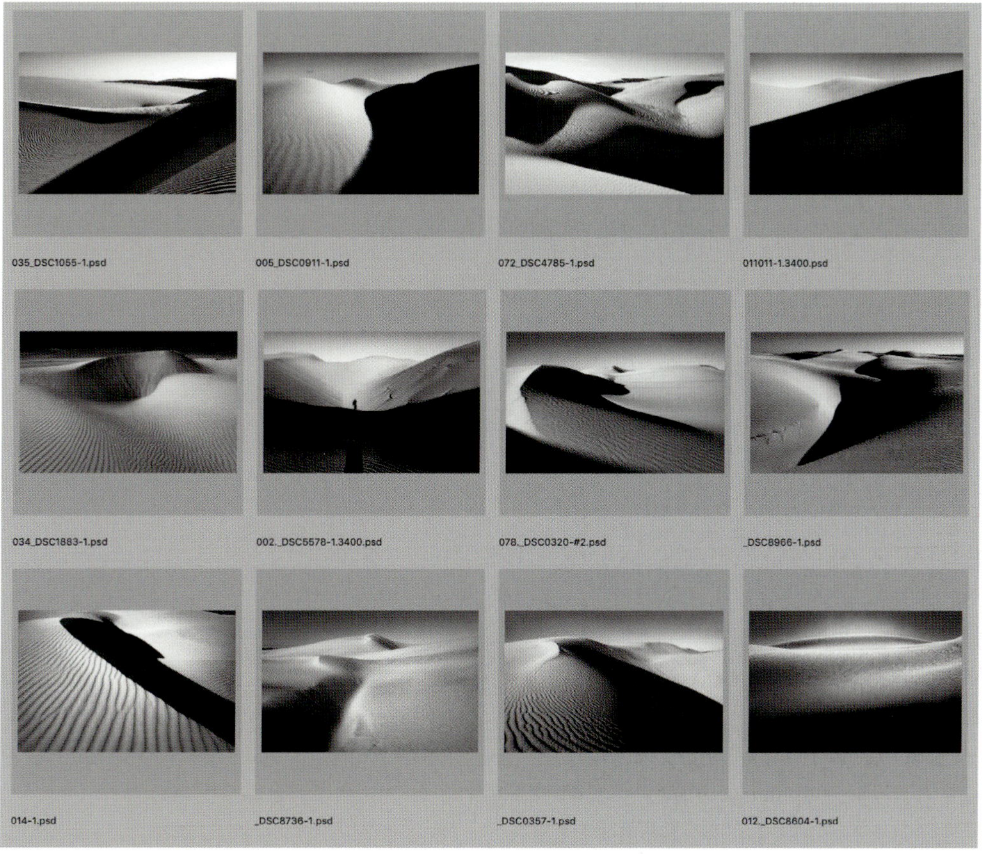

For my recent project, *Elegy for the Earth,* I use Adobe Bridge to order and sequence images for various purposes: a book, exhibitions, and web display.

of communication. Indeed, the first few seconds that a viewer observes your feed, or the short time that an art director or gallery owner may browse your initial images, often dictates if further viewing and consideration will take place—a process equivalent to the first lines in a novel or prose.

Sequencing is of prime importance in photography and represents one aspect of the medium that is often ignored. The way you sequence images depends on your intent and the platform. You may sequence images in one way for a portfolio, another for a book, and yet another for online feeds and websites. Often, the platform decides precisely how images are viewed, one to the other in linear time, page to page, or all at once in thumbnail views on Instagram, Pinterest, and other social media platforms.

Several considerations should be kept in mind when sequencing. Photography is a form of storytelling and you want to carefully craft the narrative development of your story or the clear evolution of your concept. Often, in sequences, like written essays, there are several parts: an introduction, body, and conclusion. Start by identifying the strong, quintessential photographs, the ones that can stand alone, and then take note of which images may be important as transitional movements but are not compelling enough to stand by themselves. Think about which images might function as "signature" images, the ones that can symbolize the entire project that you might use on a book cover, exhibition invitation, or on the face of your website.

Consider your intended content and message. When you bring images next to each other, you are contextualizing each photograph by virtue of its neighboring images. A larger meaning is created through the juxtaposition of images to each other that changes the way the photographs are viewed. For an obvious example, a photograph of a child with a toy or replica gun next to an image of a playground will have a different meaning than if placed next to photographs of conflict zones.

Look with your head and your heart to sense and determine the placement of images. What image might begin the sequence—one that feels like a beginning and effectively opens the theme. It should be strong enough to draw the viewer in immediately, like a good opening line. Then start moving and shifting images around, looking for resonances, contrasts, harmonies, and dissidences between images. Is there a clear narrative development, or is it a piece of visual music that you are composing?

Minor White, a master of the sequence, explains the difference between narration and evolution of meaning in non-narrative metaphoric or conceptual images: "A picture story explains and demonstrates. A sequence sustains the feeling states." He goes on to say, "To engage a sequence we keep in mind the photographs on either side of the one in our eye."

Start building the body of your sequence by shifting, moving, editing, and arranging while sensitively viewing the relationships between images. Stay aware of the visual movement of forms, the interaction of color and tone, as well as the overall feeling of one image to another. You want to move the viewer through the sequence, to guide their eyes with visual movements between shapes in the photographs. Remember, in western culture we tend to read from left to right. Let images complete each other by the forms of one moving into the forms of another. Remember that the feeling of images and their visual characteristics can help each other or diminish each other. Find the images that support each other's content and stay away from putting images together that conflict with, overwhelm, or clash with each other. Think of sequencing like composing a symphony or a jazz composition.

Build viewers to crescendos and still points, try to establish the rhythm and flow that best supports your content. Spend considerable time moving things around, trying different images next to each other or at different points in the sequence. Try to build your movements around the strong, signature images that represent the crescendo, or heart of your concerns. Don't forget the importance of editing. Should some images come out of the group? According to Zen master and photographer John Daido Loori in the *Zen of Creativity*, editing is "at once creative and critical. By cutting away the extra, you can get closer to what you intended to convey." Sometimes the entire portfolio strengthens by removing one or several images. You should be able to fully stand behind each image in the group.

In physical sequences, I use small work prints like playing cards on the floor or on a large table to rapidly shift and adjust positions. On the computer, I use a file browser like Adobe Bridge that allows you to move and re-move images around dynamically into a different order, all the while seeing all the images at once. In exhibition design, I move images around on the floor adjacent the wall on which they might be hung.

Study photography books and exhibitions to find good examples of sensitive sequencing and design. Several notable, legendary sequences are found in the history of photography. Look at *The Americans* by Robert Frank, in which he spent many months editing thousands of images into the ones featured in the book and determining the right flow of images to serve the narrative content. It's a powerful storytelling sequence. Then, look at Minor White's retrospective monograph, *Mirrors Messages Manifestations*, for an example of potent sequences that are not narrative, but metaphoric. Most of the images in the book are located within evocative, discrete sequences.

Consider your ending. Your ending should be a strong image that both forms a conclusion yet is evocative enough to leave the viewer wanting more. When they leave the exhibition or site, they should feel informed, enriched, nourished, or sparked, whatever your intent.

In literature and photography, editing and sequencing are arts unto themselves. Some people may be naturally good at it and feel affinity for this form of design. Others may have to work harder to realize the potentials of editing. Either way, consider it as a seminal, creative, and critical task in your evolution as a photographer.

Experiment

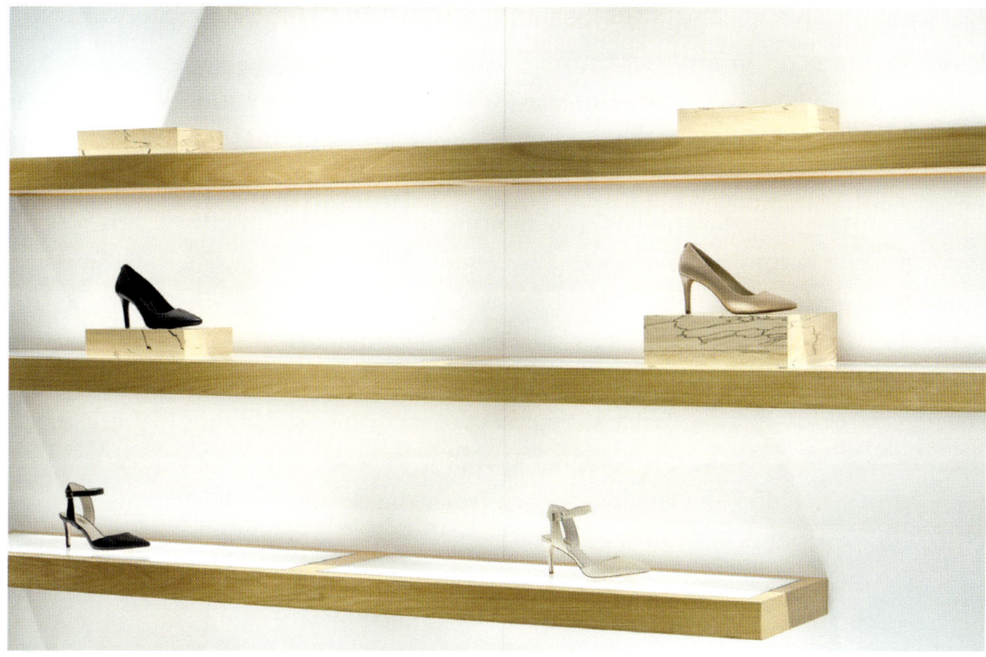

Shoe Display, from the series, *Glass Walls,* Shane Sakata
Sakata tirelessly experimented with exploring photographs of both people and objects to find images that best reflect consumer longing and consumption.

Fresh discovery forms the key to successful photographs. Wide and broad experimentation can lead to spontaneous insight and discovery. Try this and try that. Try something now and try it again. Be insatiable in your willingness to search for new solutions, innovative techniques, and heightened ways of seeing. A burning hunger for expression, experience, and experimentation separates the great artist from the dilettante. If you continue until you get there, you might discover entirely new destinations along the way.

Many practices and methods can be devised to cultivate the freedom of experimentation. You might try new camera choices or alternative processes. Historical processes such as wet plate collodion have grown in popularity over the past decade. In another example of exploring photography's past, Boston photographer Abelardo Morell turns entire rooms into a camera obscura and photographs the projected, upside-down image seen within the spaces. Try panoramas or diptychs or triptychs. Experiment with image compositing or collage—bringing multiple images together to form a single piece. Use plastic film cameras, underwater housings, and drones. If you find yourself attracted to solutions found by other photographers, don't be hesitant to try them and make them your own. Learn to steal like an artist—with joyous abandon.

You might experiment with different conceptual strategies to represent aspects of your experience and observations. Environmentalist and photographer Chris Jordan, for example, in his project *Running the Numbers*, decided that the most effective method to represent the environmental threat of consumer waste was to use overwhelming statistics. In large photographs, he fashions an extreme number of things into provocative designs on the page, including, say, photographs that depict "410,000 paper cups, equal to the number of disposable hot-beverage paper cups used in the US every fifteen minutes." Or, he shows an 80-inch photograph of what appears to be a forest of trees, representing (literally) "1.14 million brown paper supermarket bags, the number used in the US every hour."

Try on different styles and modes of expression as you might don clothing in a dressing room. Simply play with the medium. See what fits. See what highlights your natural features. See what corresponds to your unique mode of thought and expression.

Don't limit your experimentation to technique and concept. Try different observational modalities. One day, perhaps, you might look at how people move, study musculature and body language, see how activities flow within an event. Another time, you might scrutinize and savor the myriad kinds of light, both inner and outer. At other times, you can study space (both positive and negative), form, line, and color. A powerful observational experience can be found in looking at facial expressions and their relationship to emotion. Or, imagine that you just landed on planet Earth from your home planet in another galaxy. What do you see?

Experimenting with technique, concept, and observation can be inspirational and can spark inexhaustible ideas. Artists are nourished by working from a state of questioning. What if I try this? What will this look like? These questions lead to discovery. Once you uncover a style, a way of working, a conceptual exploration, or a new way of seeing, stick with it for a while. Allow it to unfold through giving it a degree of time and persistence. Broad experimentation can be a teacher, but it can also distract if you do not, at some point, follow an idea or working method through to completion. My mother would often invoke folk wisdom and ask me, due to my hyperactive disposition, ricocheting from one thing to another, "Do you want to be a jack of all trades and a master of none?"

Enjoy and endeavor to learn from your interactions with and through a camera. All art is a dialogue between oneself, one's materials, and the world. It is often a journey with only a hazily defined destination. What you see and find along the way—in spontaneous moments of discovery—often form the shape and content of your work. When I began this book, I only knew about a dozen of the titles and intended content of the essays. As for the rest, one thing led to another, and another, and, once I was fully engaged, moments of insight and intuition would appear that helped guide my path to completion.

Passionate, engaged people maintain many interests and are rarely bored. It's far better to struggle to focus your wide interests than it is to be bored and cynical. Look around you. Look wide and deep. Try different things, have different experiences, follow the threads of your enthusiasms and passions. Photography leads you into the world; through it you may have the experiences that help define and shape your work and your life.

Become the Camera

A camera is only a tool for expanding your always-available sight. Your eye, mind, and memory form the heart of your vision—and are the principal tools for visual expression. In reality, you are the camera. The eye and mind give us the power of observation and the ability to know the world—and oneself—through direct perception in the present moment.

The camera can remind us not to take the gift of sight for granted. Don't rely on it for every observation. The richness of visual perception is food for the psyche. It helps us better understand the thing seen, to generate action in accordance with our observations, and gives great pleasure. The eyes stand at the intersection between the inner and outer worlds, and both receive and reveal. Seeing then is an action and a force that links us more fully to the world.

Learn to use your eyes well. When looking at something, say a person or a sunset, just watch. Stay in tune with the moment-to-moment impressions that you receive. Savor them. Take them in with relish and deep appreciation. Let them impress themselves upon your being. Let them become a form of nourishment and an education for the heart and mind. Let them interact with you inwardly and let their power change you. Let sight teach you to see what is. Don't let the camera impede the action of seeing.

I am often dismayed in art museums by not being able to see and contemplate a work of art due to numerous people jockeying for position with cell phone cameras. Multiple screens popping up and down get in the way of extended viewing. These camera viewers hardly pause to take in the painting or sculpture. All they do is click, as if to say, "been there; done that." Psychology researcher Linda Henkel at Fairfield University in Connecticut has studied this phenomenon.

In an experiment, she took 28 undergraduates to an art museum and identified thirty objects for viewing by the students. With half of the objects, they were asked to merely observe. With the other objects, they were encouraged to view and take pictures with their cell phones. The next day, she tested their memory and recall, and the results were unambiguous. The participants were less accurate in identifying the objects they had photographed, and more able to recall the visual details of the artworks they had merely observed. Henkel has called this the "photo-taking impairment effect."

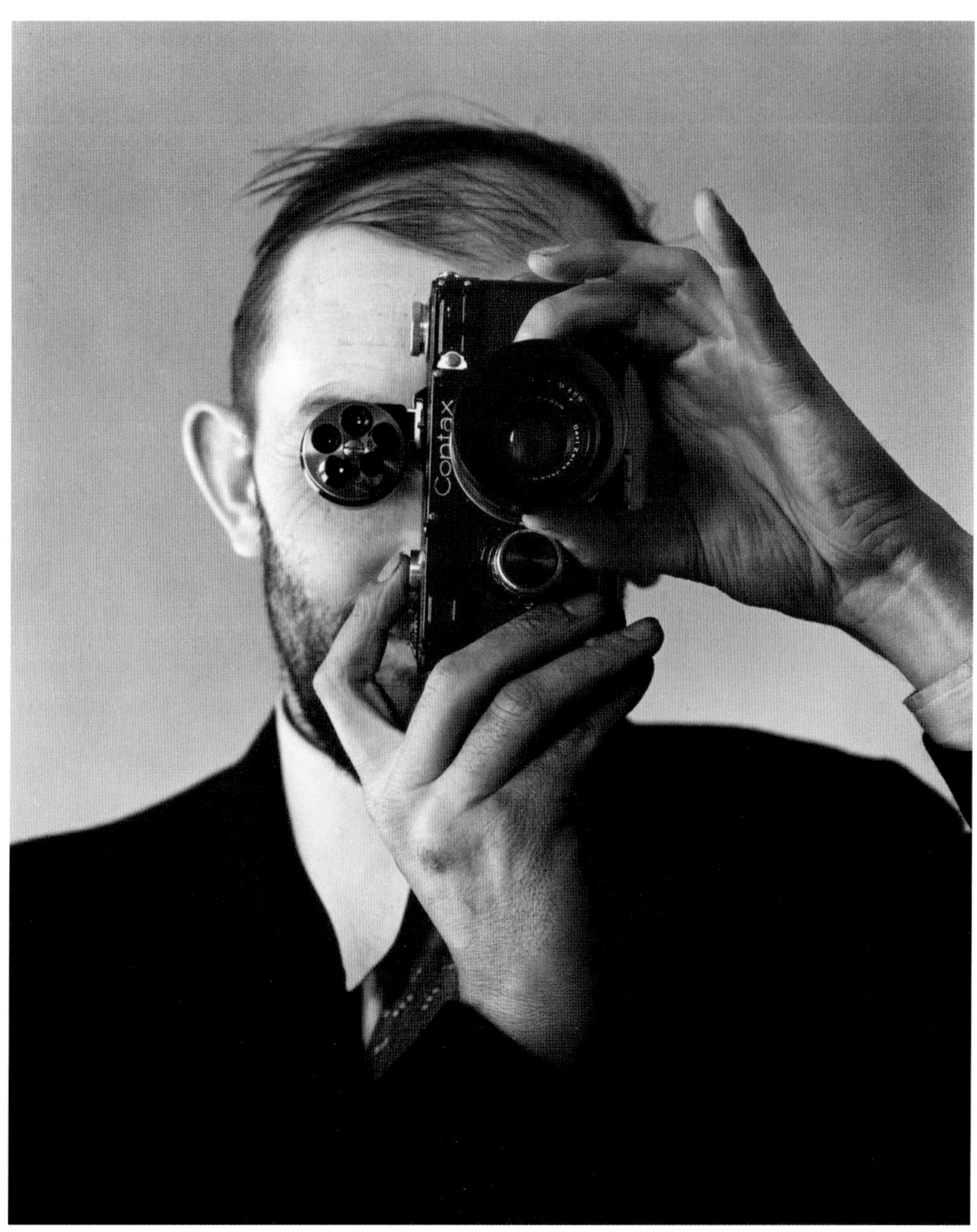

Ansel Adams, Just after He Got the Contax, 1936.
Photograph by Edward Weston

Henkel explains: "These results show how the 'mind's eye' and the camera's eye are not the same. When people rely on technology to remember for them—counting on the camera to record the event and thus not needing to attend to it fully themselves—it can have a negative impact on how well they remember their experiences."

This study verifies common sense and has obvious consequences for photographers. However, what if a viewer does both: fully contemplates an object and works with it through a camera? Can the camera serve to intensify one's experience of the world rather than impede it? Fortunately, Henkel performed a second study. In this, she found that through interacting with an object through a camera, by changing positions and zooming in on details, it preserved memory and recall. Students reported greater memory not only for the part of the object that was zoomed in on, but for the look and feel of the entire object. This second study is heartening and confirms that active camera work can serve to heighten seeing and not diminish it—but it must be active, not merely using the camera as a substitute for experience.

Become the camera. Photography serves your vision, not the other way around. The camera is an inanimate object—a mere tool for the sight of the mind. The camera itself is not worthy of being obsessed over, its type and quality; and taking pictures is certainly not so important that it should interfere with the human lens of eye, mind, and memory. The world itself deserves our deep perception much more than any electronic device in our hands. The real world contains more depth and fascination than what can be mediated on any type of screen.

Active seeing links your psyche to the thing seen. A relationship is established; impressions enter your being and feed your mind and actuate your emotions. And, as modern physics teaches, the presence and action of the observer changes the nature of the observed. When you regard something closely, it becomes a part of you. And you become a part of it. Seeing can teach you to let go and surrender your ego encapsulation; to sacrifice your tight boundaries for the sake of the interaction of perception, the exchange of energy that takes place between seer and seen.

Seeing is a call that requests our response. Sometimes the affirmation of offering our attention is enough. At other times, we are called to contemplate the thing seen, to place the impression deep within our being, and strive to understand or formulate our view from the mind's eye. Very often, what we see spurs us to direct action, such as when observing a friend in need or perceiving the dynamics of an event—personal, social, or political—of which we are a part. And sometimes the legacy of images from the camera eye becomes the ideal manner to interact with the observed.

When taking care of a child, or interacting with a partner, or standing in front of the *Mona Lisa*, your attentive presence is given through your eyes—and touches your mind and heart. You give and receive. Moments of deep attention, of being in the here and now, heal the detrimental effects of the illusionary separation of self and other, seer and seen. The work of the eyes has far reaching consequences in our lives together on this planet. We are less prone to harm that which we are. Seeing can engender unity, responsibility, and deep caring.

Music of the Spheres

I find this to be an exceedingly beautiful, evocative phrase, even though I do not fully understand what it means. I intuit its meaning to refer to the sound of worlds. As a photographer, I do have the experience of both the silence and sound at the heart of things, a kind of vibration I hear occasionally with my inner ear in looking at scenes and works of art. It brings me more fully into the moment and synchronizes my perceptions with the observed.

Perhaps because I lost an eye and my vision is physically not so keen, I have developed a kind of "sonar" that allows me to navigate through space and perceive the sounds of the world, sounds that I don't physically hear as much as they resonate in my inner ear. With that said, I find it very difficult to gracefully navigate space in very noisy or chaotic environments. These experiences have taught me that all of the senses, inner and outer, are deeply related in a unified field of awareness. I firmly believe that all people, especially artists and photographers, can learn to employ all of their senses while looking and working. Actively listening to what you see can "tune" your awareness to the inner tone or essence of the thing seen.

Everything has its own music, its own vibration; and it is something you can endeavor to photograph. It comes as no surprise that some photographers consciously cite music as a powerful influence on their work. As a young man, Ansel Adams agonized whether to pursue a career as a classical pianist or to realize his professional leanings toward photography. While he chose photography, he maintained his passionate involvement with music throughout his life and saw the two disciplines as deeply allied. And Beat writer Jack Kerouac invokes the music of jukeboxes and funerals in describing the photographs of Robert Frank in the first line of his introduction to Frank's book, *The Americans*. "That crazy feeling in America when the sun is hot on the streets and when the music comes out of the jukebox or from a nearby funeral, that's what Robert Frank has captured in tremendous photographs...."

"What is the sound of the day?" is a question photographer Nicholas Hlobeczy often asked workshop participants. Listening can expand seeing and vice versa. As an experiment, try listening to the sounds of what you see. This tone, which is invisible to the eyes, can teach you about the essential nature of your subject and can deeply inform how

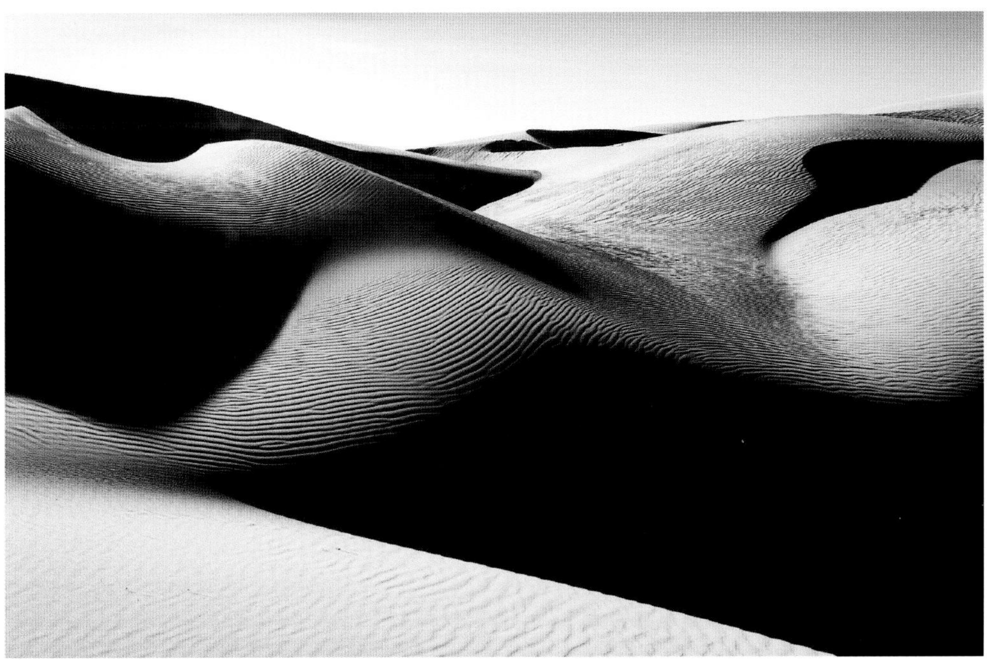

Oceano Dunes #14, California, 2018, David Ulrich

you approach it through a camera. The question also arises: what is your own sound, at different times, and can you find the corresponding vibrations in the world, like a tuning fork that reverberates with sympathetic vibrations? The camera eye seeks resonance.

How might this help in your photography practice or even within the circumstances of your life? Active listening plays a major role in communication, in the development of empathy, and in the central need between people to understand each other and learn from other viewpoints. Listening to the sounds of things, their inner or outer vibrations, can link you more fully to what is in front of you as well as deepen and sharpen your response through a camera. Silence can open your heart and mind to the reality of what is.

Several times while photographing the canyons of Utah, I came in touch with the exquisite silence of the land. I felt the nameless source of what animated the ancient rocks, trees, and sky. I took in through my inner ear the presence of life; and ironically it came through stillness and silent vibration, barely perceptible but profusely musical nonetheless. I experienced my own sense of "I am" that was no different than the sacredness of what I perceived. One of my teachers, D. M. Dooling, founding editor of *Parabola* magazine used to say of these moments, "I am a part of it and it is a part of me."

Since 1998, scientists have been exploring the "hum of the earth," or a low frequency sound that some are poetically calling the song of the world. It's an intriguing concept with multiple dimensions. Does everything have a hum, a song? Can this song be represented through art and photography? For centuries, artists have attempted to depict the sublime, or rather, those aspects of the world that inspire wonder, grandeur, and awe.

In my own work, the sheer force of the mystery and beauty of Hawai'i captivated me for many years—and eluded capture with a camera. What kept me coming back again and again was the illusion that it could be contained within a picture frame. It's what we do as artists. Our deepest visions are unrepresentable, but the power resides in the striving, the graceful effort to crystallize something that forever resists distillation. Nature is too big, too unknowable and multidimensional to be contained by a camera lens. The highest mysteries cannot be reduced to human knowledge. The mind cannot grasp their dimensional meaning. But we try. What is seen in an artist's work is a pale reflection of a search for truth, an echo of the song of the world. Grace is the descent of the incomprehensible into human scale.

The Art of Inseeing

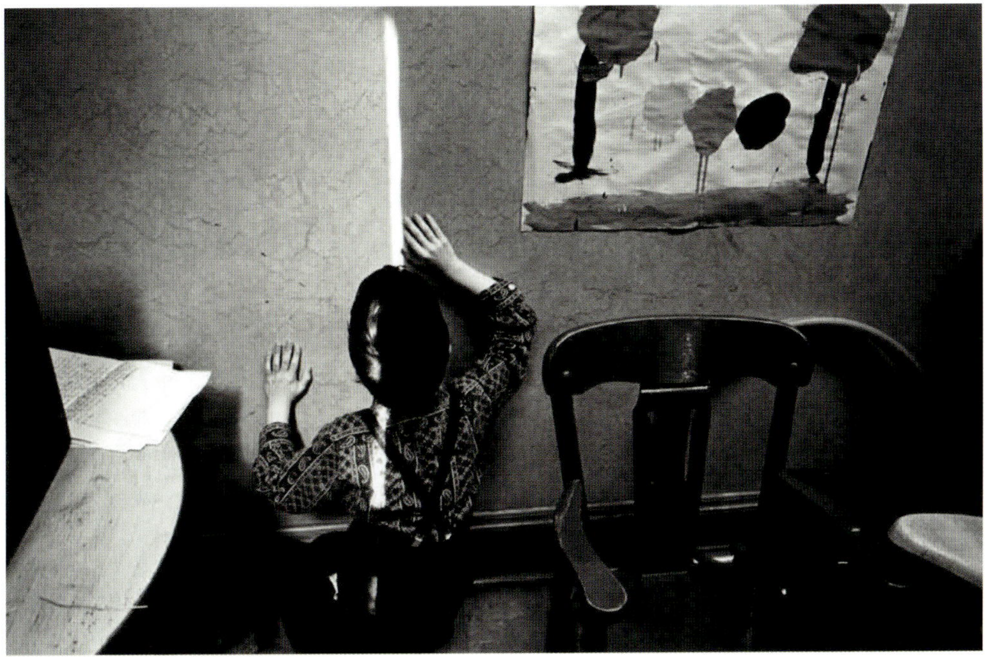

Blind Boy, Charles Harbutt

Much photography depends upon penetrative perception in the moment. Seeing into the heart of things—to feel and know them from the inside out—is a learned capacity. The degree to which we are able to embody the art of inseeing creates the measure of our sensitivity and awareness as both artists and moral human beings in modern society. On the website *Brain Pickings,* Maria Popova writes, "Empathy, an orientation of spirit decidedly different from sympathy, has become central to our moral universe."

In the late 19th century, philosopher Theodor Lipps advanced the then-novel hypothesis that the power of art's impact on a viewer did not originate in the work itself but rather in the act of beholding. Viewers can "feel into" a work of art and experience its movements and resonances within oneself. It draws the observer into their own body and engenders a sense of empathy that triggers an experience: how the work of art resounds within oneself. Freud appropriated this concept and believed that doctors should embrace empathy as a potent means of understanding patients. And modern culture has adopted empathy as the principal tool for linking oneself with others; to stand in another's shoes; to feel their reality within one's own body and feelings. The art of inseeing has powerful repercussions for photographers' dialogue with the world.

We do not look at someone; rather we feel into them. We do not merely observe a tree; we sense its outstretching movements and livingness within oneself. Try placing your attention within an object—or a person—and experience their postures, moods, expressions, and even thoughts within your own field of awareness. Allow their being to act on your own. Use your body and feelings to understand them from the inside-out as you might approach a work of art. If you stay inwardly silent, suspend your own opinions and preconceptions and offer them your attention, you may experience a profound blending of energy, an interpenetration of your being with another, a linking of life to life. Your livingness resonates with theirs. This type of intentional awareness gives respect for others in a way that harming them would be tantamount to harming oneself—likewise with the Earth. And we learn to appreciate and empathize with other ways of seeing and thinking. With empathy, we give up the divided, isolated self.

One of the great aims of photography, and indeed much art, is to show the world to itself. In the hands of a perceptive observer, the camera can reveal the nature of what is and reflect that representation back to society. Visionary perception is nothing more than seeing into the multiple forces and dynamics present in individuals, nature, culture, and society itself. Artists and photographers reflect their perceptions back into life for the benefit of the many. Society needs its artists, and, for true equality and justice, others need and deserve the quality of empathy that can be learned by each of us.

The camera lens stands at the intersection between two worlds: the inner and the outer. To see into things with a camera serves to heighten your awareness of outer conditions and people, and brings them into oneself. It announces life to itself. Can you capture the heart of a thing, the character of a person, the meaning of an event with a camera? Can your photographs bring depth, presence, and penetrative insight to the viewer?

Rather than using the camera to seek "likes" and the admiration of others, can we use photography to serve and heighten sight and insight—to create a bond with the

   THE MINDFUL PHOTOGRAPHER

subject? If we employ the camera as a tool for respect, the act of photographing becomes a linking, the forming of relatedness with the thing seen. Seeing into things that are life affirming reminds the viewer of the beauty and natural order of life. Regarding the pain and suffering of others, or even of the Earth; by internalizing their distress, the resulting photographs that reflect our experience can awaken conscience and spur positive action in a viewer.

Rilke, who was acquainted with Lipps and Freud, writes in *The Notebooks of Malte Laurids Brigge*, "I am learning to see. I don't know why it is, but everything enters me more deeply and doesn't stop where it once used to. I have an interior that I never knew of…"

Fifty/Fifty

After you have taken the photograph, the process is not yet complete. You still need to realize your intent and vision. Most photographers define a workflow that involves some measure of both camera work and post processing on your device, computer, or in the darkroom. For me, the ratio is around half and half between what can be realized in the camera and what elements of visual expression are furthered and interpreted with imaging software.

When I worked mostly in the darkroom, I was touched and amazed by the visual alchemy of light, silver, and chemicals that unfolded an image to an expressive state. Now, most of my workflow is digital and the tools are vastly more flexible and powerful than the darkroom's magic. On the computer, I use Adobe Lightroom and Photoshop for processing of images; on my iPhone, I prefer Lightroom Mobile. With either my professional camera or my phone, I capture images using the RAW format, which holds thousands of times more color depth and tonal dimension than the default JPG format. If you don't know and use RAW format, I recommend that you experiment with it. The results are vastly superior to JPG.

Photography is an inherently plastic medium. Through the combination of camera and software, you partake in a transformative alchemy between what you see with your eyes and what you intend or want in your expressive statement. Sometimes you know in advance what you want but often you discover an image's potential through experimenting freely with post-processing options. Balancing color, maximizing tonal dimension, enhancing light, and strengthening relationships between form and content through cropping, perspective adjustments, and spot or blemish removal; these all form the expressive potential of image making. Through software or the darkroom, you achieve the vision of your mind's eye, which may differ a little or a lot from the retinal image in your eyes.

Photographic artists make a distinction between global image editing (working on the entire photograph) and local editing (where you work on details or parts of the photo). You would be well served by becoming conversant with both dynamics. After adjusting the color and tonal range of the entire image, you may find parts of the photograph that are out of balance; perhaps too dark, too light, not enough versus too much contrast, or maybe in need of a different color treatment than the rest of the photo. In the darkroom, these local controls are known as burning and dodging; with software, they are known as selective adjustments.

I can spend hours refining and distilling an image on the computer. For me, it is akin to writing in which the first draft tumbles from my pen freely and spontaneously, but the work of editing, of re-working and strengthening takes place over much longer periods of time. Others do more work in the camera than in software. Find your own way.

One of my students, who is also a musician, spoke of the clean satisfaction when you find just the right chord, or just the right color and form in an image. She said, "It feels right and touches something, precisely here," as she pointed to her solar plexus. With image editing, you don't stop until you are intuitively done. Something in you knows when the expression is complete. Be careful not to overwork it from your ego. Find the balance dictated by your natural wisdom. Striving for mere effect is the mark of an

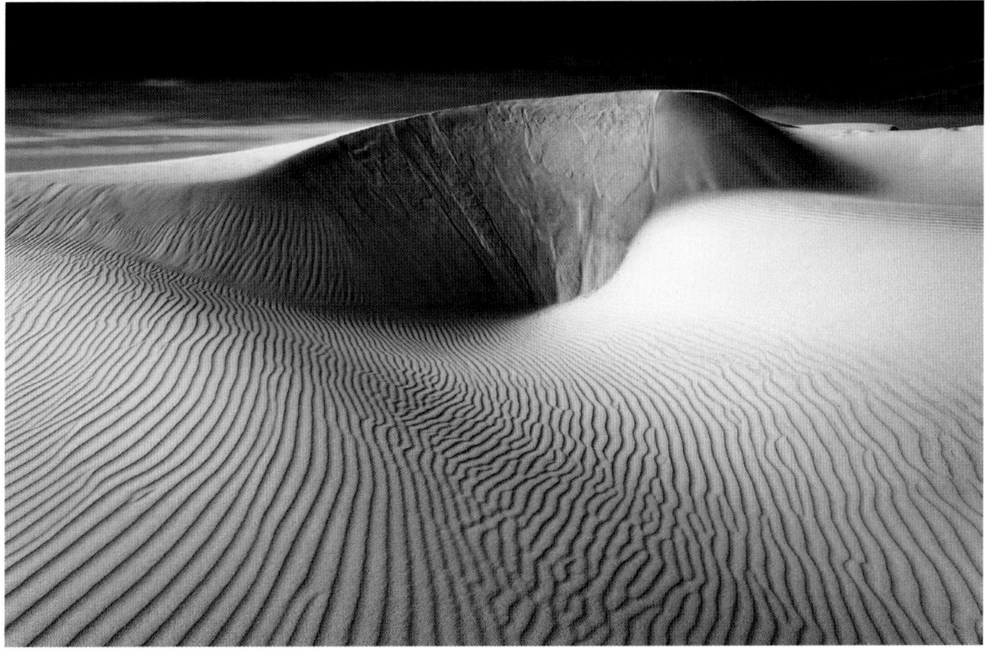

Oceano Dunes #34, California, 2018, David Ulrich

inexperienced beginner. Subtlety goes a long way toward the viewers comprehension and satisfaction.

What you seek is an intentional balance of the elements in the image according to what you are trying to say. You interpret your vision and ideas through sensitive work with software and tools until your intent shines forth in living clarity. Don't shirk from spending the considerable time necessary to master the tools of post processing. It can help ally your vision with the tools needed to communicate your expressive intent to others—to pave the way for clarity and fullness of expression.

Several exercises that we give in photography school can help. First, make four to six completely different expressive statements from one negative or file. Use cropping, tonal and color relationships, and selective adjustments, but you cannot use compositing or extreme manipulations. This exercise can teach you about the many expressive possibilities of a single image. The second exercise is to "trade" negatives or files with a partner. You process their image as you see it and feel it. They, in turn, work with yours. Then you share results. You may be amazed over how differently you each view and express the visual potential of the same file or negative.

As you learn the craft, discoveries are made in process and your mind opens to what is possible to achieve with expressive means. Your potential widens and broadens. You begin to appreciate the remarkable alchemy that is possible with materials and methods that form the transformation between an incomplete, vague idea and the richness, fullness, coherence, and presence of a living work.

Creative Mind and Not Knowing

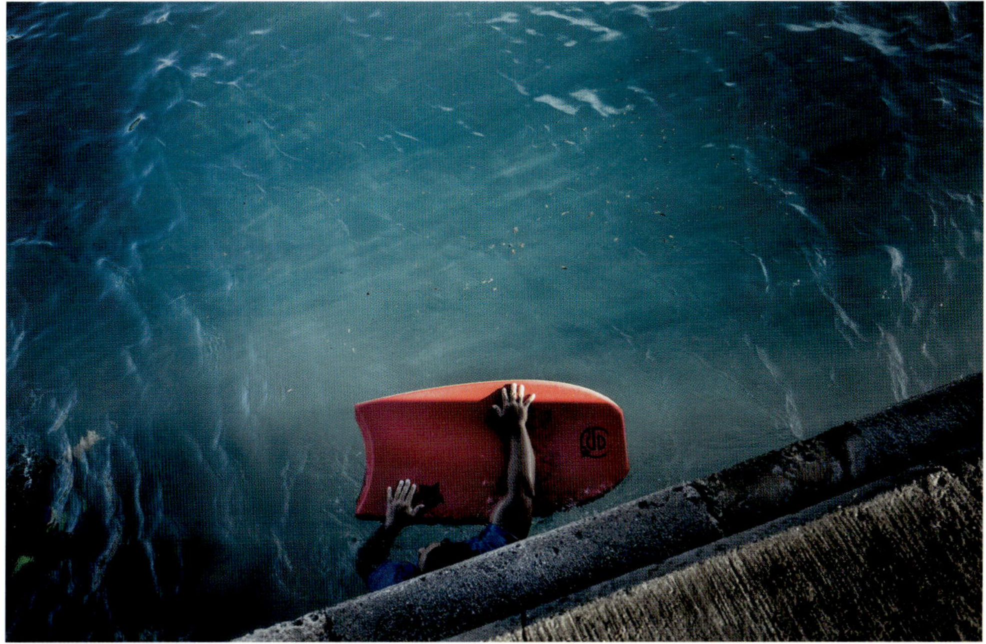

Waikiki, 2015, James Knudsen

Photographers often spend a disproportionate amount of energy thinking about and even obsessing over tools and equipment. Does it help? Maybe just a little. Having the right camera or the ideal lens can help make successful photographs. However, this is a limiting and partial attitude. I believe that the pivotal concern that should greatly supersede the quest for more stuff is finding the right frame of mind and cultivating the necessary skills to help us see and work.

What is the ideal working state of mind and how might we achieve it? Artists and photographers have long sought the magic elixir within which creativity can sprout and bloom. To the extreme, some have tried drugs and various kinds of indulgence or privation: alcohol, lack of sleep, celibacy or promiscuity, and fasting. Others don't think about it at all and come as they are into the field or studio. Certain enduring factors for a working state of mind have emerged from the experiments of creative individuals that are time-tested and reliable.

The first is the advent of a quiet, receptive mind. Stillness of mind does not just appear on its own; we must aim in its direction. Attentive seeing and focused creativity cannot take place in the carnival of the mundane. Reduce distractions, try to clear your mind of shopping lists and daily ephemera and learn to find disciplined focus. Sometimes I work before the daily intrusions begin to dominate; at other times, I take care of urgent tasks before getting to work on a creative project. The one thing that helps me the most comes through the inward attention cultivated in sitting meditation. Buddhists know this state as mindfulness or *vipassana*.

In the mindful state, we strive to merely accept what is. We cultivate what some call the impartial witness or what Krishnamurti calls "choiceless awareness." It's the part of the mind that is large and broad, that is capable of embracing thought and emotions with detached interest. In mindfulness, we do not seek to change things. We strive to see and know what is. Ironically, once the light of awareness is let into the dark places, change does begin to come about naturally. Certain processes in the psyche can take place only in the dark, hidden recesses, apart from conscious awareness. In mindfulness, we observe the mind itself and bear witness to the often raging and ranging thoughts, as well as become aware of reactive emotion. Ironically, this action of becoming aware of thought and emotion has a calming and quieting influence. The rapidly thinking, associative mind does not go away but it occupies less space in our inner landscape, freeing more attention to devote to finding creative focus.

Attentive seeing and focused creativity cannot take place in the carnival of the mundane.

I have verified this repeatedly. I tend toward a hyperactive disposition of both mind and body—and am easily distracted by shiny devices, news feeds, and inner conditions. I feel pulled here and there constantly and, like a child, cannot effectively discipline my peripatetic nature. So where does that leave me? Punishing my body and mind into submission feels demeaning and rarely helps. For me, inward attention, being aware of the direct experience of the here and now, coupled with self-observation or the cultivation of the mind's witness, acts much like tightening and tuning a guitar string. My anxiety lowers, my body and mind more fully enter the present moment, and a certain creative sensitivity becomes evident in my inner state. I am more responsive, focused, and steadily energetic in my creative work.

The mind quiets of its own accord through mindful awareness. Rather than the fractured mind that is drawn here and there, my mind and seeing become sharper-edged tools for creative application. My mind also opens to new possibilities, new directions, and intuitive guidance from its deeper regions. I enter the flow state, in which endorphins are released, the work gathers its own momentum, and the interaction with tools, materials, and ideas stimulates discovery and leads toward clarity.

One of the hallmarks of a clear, receptive mind is found in the paradoxical Zen concepts of "no-mind" and "not knowing." In the state of not knowing, we strive to suspend our fixed opinions, immediate judgments, and preconceptions. We maintain a healthy curiosity and attentive interest to the ever-changing here and now. New, creative discoveries cannot be made in a mind overfilled with opinions and speculations. Instead, the mind can be open and can cultivate an enthusiastic, child-like wonder. The mind inquires rather than thinking it knows. Active questioning forms the ideal creative working state. From this standpoint, we can make new discoveries, have a fresh, untainted view of the world, and use the camera for one of its most righteous aims: to learn to see what is.

The mindfulness of no mind encourages a spontaneous, instinctive, and intuitive way of working. We learn to depend upon the wisdom of the body, the subtle ways of knowing of the emotions, and the intelligence of instinct—rather than relying strictly on the rational, plodding disposition of the head brain. Try to look and see without thought. It is hard to stay open and rigorously suspend preconceptions—to let the mind become a blank slate. Try to approach the world with the question: what will I learn today? Try to work with the camera or post processing in a state of inquiry and free, even wild, experimentation. Try to be still and mindful. Allow the moment to unfold without your opinions of how something should happen. Dance with the world, and don't always try to lead. Intuition prevails when we learn to stop thinking so hard and knowing so much.

Be quiet.

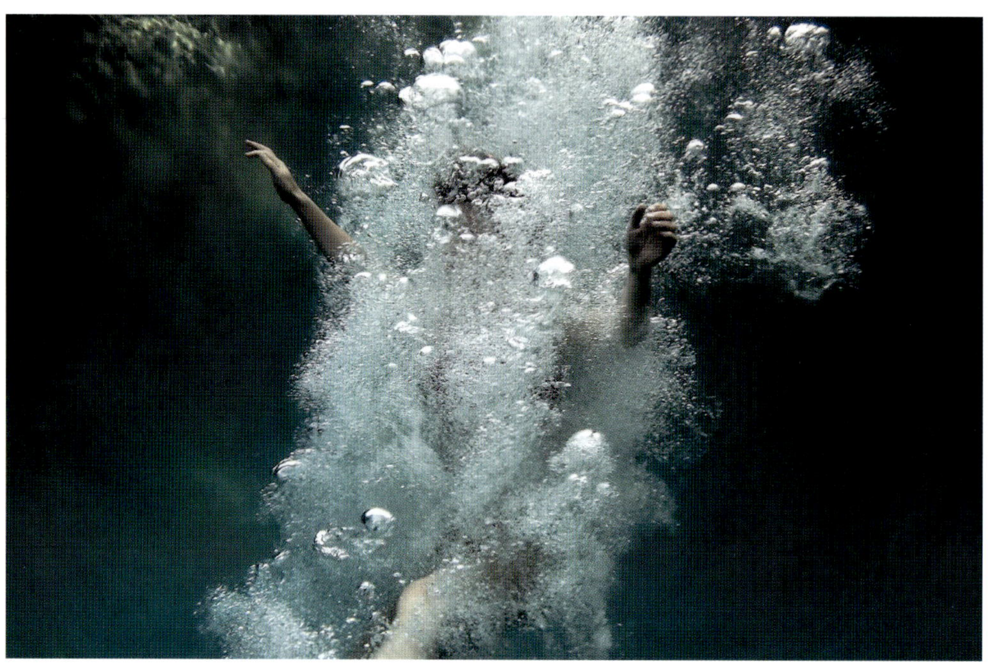

Untitled, from the series *Laws of Silence,*
Jennifer McClure

Trust Your Process

Self-doubt. Fear. Insecurity. Inadequacy. Not being good enough. Marginalization. Disempowerment. Depression. Despair. Cynicism. Egotism.

Which of this laundry list of common conditions distorts your belief in yourself? Let's be honest. We are all plagued by some measure or combination of these traits. We all have our personal brand of demons to battle and someday vanquish. The creative arts, because of their insistent necessity on going inward, place us squarely in the sights of our fears, doubts, and insecurities. Our only hope to be successful in photography or any art is to learn to be unabashedly what we are, flaws and all. We cannot destroy our demons all at once, but can accept our circumstances as part of our unique identity.

Everything that you are is fodder for your creative work. Do not run; do not hide from your gifts, your shortcomings, and your background. Make them part of your creative approach. I can think of numerous bodies of photographic work that are like visual diaries, exposing one's struggles, dismaying conditions, and triumphs to the light of day and sharing them with others. Your experiences can affirm others who share similar trials. One powerful project that comes to mind is *The Notion of Family*, LaToya Ruby Frazier's exploration of the legacy of racism and economic displacement in the downturns of her Rust Belt hometown, the small steel town of Braddock, Pennsylvania. In another highly personal project, *Laws of Silence*, which reads like a visual journal, Jennifer McClure examines the nature of her own life that goes against the grain of the American Dream and the life she "was programmed to live."

Don't be afraid to be real. Trust who you are. Each of you arises from your own blend of circumstances and has unique gifts. There is nothing new under the sun to photograph. Therefore, your unique vision and expression can grow authentically from yourself. There's no one else on earth with your particular mixture of talents, gifts, obstacles, and unique insights. In teaching photography, I find that there is some quality in every person's work that is alive and memorable. One or two stunning images, with depth and grace, populate their portfolios. Mostly they can't see them and, when the unique goodness of those images is pointed out, they don't believe it.

For years as a Department Chair in an art school, I would view the work of potential incoming students in their admission portfolios. These students were applying to school for art, design, and photography. Several prominent art schools had admission requirements to draw or render a bicycle or an apple. In every portfolio, there was a meticulously drawn or photographed bicycle or apple, as well as other technically sound but quite boring drawings or photographs. Usually in the back, or tucked into a side pocket of their portfolios, I observed stray papers peeking out from the leather binding. These were the drawings or photographs their art teachers (or parents) advised them against showing me.

I want to see *these,* I would say to the prospective student while pointing to their hidden piles. What I found were visual diaries, unrehearsed sketches and images from their lives and loves, spontaneous experiments, and depictions of interactions with friends. There were imaginative dungeons and dragons, goth, animé, costumes, visual lamentations of heartbreak, angst, and loss, as well as drawings and photographs that rejoiced in their home, their surroundings, and the simple details of their lives. They, of course, quivered when exposing these images for fear that what they really are isn't good enough. These sketches and photographs *rang* true; they were songs of being and becoming. And they drew me in.

The bicycles and apples kept me at a distance, bored and sitting back in my chair. The messy, spontaneous sketches and photographs had me leaning forward, moving in with rapt interest and delight. Authenticity, in whatever the content, speaks of one's personal truth and heartfelt observations. And the viewer can immediately recognize the nascent brilliance of transparency and soulfulness.

Take ahold of your vision. It's yours and yours alone. Don't try to be good, just try to be real. Each person has some genuine place of genius in their constitution, and you are not going to find it by trying to please others: teachers, parents, admission committees, or peers. Trust your own process. Take responsibility for everything that you are or are not. Your joys, struggles, trials and tribulations, longings, obsessions, and passions are all fair game for your creative exploration. Oftentimes, when an artist delves deep into their own life, and is unflaggingly honest with their perceptions, it moves outward and strikes a chord of resonance in the viewer. It changes things for the viewer, sometimes a little, sometimes a lot. Learn to discriminate your authentic perceptions, your gems, from those images that imitate the masters, or are merely the mind's digestion of popular photography tropes.

Claim your unique brilliance. Learn what it is. Do not fear who you are. Be yourself. Natalie Goldberg writes of what her teacher, Katagiri Roshi, said to her. "We are all Buddha. I can see you are Buddha. You don't believe me. When you see that you are Buddha, you will be awake. That's what enlightenment is."

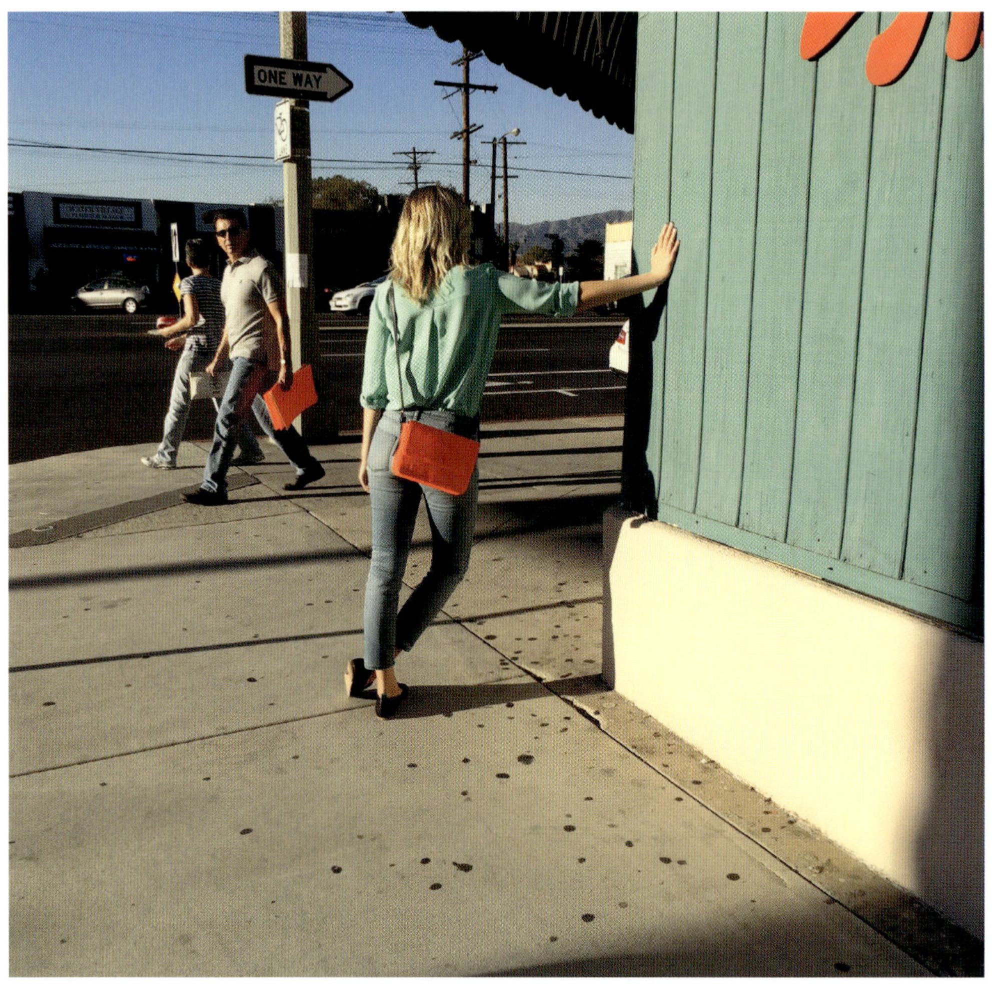

Coral Reef Chinese Restaurant, Glendale Boulevard, Los Angeles, California, January 17, 2015
Instagram © Stephen Shore. Courtesy 303 Gallery, New York

Digital Life

Are you a digital native who grew up with computers and devices at your fingertips, or did you come to the silicon banquet later in life? I am the latter and many of my students are the former. Both conditions hold their inherent benefits and challenges. If you grew up in the past twenty-five years, it is likely that digital technology seamlessly integrates and inserts itself in all areas of your life: educational, professional, social, creative, and even romantic. For those of us who came of age in the mid to late twentieth century, our life was analog with papers and pens, books, libraries, newspapers, film and darkrooms, letters written by hand, and actual telephones. Many came to the digital revolution kicking and screaming, with our fingernails scratching across the floor.

At first, I strongly resisted the advent of digital tools. I viewed them as robotic and dehumanizing. I have long realized and accepted that all tools are extensions of the capabilities of the human body. The camera is an extension of your eye and brain, the pen and paper an extension of your hand and mind, and the darkroom functions as a metaphor for the alchemy of imagination and the power of visualization. After getting my first computer in the early 1990s (a Mac laptop), I felt a strange resonance and inward satisfaction with its electronic streams of bits of information. In a moment of realization, I understood that digital tools are potent metaphors of our brains and nervous systems. I became an immediate devotee.

All art forms, including photography, are manifestations of materiality and representations of material culture. We bring our visions, concepts, and perceptions to life by giving them form and substance. This takes place within the context of an attentional flow between the artist and world, and between the artist and their materials and tools. Analog and digital tools both have a place—albeit a different one—in the broad matrix of attentional flow and materiality.

Attentional flow is often impeded by distraction and identification with our devices that propagate a near constant barrage of generally trivial information. But with a responsible attitude, digital tools can enrich and heighten the attentional flow.

Digital technology offers a freer and more subtle form of materiality. No longer limited by the need for such things as gathering tools, cleaning your desk, or buying and loading film, digital warriors can respond spontaneously to the moment—with attention and freedom. You can take photographs at the speed of your body's ability to respond to the moment. You can view, edit, and publish photographs without the need, say, for preparing darkroom chemicals or waiting to view images until the film is developed. There is an immediate form of feedback, a dopamine boost, that can help you analyze and revise your point of view at a moment's notice.

In the past, when I would travel, it often took weeks or months before I could see the negatives, make contact prints, and evaluate my findings. If I needed to revise and re-shoot, sometimes I couldn't; at other times, I'd need to wait long periods of time to return to the subject. These days, with my device on my person at all times, I can write when inspiration strikes, when the digestion and contemplation of ideas results in insights and even sentences bubbling up while I'm shopping or walking or taking care of mundane tasks. I can also photograph anytime and anywhere without the need to carry cumbersome equipment with its complicated and time-consuming set-up.

The clear and present danger of technology, however, lies in its seductive draw, its ability to steal our attention and create forms of attachment unheard of when Buddha walked the earth. We need to fervently resist this powerful form of technological addiction that can make us into reactive machines instead of people. The struggle between the cultivation of our free attention and resistance to our attachments form a major part of all inner teaching traditions. The world and people, as well as our own body and mind, deserve our attention; we cannot allow the gift of awareness to be squandered and plundered by inconsequential and trivial message feeds, the plethora of trite, narcissistic images, or the daily barrage of impressions from social media. We need to strengthen and expand our capacity for attention and not give in to the constant distraction of a peripatetic mind. Attention begets attention. Through our intent, we can also help others gain attention.

Resist the powerful draw of your alluring device. Learn to engage the struggle between desire that grows from attachment and your intent to strive to be present: to oneself, to one's surroundings, and to others. Intent is a powerful tool for growth and evolution. Often it is enough to be present to the mind's witness. When we see and watch our constant turning toward our devices, the seeing itself has force; it distances our consciousness from the habitual activity and creates a measure of inner space. It helps free up our attention for more important purposes.

> **The clear and present danger of technology, however, lies in its seductive draw, its ability to steal our attention and create forms of attachment unheard of when Buddha walked the earth.**

How can analog tools assist our creative growth? All forms of analog tools are primarily physical in a way that directly engages the body. Writing with a pen slows you down, synchronizes the hand and mind to a human pace, and the appearance of the words themselves have expressive materiality; your style of penmanship creates another layer of communication and transmission. Photographing with film encourages a disciplined approach. You take fewer pictures. Film costs money and takes time to process in the darkroom. With a film camera, you need to be attentive and sure of yourself—bringing a nimble quality of attention to the moment, since you often take far fewer photographs than with a digital camera. Each moment, each shot, needs to count. In true Zen fashion, you need to be physically present to the moment—whole and undistracted.

Same with the darkroom. Stephen Shore, photographer and director of the photography program at Bard College, said in a recent interview: "I don't have a prejudice against digital—that's all I use now—but I'm convinced that there are certain things, very hard to describe, that are learned by doing darkroom work. It makes a lot of decisions *physical*. You learn to look at light in a way that you wouldn't if you just used a slider in Photoshop. Turning a dial, pressing a button and exposing it, taking out the processing paper and looking at it—people get a more visceral sense of the decisions they make by working in analog."

I have to admit, experience in the darkroom helps tremendously with learning Photoshop and other digital tools. I also highly recommend that photographers learn to draw or at least experiment with drawing. Take a pencil and sheet of paper and draw something. You'll find that drawing helps, like no other discipline, to synchronize the hand and eye, and to correlate your perceptions *and* your feelings with such things as the weight of a line, the movement of a form, the qualities of volume and space, the nature of light, and the relationship of objects to others in its environment. The sheer physicality of drawing helps to release your creative flow.

Finally, what about publishing and exhibiting your images? The analog world of photography required that we print, matte and frame, and present our work to others. Considerations of size, print quality, paper choices, and presentation methods all contribute to the final expression. I at least recommend that digital photographers learn to print their images. The interpretative action of printing and the multiple decisions that need to be made is an art form unto itself and a way of learning about the expressive potentials in an image. You are left with a physical object—that can be hung on a wall, sold, and serve as an object of contemplation for others in a way that digital feeds cannot begin to match.

However, digital tools open the door to many other possibilities, including global dissemination of images with an almost immediate turn-around time between making an image and publishing it. Instagram, Facebook, Snapchat, and other services are primarily *publishing* platforms. Unlike traditional galleries and books, with digital tools, you have the opportunity to curate your own images guided by your intelligence and conscience. What type of food are you offering the viewer—the junk food of ego delights or a nutritious, life-enhancing meal. Do you want to engender admiration or provoke thought?

What I find encouraging is the manner in which many photographers are exploring the creative potential of these powerful, new publishing platforms. For example, Stephen Shore's Instagram feed was part of his recent retrospective exhibition at MoMA. In another example, *Time* magazine's Instagram photographer of the year is Melissa Spritz featuring her project, *You Have Nothing to Worry About*, that explores images of her mentally ill mother. Alexandra Genova of *Time* observes, "Spritz takes the viewer on a captivating and unflinching journey with images that reflect the complexity of mental suffering through the lens of someone who cares deeply for her subject." These projects have depth and bring insight through a digital platform.

In an excellent and controversial TED talk by Jia Jia Fei, titled *Art in the Age of Instagram*, she makes the startling statement: "In the pre-digital photography era, the message was: This is what I'm seeing. I have seen. Today, the message was: I was there. I came, I saw, and I selfied." I don't know about you, but I find this very disconcerting. We deserve better than this.

Rather than allowing digital tools to be reductive, can we use them to expand our experience and deepen the nature of the mind. Selfies have their value, but do they ascend to the level of selflessness or help us understand and integrate the Buddhist concept of no-self into our core being? Does our identification with and celebration of a very limited range of existence—the ubiquitous *me*—that often ignores the other or the unity of all things, serve the evolution of the human mind for generations to come? And isn't that very evolution of consciousness meant to be part of the purpose of art and photography?

Steal Like an Artist

I have great appreciation for the nuances of United States copyright law. Under the current law, a free exchange of ideas, techniques, and styles of expression are allowed and indeed even encouraged. Only actual works or the physical manifestation of ideas are protected by law. And the fair use clause of copyright law even allows for a dialogue with actual works of art for the purposes of transformation, parody, criticism, and education.

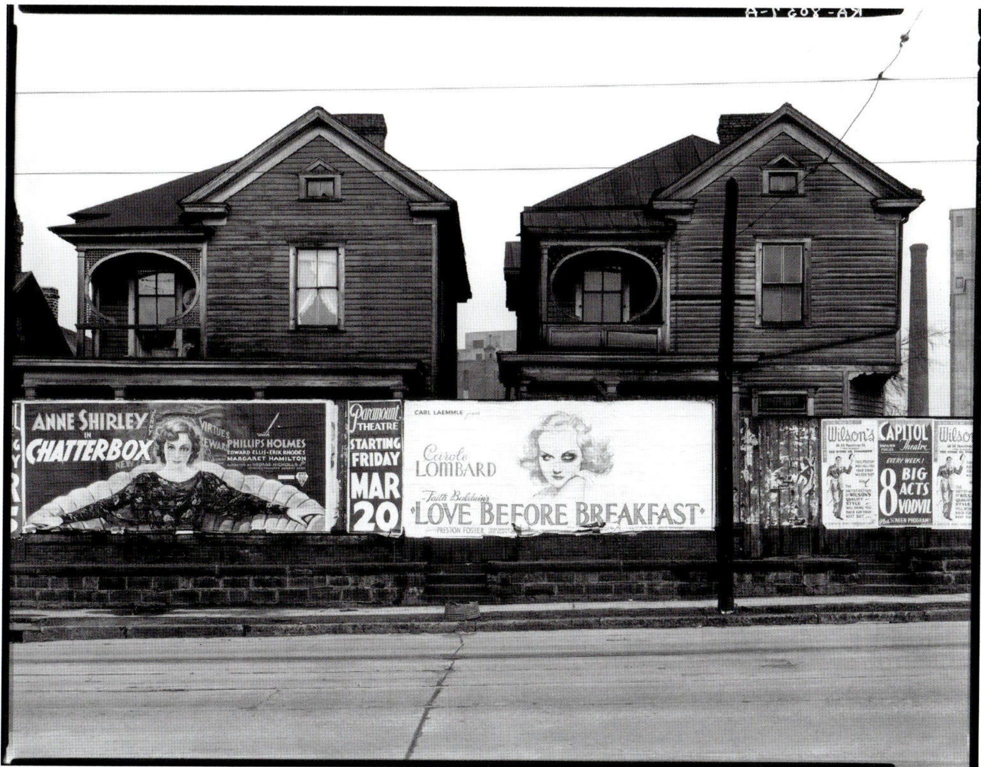

Billboard and Frame Houses, Atlanta, Georgia, 1936, Walker Evans

Many contemporary photographers cite Walker Evans as a primary influence on their work due to his dispassionate gaze and vernacular images of American culture.
Courtesy: Library of Congress, FSA/OWI Collection

What this means in practice represents a powerful benefit to artists and creative individuals. We can borrow freely from each other in the form of ideas, techniques, styles, genres, and approaches to the medium. Indeed, we are, at heart, historical creatures. We build upon the discoveries of the past and add our own insight to the mix. We study the artists from the multiple histories of art, photographers from the history of the medium, and read the great literature of the past few centuries—and unreservedly open our minds and allow ourselves to be influenced. And finally, we can use the accomplishments of others as the threshold of our own unique explorations.

I tell my students frequently, *learn to steal like an artist.* Do not work in a vacuum. We have ready access to global histories of art, photography, literature, architecture, ritual, dance, and music to inform and inspire us. I can tell immediately in looking at student work if they have a background of looking at serious art and photography (not just Instagram or popular photo magazines), reading great literature, and listening to something more than the top 40 in music. Their work has greater depth, empathy, and sophistication and enters more cleanly into the dialogue of our times.

Read, look, and learn. Gather your influences into a bouquet that you place in a prominent place and look at frequently. I keep folders and bookmarks of essays, articles, images, and websites that influence and inspire me. Seed your unconscious. Choose your influences as carefully as you mind the food that enters your body. Nourish your psychic space with photographers, images, and bodies of work that you aspire to and want to emulate. Don't worry about imitation for now. As you work through themes and ideas inspired by others, you cannot help but to add yourself to the mix. It is natural and normal to respect and learn from history; it is inevitable that you will find your own way, your own path of navigating through your multiple influences into a unique blend that represents your concerns, ideas, and growing style.

The fact is that there is nothing on earth that is completely individual. We are all in relation to something. As artists, we plumb the deep commonality of our humanity and the multiple legacies of the past, present, and future found in many forms: our genetics, our background and conditioning, our destiny, our unique experiences, our societal/ artistic influences, and the hopes, dreams, and aspirations of ourselves, others, and our communities. We are a link in the great forward movement of history, and we must find the place that we occupy in the ongoing dance of time.

Steve Jobs once said, "Ultimately, it comes down to taste. Try to expose yourself to the best things humans have done and then try to bring those things into what you are doing."

Art Is a Lie
That Tells the Truth

This statement is attributed to Picasso. Photography is an interpretive medium. Through the eye and mind of the photographer, a subject is removed from the larger context from which it was found. What the photographer decides to include or not include in the frame, which precise moment they choose to snap the shutter, and their choice of lighting and post-processing options are all highly transformative choices.

Take Dorothea Lange's iconic image, *Migrant Mother*, as an example. It is widely believed that the photograph depicts a destitute mother from a pea picker's camp in Central California. Dorothea Lange wrote in her notes that formed the official, but rarely used, caption. "Migrant agricultural worker's family. Seven hungry children. Mother aged 32, the father is a native Californian. Destitute in a pea pickers camp because of the failure of the early pea crop. These people had just sold their tent in order to buy food. Most of the 2,500 people in this camp were destitute. Nipomo, California, 1936."

The actual facts are that Florence Thompson, the subject of the photograph, was returning home with her husband and children after a period of farm work. They had a flat tire and Thompson's husband and older son went into town to have it fixed. Florence awaited their return at the pea pickers camp. However, Lange wrote in her notes for the photograph, "She had just sold the tires from her car to buy food."

The facts are evident. Thompson and her family were poor but not destitute. They had work, a home, and they owned a car. However, the resulting photograph became a symbol for the great depression, reflecting both human dignity and suffering. In the eyes of many, and maybe even for Lange, a destitute subject could tell a better story without the inconvenient and nuanced narrative reflected by the actual facts. The photograph *Migrant Mother* became a potent symbol for the great depression. Art is a lie that tells the truth.

Photography is a subjective endeavor that can lead to collective awareness. At its best, it can lead to the kinds of truths that are deemed self-evident through the agency of basic decency and human conscience. These truths are potent but few: the fundamental need for equality for all, our sentience and mortality, our need for human connection,

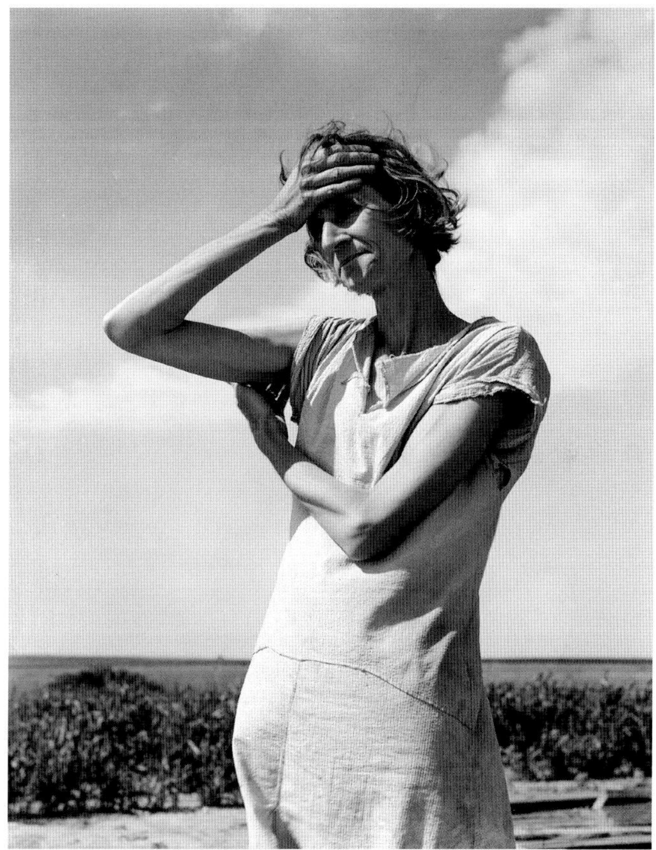

Wife of a Migratory Laborer with Three Children. Near Childress, Texas. Nettie Featherston, 1938,
Dorothea Lange

In Lange's original title and caption, she gives the name of the subject and her circumstances. All too often, Lange's photographs become symbols of the great depression and eclipse the specific lives of the subjects.

Courtesy: Library of Congress, FSA/OWI Collection

and our interdependence with the Earth and others. The use of metaphor in a photographer's work can transform a subject from the specificity of fact to the "untruths" of a highly personal yet broadly relatable collective expression. Writer Paul Theroux contemplates this phenomenon, "There is a paradox…the deeper I have gone into my own memory, the more I realized how much in common I have with other people. The greater the access I have had to my memory, to my mind and experience…the more I have felt myself to be a part of the world."

When you re-contextualize an image by taking it out of the flow of time and divorce the subject from its larger surroundings, you are influencing the viewer's experience based on your artistic intent. This creative license should be governed by integrity, compassion, and social awareness. As image makers, we strive to balance personal expression with civic responsibility.

Think carefully of what you photograph, why, and how. Meaning in an image is often seen by others based on their worldview, their experiences, and their associations. Your work is a dialogue with your audience. This is part of the enduring power of artistic expression. Be mindful of your journey toward truth, not the journalistic aim of impartiality or any kind of non-verifiable objective truth, but in striving to be true to the integrity of your experience expressed through the transformational nature of the medium.

Mostly, try to be honest.

Use Irony Sparingly

Irony dominates much contemporary fine art photography. The classical definition of irony revolves around the notion that things are not always what they seem; that there may be an opposite meaning in an image that belies its superficial depiction. As a literary device, irony speaks to those in the know by subverting or contrasting meaning through words that are contrary to expected beliefs. In Shakespeare's *Julius Caesar*, when Mark Antony states several times in his funeral oratory that Brutus was "an honorable

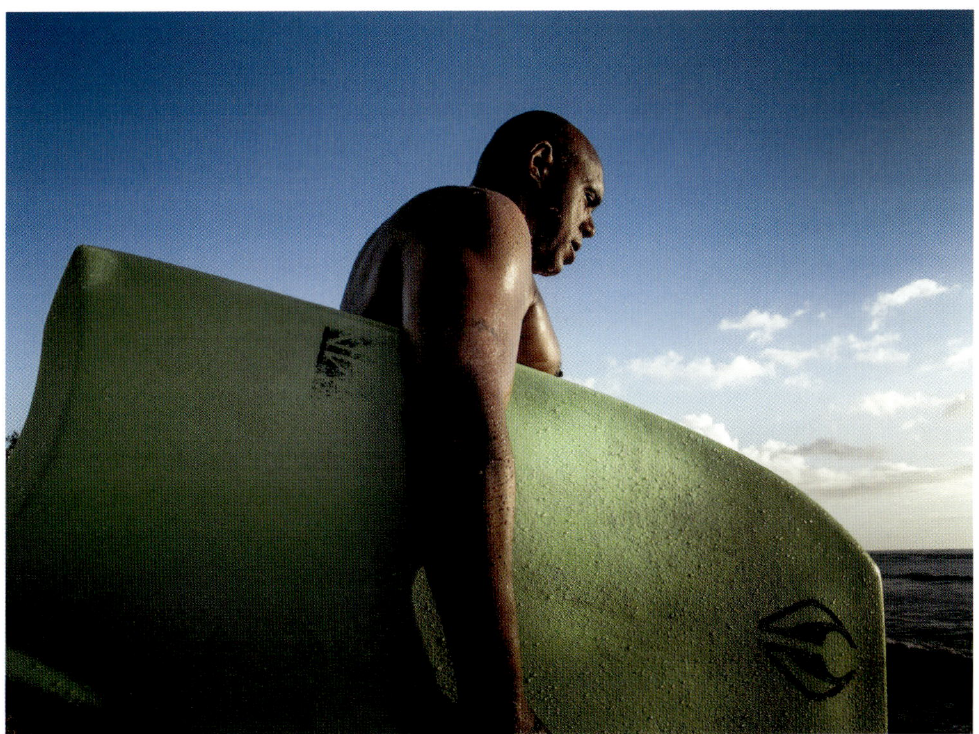

Waikiki, Hawai'i, James Knudsen
A strong element of irony can be found in this photograph of a man on Waikiki Beach, reflecting the photographer's intent to highlight the dark side of paradise.

man," we know that he is using sarcasm as an ironic tool to refer to the scoundrel-like nature of Brutus.

How might irony be employed as a powerful tool in photography? Situational context often forms the boundary between straightforward expression and ironic meaning. An obvious and striking example can be found in Margaret Bourke White's photograph *Breadline During the Louisville Flood, Kentucky, 1937.* The mostly black welfare recipients standing in the breadline are contrasted by the larger-than-life propaganda billboard behind them that depicts a glowingly happy white family in a new car coupled with the text, "World's Highest Standard of Living: There's no way like the American Way."

In another example, Richard Avedon traveled the American west with an 8×10-inch view camera and photographed its residents on a commission from the Amon Carter Museum in Fort Worth, Texas. In light of these portraits, Avedon makes the comment, "The photographs have a reality for me that the people don't. It's through the photographs that I know them." The project subverts any vestige that the viewer may have about the romantic frontier of the American west and the noble, pioneering spirit of its people. The people portrayed are misfits, drifters, blue collar and droll, with a pall hanging over almost all of them. One reviewer, Richard Bolton, commented, "Here is a new age—postindustrial, postalienation, posteconomic despair." In one photograph, a cherubic overweight boy cradles a large rifle, and in another a ruby red-lipped, despair-ridden woman, possibly a waitress, poses with a splash of dollar bills held close to her chest.

Herein lies my concern with an excessive use of irony. All too often it speaks only to those "in the know," the educated elite, and is infused with a sense of moral superiority to those depicted. I suspect that liberal ignorance and a blind eye to the decades-old conditions and needs of the working class in red states contributed greatly to the results of the 2016 election. I think all too frequently we don't strive to understand and empathize with those in front of the camera; rather, as photographers, we often use them as actors on a stage to confirm our own opinions, biases, and critical standpoint. I question why, for example, so many young photographers are drawn to photograph the homeless and the dispossessed.

Nevertheless, irony is a powerful tool in the hands of sensitive artists and photographers. It encourages nuanced expression that ignores neither history, tradition, and beauty, nor denies the forces of modern reality that subvert idealism and outdated myths. Things *are not* as they appear and have multiple and sometimes contradictory layers of meaning. Both the appearance of things and their underlying dynamics can be rendered in a photograph.

In other images from the western states, two of the photographers included in the seminal *New Topographics* exhibition—Stephen Shore and Robert Adams—employ considerable irony in their cool, dispassionate observations of the man-altered landscape. Unlike their forebears of Ansel Adams and Edward Weston, who lived in an era when pristine nature could be found, and representations of the land incorporated an idealistic and spiritual dimension, the *New Topographic* photographers focused on the haunting and minimal beauty of suburban tract developments against majestic peaks, roadhouses and gas stations, motels and drive-in culture. The powerful irony occurs due to the deep attention to form, craft, and suffusing light that Shore and Robert Adams can masterfully convey. The images subvert the earlier, romantic landscape tradition by having similar exquisite beauty and formal coherence, but have as their subjects the difficult and uneasy intrusions of humans into the once-mythic frontier.

Irony, as a tool in the hands of intelligent and caring photographers, can remind us of what we have lost, represent where we are as a culture, and disrupt some of the outworn mythologies that still govern part of our societal lives, such as the "American dream," the "Marlboro man," and "manifest destiny." It can invoke in images the powerful words of James Agee on photography's potential to represent "the cruel radiance of what is," a phrase that itself conveys considerable literary irony. Use it with intelligence, conscience, and empathy.

Embrace Paradox

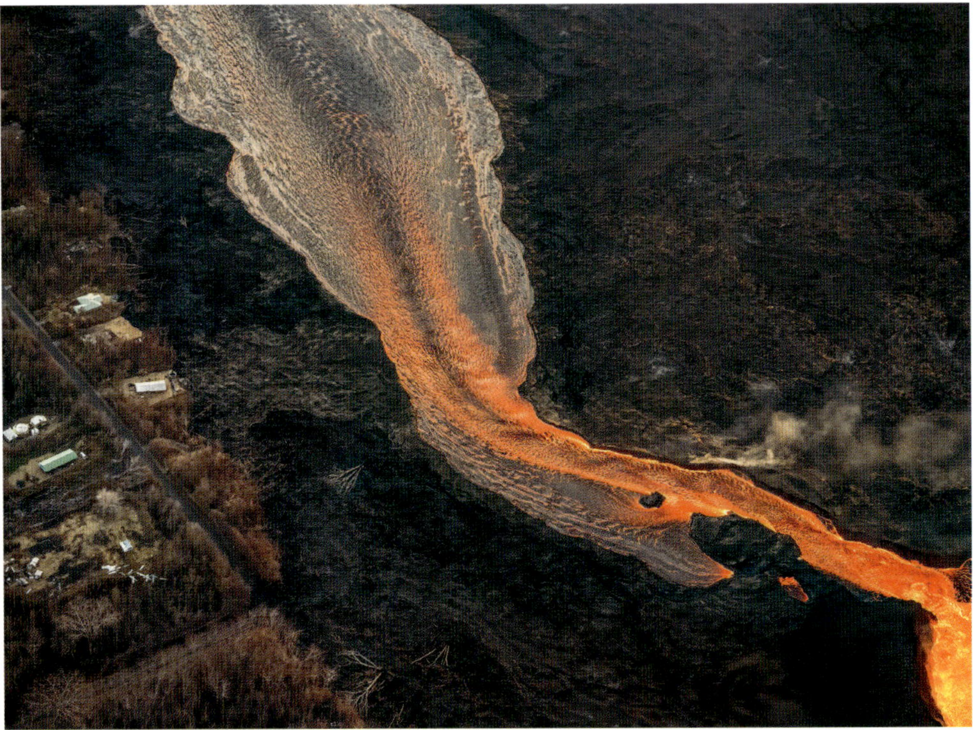

Fissure #8, Kilaeau Volcano, Hawai'i, 2018, Leslie Gleim

Photography and art place us in front of some of the great, unanswerable questions of existence—and then reflect our reply. Who am I? What is the nature of our lives individually and collectively? Both irony and paradox address, though differently, the contradictory dynamics at the heart of most phenomena, that all things hold opposing tendencies and conflicting aspects that are often impervious to casual observation and cannot be explained and represented through shallow thinking.

While irony, in art and photography, refers to the difference between appearances and content, paradox reveals the inherent contradictions and the irreconcilable differences present in a subject that defies logic and neat categories. Most things are neither exclusively good or bad, dark or light, beautiful or ugly, or energy or matter. They are both, and more. Through deep perception, photographers can employ paradox to reveal the many dimensions of the subject and the mysteries of both human and natural life.

I am reminded of Richard Avedon's portrait, *Marilyn Monroe, actress, New York, 1957*, that I often show in classes to illustrate the power of paradox. In the portrait, Marilyn wears a low cut, dark-sequined dress, with her white skin glowing against her dark, glittery clothing and the luminous, grey background. Her smooth skin, voluptuous figure, tousled hair, and parted lips reveal sensuous attractiveness, while her downcast, sad eyes and the childlike fragility of her posture reflect her troubled nature. Avedon was able, in a masterful single portrait, to convey her beauty and tragedy simultaneously, both at once. Paradox can convey mystery and different dimensions of a subject in a manner that suggests what lies beyond the picture frame.

Many photographers make compelling photos of ugly, difficult things: industrial settings, intense sunsets from polluted air, and the chaos of modern urban life. By making order from the profane and the disagreeable, we are presenting viewers with a kind of truth, that nothing is just this or that, and that opposing characteristics can be resolved and integrated. Thus, art becomes a metaphor for potential unity and wholeness in a broken world. In his eloquent book, *Beauty in Photography*, Robert Adams writes: "Photography ought to start with and remain faithful to the appearance of the world, and in so doing record contradictions. The greatest pictures would then—I still believe this— find wholeness in the torn world…. art is a discovery of harmony, a vision of disparities reconciled, of shape beneath confusion."

The paradoxical nature of photography becomes evident in mass communication with certain kinds of pictures that can help in engendering awareness and fostering change in conditions that demand societal attention. Who wants to look at suffering, starving people, or pictures of violence and death? Yet we look. Compelled through the photographer's mastery of form and color, drawn to the seductive vitality of the subject and image, we are taught, informed, and made aware of injustice and suffering. The photograph demands our attention. Hopefully, the expanded awareness on the part of the viewer can help change things for the better. Consciousness is a transformative force in the world. To find dignity in the commonplace, goodness and strength in the downtrodden, and humanity in the casualties of strife represent some of the paradoxical powers of the camera.

As a landscape photographer, I often choose to represent the intelligent and sublime design of nature against the backdrop of the outsized human footprint on the land. Some of what are, for me, my strongest images contain this paradoxical mystery of death and life, natural order and the devastating impact of human desire. I simply want to present the paradoxical facts and leave judgment to the viewer.

In like fashion, photographer Leslie Gleim portrays the awe-inspiring creative force of the Kilaeau volcano in Hawai'i that has created thousands of acres of new land, contrasted against the destruction of hundreds of homes and businesses by molten lava. Canadian photographer Edward Burtynsky photographs the evidence of industrial waste and environmental damage from refineries, quarries, mines, recycling yards, large scale agriculture, and other interventions on the land. His photographs are as majestic as they are horrifying. They scare us yet compel our gaze and remind us that we created and continue to augment these fearful residues of irreversible planetary damage.

He writes: "These images are meant as metaphors to the dilemma of our modern existence; they search for a dialogue between attraction and repulsion, seduction and fear. We are drawn by desire—a chance at good living, yet we are consciously or unconsciously aware that the world is suffering for our success. Our dependence on nature to provide the materials for our consumption and our concern for the health of our planet sets us into an uneasy contradiction. For me, these images function as reflecting pools of our times."

If there is truth that we can find as artists, it can only be approached through the recognition of the deep paradoxes inherent in our own lives and in the life surrounding us.

Know When to Be Tender,
When to Snarl,
When to Shout,
and When to Whisper

I am a Boomer and love Bob Dylan. It goes with the territory. Dylan knows how and when to snarl in his nasal, searing voice. Think of *Positively Fourth Street* that begins with a roar, "You've got a lot of nerve to say you are my friend." And Dylan can equally be tender and endearing as in songs like *Tomorrow is a Long Time*. He sings, "There's

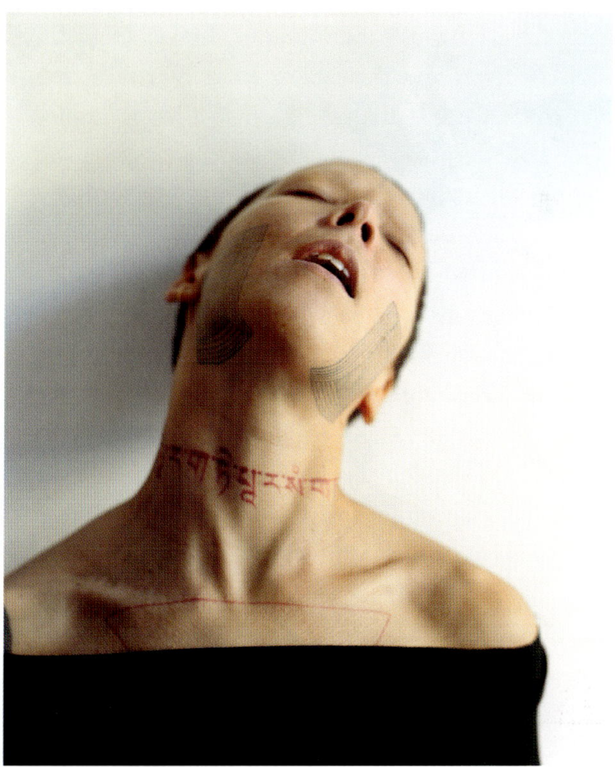

GERMANY. Berlin. 2018. Michelle, from *I Know How Furiously Your Heart is Beating,* Alec Soth

beauty in the silver, singin' river.…But none of these and nothing else can touch the beauty that I remember in my true love's eyes."

What is it about popular photography (including Instagram) in which the range of expression seems so narrow? Many photographers are willing to show beauty, highlight pleasing shapes and forms, engage in endless self-display, and even touch the surface of social justice and environmental issues, but really don't want to be viewed as being negative or confrontational. Many pictures seem so tame. Pictures from amateur photographers in our bi-monthly public critiques often seem like Hallmark cards, full of clichés and tired tropes. Or, from more experienced photographers, aware of the contemporary practices in the medium, they have adopted the "deadpan" aesthetic so prevalent in today's art photography.

In the deadpan aesthetic, subjects stare expressionless into the camera lens. Often evident in the photographs is a conscious lack of sentimentality and engagement; the subject just stands there without overt involvement from the photographer. Susan Sontag traces the prevalence of this trend in portraiture to Diane Arbus. She writes, "The authority of Arbus's photographs derives from the contrast between their lacerating subject matter and their calm, matter-of-fact attentiveness. The most striking aspect of Arbus's work is that she seems to have enrolled in one of art photography's most vigorous enterprises—concentrating on victims, on the unfortunate—but without the compassionate purpose that such a project is expected to serve. Her work shows people who are pathetic, pitiable, as well as repulsive, but it does not arouse any compassionate feelings. For what would be more correctly described as their dissociated point of view, the photographs have been praised for their candor and for an unsentimental empathy with their subjects."

If we follow this trend forward, we see the vacant eyes, robotic stares, and androgynous poses, devoid of feeling and even basic humanity, of fashion photography since the 1980s. Deadpan has become a prevailing look and art photographers have often eschewed emotion for the dissociated gaze.

Excuse me, but I want to say, screw that. Where is your mercy, your sympathy, or your anger and outrage? Where lies your undying love and passion and longing? Where do you find your bliss, or your tender, raw suffering, or your broken heartedness at the state of this, our only world. I want to see feeling in your images, not sentiment or new-age sweetness, but genuine, deep, emotion that grabs you by the throat and won't let go.

Certain photographers and bodies of work are considered great and have stood the test of time because of the range of their voice and the breadth of their expression. Robert Frank's *The Americans* forms the example that prompted this essay. His sympathies for the everyday, common people of America shine through with tender mercy on every page. His disdain for the aristocratic members of society (celebrities, town fathers, nouveau riche) are the subject of his profound snarls. There is no deadpan in his book. He is kindred to Bob Dylan in his poetry and feeling. His lonely elevator girl is like Dylan's *Sad Eyed Lady of the Lowlands* and has inspired common sympathy for our human condition for generations now.

Positive change is starting to take place in photography. The deadpan aesthetic has dominated much photography for decades now, since the seminal exhibition *New Topographics*, and involves channeling emotion through the mind and an impassioned lens. In art photography, feeling can too often be viewed as mere sentiment. Alec Soth's debut book, *Sleeping by the Mississippi*, contains portraits of normal yet strange-around-edges people (seemingly inspired by Arbus) that gather in communities adjacent to the river. Soth maintains an impassioned view. His gaze and their gaze interlock in a mutual dance of distance and cool regard. Eventually, Soth found that "being this reserved person interacting with other people almost started turning into the subject of the work itself."

When feelings grab you by the gut, pick up your camera. Show us your anger and outrage, your tender sympathies, your loves and antipathies.

Soth took a year off from working to meditate by a lake and reassess his life and working practice. He underwent what he calls "a full-on mystical experience," and had "this sudden realization that everything in the universe was connected."

"I know it sounds hippy-dippy, but it was incredibly intense. I was tearful and simultaneously filled with this almost overwhelming sense of joy." He began a new body of work, with a title taken from a line in a Wallace Stevens poem, *I Know How Furiously Your Heart is Beating*, in which he makes a series of portraits of people in their personal spaces that are hauntingly intimate and full of a profound sense of empathy. Soth claims he is "trying to incorporate a little more of the sensitivity I felt when I was on my retreat from work. Photography is not essentially a sensitive medium, but I've come to realize that sensitivity matters. It really does."

How do you convey feeling in your work as a photographer? Can you move beyond mere superficial sentiment to something that really engages you? There are several tools and methods that I incorporate in my creative practice and recommend to my students.

The first is to work in silence. When Soth makes portraits now, he experiments at times with complete silence between photographer and sitter. Engagement can deepen in a space of silence. The non-verbal encounters based on sensation and feeling can shine through in a special way. Even when photographing objects, try to turn off the endlessly commenting and categorizing nature of verbal thought. Feeling and sensitivity can deepen in this wordless space.

When feelings grab you by the gut, pick up your camera. Show us your anger and outrage, your tender sympathies, your loves and antipathies. Don't be afraid to be real, vulnerable and touched by something of someone. When do you need to shout from the rooftops and when do you want to take us aside and whisper in our ear?

One of the common mistakes beginning photographers make is trying to represent feeling from the outside looking in—by photographing those in a state of sadness, joy, conflict, or suffering. When *you* experience these emotions, what do you feel like on the inside and how does that affect the way you see the world? When you feel sadness or joy or outrage or hope, simply pick up a camera. Again, see how you see differently in different states of mind and being. Expand your range of photographic expression.

Look at photographs by Diane Arbus and Lisette Model. Study Robert Frank's *The Americans*. Look at Sally Mann's intimate explorations of her own family, her elegiac images of death and the southern landscape, and her wrenching images of the degradation of her husband's once strapping body from muscular dystrophy. And finally, look at the highly collaborative portraits by Lydia Panas. She says, "I am inspired by people who are honest with themselves.... As we quietly look at one another during a photo session, we get to a point where we drop our facades, and for those moments, we understand each other perfectly."

Study Alec Soth's book, *I Know How Furiously Your Heart is Beating*, to witness a shared intimate space, a collaboration of compassion between sitter and photographer.

"Sharpness is a Bourgeois Concept"

This quote from Henri Cartier-Bresson captures aspects of the film-versus-digital argument. By modern standards, many of the great photographs from the film era are grainy, unsharp, and lacking in extreme resolution. But have you ever looked at a photograph by Cartier-Bresson or Robert Frank and placed your nose against it to examine its critical sharpness? I doubt it. You take in the overall look and meaning of the image viscerally, emotionally, and thoughtfully. Many film photographs are simply softer than their

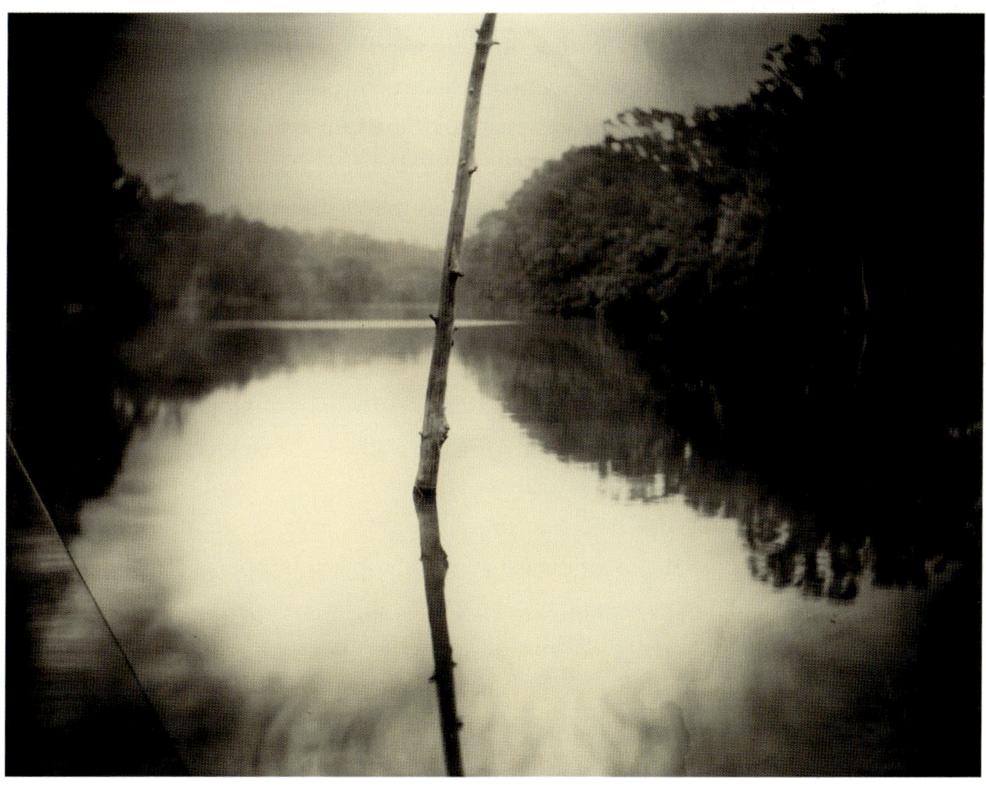

Deep South, Untitled (Stick), 1998 by Sally Mann
Tea-toned gelatin silver print, 40 x 50 inches, (101.6 x 127 cm) (unframed) Edition of 10
© Sally Mann. Courtesy Gagosian

digital counterparts. Lenses were not as good, darkroom technology had its flaws, many shots were handheld with slower films, and, as a rule, photographers were concerned with the subject and not obsessing over cameras and lenses.

Inexactitude and imperfection are often intentional components in art, mirroring the human condition. Many digital photographs can feel clinical and sterile, over-sharpened and falsely perfect. In the hands of inexperienced and insensitive practitioners, they feel synthetic, like specimens of too much cosmetic surgery, and strike the audience with a blow to the eyes without penetration into the psyche of the viewer. High impact imagery prevails in the popular photography aesthetic with attempts to "strike" the viewer with a strong—one could even say overdone—look and feel. For sophisticated viewers, these images come off as hammering to the senses, much like a constant diet of heavy metal music.

Can we instill in a photograph the aim of presence or the representation of raw humanity, full of contradictory imperfection? The messy spontaneity and deep ambiguity of real life cannot be rendered in faultless resolution. Our eyes even see in a particular fashion, sharp in the central vision of the macula and blurring out as the retinal image moves to the edges of the visual field. This is why, I believe, some photographers are drawn to plastic, toy cameras like the Holga and Diana and soft-focus lenses or use long exposures and slow shutter speeds to render motion and not freeze it. During the film era, many photographers sought intentional grainy results and an impressionistic rendering of the subject. These kinds of imperfect and unsharp renderings often suffuse the subject with light and atmosphere, much like the way we actually see the world.

The messy spontaneity and deep ambiguity of real life cannot be rendered in faultless resolution.

In the hands of skilled practitioners, sharpness does have its definite place in the pantheon of photography. The tonal precision and sharp acutance of, say, Ansel Adam's landscapes or Andreas Gursky's zeitgeist imagery can be awe inspiring. Or, it's hard to image a soft, blurry rendering of Edward Weston's modernist shells and vegetables. Many contemporary photographs of the land depend on verisimilitude and an intensification of the subject, rendering every detail as worthy of consideration. However, precision forms one, but only one, expressive tool in the hands of photographers.

When making images, pay attention to the quality of lenses and the digital editing process. Contemporary lenses can be blazingly sharp and photographers devise methods in software to accentuate that sharpness even further. Digital cameras in JPG mode

     THE MINDFUL PHOTOGRAPHER

and scanners often have automatic sharpness built in. Indeed, some popular high-quality film scanners require the sharpness to be turned down to a negative value, like minus thirty, merely to turn off the automatic sharpening. Likewise, images made with an extremely sharp lens require minimal sharpening in software, while photographs made with moderate-quality "kit" lenses, those that are sold with the camera, require more aggressive sharpening. In my experience, over-sharpening is a much greater danger than under-sharpening. With sharpening, often, less is more.

Over-sharpened images look "crunchy" and brittle; they often lack nuance and sensuous gradation. A sure sign of digital over-sharpening is when you see whitish halos around the edges of things in the photograph. Look at photographs in magazines and on websites to see how prevalent the over-sharpened look has become. Learn about and pay attention to sharpness. There are numerous effective methods to enhance sharpness without killing the sensuousness, subtlety, and nuance of the image.

I think that anyone seeking to make a career in photography or to pursue it with a degree of seriousness should have the experience of making images with film. Both film and digital images have their own strengths and unique qualities. My argument has always been to embrace both film and digital technologies. Film has a natural kind of depth, presence, and dimensionality of color and detail. Digital technology offers ease of use, economy, and, when using RAW format, a dynamic range of brightness that approaches and can exceed many films. But they feel different. Use what works for your intent and your desired look but learn the processes well. Skilled photographers can work in both digital and film without the viewer knowing the difference.

Most photographers use, more or less, the same camera today: a handheld digital SLR or mirrorless camera with rectangular proportions, sharp lenses, and a sensitive sensor. Study photographs made with film (square and rectangular format), view cameras, digital technology, sharp lenses, toy cameras, and soft-focus lenses. Too much control can be overrated. Some photographs live within a space of intentional imperfection. Look, for example, at the resonating mystery of suffused light and exquisite darkness in Sally Mann's southern landscapes made with an old 8×10 view camera, replete with light leaks and employing soft-focus, damaged lenses. In these images, serendipity rules.

Chance is part of every artist's methodology, whether intentionally embraced or not. Sally Mann says of her images, "I'm so worried that I'm going to perfect [my] technique someday. I have to say it's unfortunate how many of my pictures do depend upon some technical error."

Learn to Love the Questions

Artists often work from questions, not answers. If you read what artists say about their work, take careful note of their verb choices. They investigate, explore, interrogate, inquire, study, examine, research, and probe. Many find delight in the state of not-knowing and looking into the nature of things. Answers can all too often be limiting and a form of entropy; they serve to close off the living questions that lead to ongoing discovery. One of my first photography teachers gave us a few powerful words of wisdom. While looking at a photograph, a scene in the world, or even another person, he would advise us to stay open to new and fresh discovery, to stay in touch with our

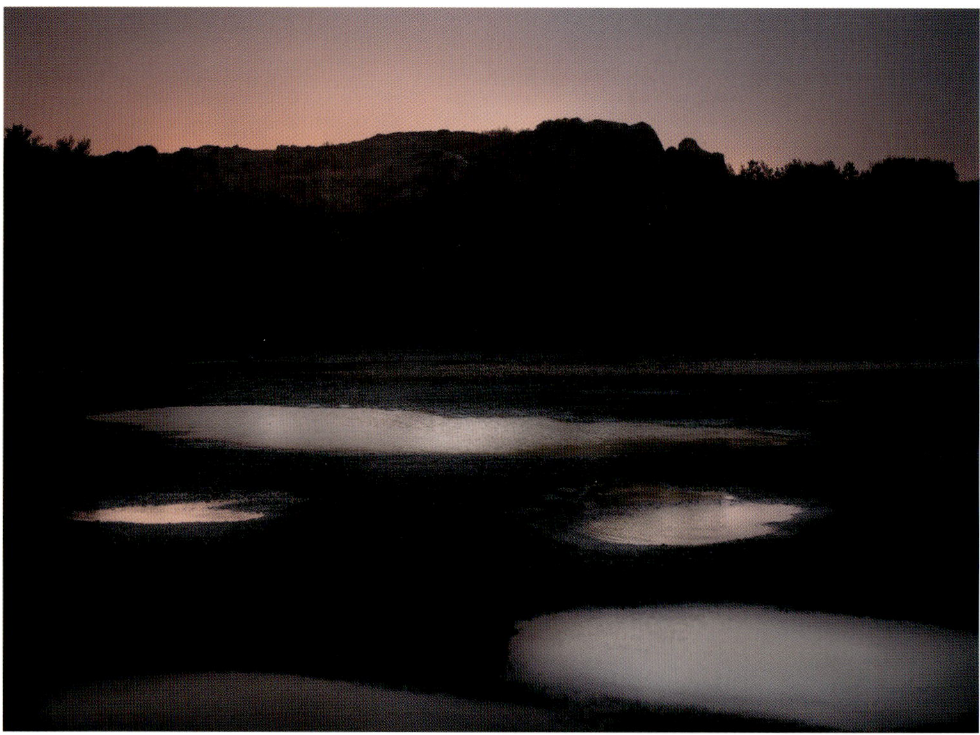

#11749-1004, from the series *Bright Black World, 2017,* Todd Hido,
courtesy Bruce Silverstein, New York

unfolding perceptions of something over time. He would often ask, "and what else?" When we thought we knew, when we figured something out and identified the meaning of an event, person, place, or thing, he would often remind us of the question, "and what else?" When we made a photograph that summarized what we had in our mind or heart, he would then also ask, "and what else?" This single, resonating question gave rise to multiple discoveries.

In my experience as an artist and a teacher, nothing is more restrictive to the arts and deadening to the power of the human mind than a fixed, unflinching agenda. To stay open and question is essential to live and grow. As a department chair in academia for many years, I often needed to navigate conflicts between liberal and conservative students and faculty with strongly held points of view. In one notable instance, a former soldier from the first Gulf War returning to college on the G.I. Bill attempted to interrogate and resolve his experiences with violence and death in the college classroom. He used ammunition (with the gunpowder safely removed) and army medical supplies to symbolize the heart-rending triage necessary on the battlefield. His work both questioned the necessity of war as a means of solving problems and protested the human cost of armed conflict. Mostly, he acknowledged through his work the sacrifices his brethren had made in following the code, "no one left behind."

Most of the students and the faculty member resisted the work strongly and rejected it out of hand because it violated their own beliefs about war, class, and race (the student was white; the brethren who saved his life was African American). The title of the piece was *The Soldier's Code* and students found it "disturbing," "romantic," "simplistic," and "racially charged." The liberal faculty member could not even consider the merits or problems with the work itself and expelled the student from her classroom because the work "reeked of violence."

As I intervened and questioned the student, I found him to be sincere, thoughtful, and, above all, open to feedback. He held in his mind what I determined to be an extremely powerful question: why me? Why did I live while others did not survive? What can be made of this experience to educate others about war, violence, and brotherhood? He understood the issues of race and class in who is called to fight a war and I found him to be highly sensitive with an open mind and a spirit of service. How might his painful experience help others? He was a conservative individual willing to risk the discomfort of facing differing attitudes and points of view. He consciously enrolled in a liberal art school to challenge his mind and meet opposition for the sake of growth and discovery. I wish I could say the same about the others in his classroom.

Poet Rainer Maria Rilke writes in *Letters to a Young Poet*: "Try to love the questions themselves."

"Do not now seek the answers, which cannot be given you because you would not be able to live them. And the point is, to live everything. Live the questions now. Perhaps you will then gradually, without noticing it, live along some distant day into the answer."

Taken together, photographs that comprise a body of work often shed light on the investigations of a photographer and offer ever increasing questions. In his book, *Bright Black World*, Todd Hido explores the meaning of a word from Nordic mythology, *Fimbulwinter*, which translates as "endless winter." In photographs from Northern Europe and the North Sea of Japan, Hido attempts to "photograph the darkness that I see coming." He opens the book with the working question: "It's been said that Inuits have many words to describe white. As the polar snow caps melt faster than we ever imagined, I wonder how long it will be before we have as many words to describe darkness."

In my experience with making photographs, even when my originating concept that motivated the work is extremely clear and well-defined, I *always* find that fresh discoveries and new perceptions in the moment serve to shift the nature of a growing exploration of the subject. Keep your opinions in abeyance for the time being. See what arises from treating each subject and each working session with an inquiring spirit, open to new realizations that can come from the corner of the eye or the depths of the mind.

The Wisdom of Chance

Chance occurrences, technical mistakes, and spontaneous, unplanned discoveries are all part of photography's enchantment. Every photographer I know credits providence, or accident, as the source of some of their enduring images.

Serendipity does not arise on its own; it builds on the back of our serious efforts. To be sure, sometimes accidents happen. But more frequently, we pave the way for providential images through conscious work over long periods of time. We prime the pump of discovery by seeding the unconscious and the intuition through intention,

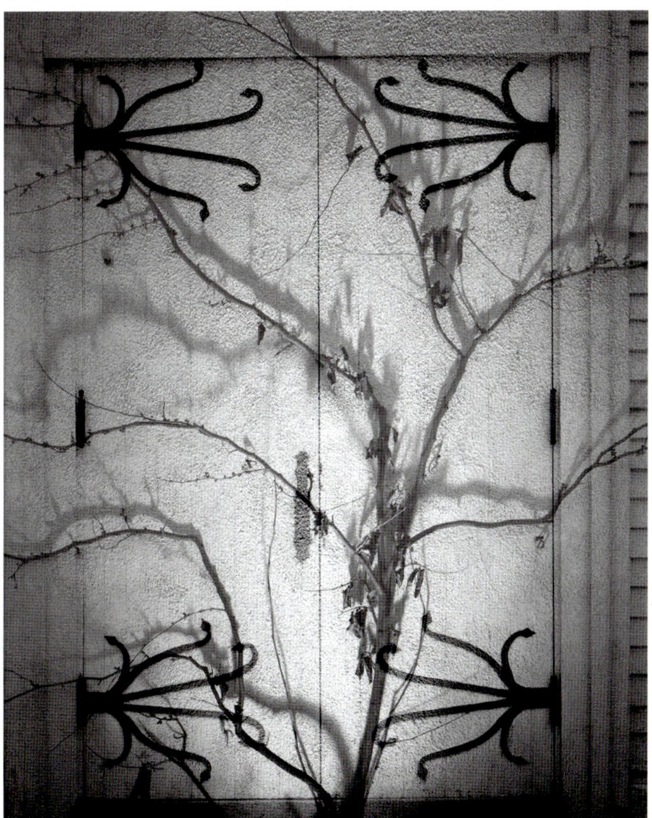

York, Maine, (double exposure), David Ulrich

considerable thought, and a good working ethos. The unconscious, when it does offer moments of stunning clarity and insight, has its own mysterious ways and unknowable order.

Most "accidents" that have occurred in my own work were preceded by purposeful experimental procedures and ways of working. For example, "unintentional" double exposures, seemingly accidental, happened during a period of time when I was exploring how multiple images might be integrated into a single frame. Fellow photographer in Hawai'i, Franco Salmoiraghi, has shot over and developed decades old-rolls of exposed but unprocessed film as a means of opening to the unanticipated wisdom of chance.

I recommend several tools to my students as a means of leveraging chance and lubricating their intuitive capacity. The first is to photograph regularly *without* looking through the viewfinder. Shoot from the hip, or overhead, or from the side. Look at the subject and intuitively frame with the mind's eye but stay loose and untethered to the viewfinder. Several discoveries can be made. The chance and random juxtapositions within the frame, that you *never* would have consciously considered, can teach a great deal about the fluid dynamics of composition and visual tension. You'll open your eyes to myriad possibilities with the frame when you return to the viewfinder. Second, you might realize how boring and conventional the standard eye-level view can be and how it limits your possibilities for visual originality and fresh standpoints. And third, it loosens your eye and mind by connecting spontaneously with the subject, bypassing the usual tight labor of overly careful, overly planned, self-conscious framing.

Another exercise I find enlightening and awakening of much chance-like, photographic possibility is to simply turn the phone camera on wherever you are, in stray moments, and in whichever direction the camera is already pointing. I discovered this by walking toward a subject I intended to photograph and turning my phone camera on in preparation. Sometimes I have been stopped in my tracks by the unexpected views that pop up on the phone's screen. These have often resulted in more interesting images than the one I initially sought.

Although I am careful in how I give this exercise now due to safety reasons, I recommend that you try and let your feet or your car dictate where you might end up to take photographs. Experiment with this at your discretion. Get into your car, or go on foot, and just drive or walk somewhere new. Let your feet guide you. Allow your inner senses to determine where to turn, how far to go, and try to keep your destination unplanned.

See where you end up. Take out your camera, wherever you are. Make images whether or not it is a place you would normally find amenable to photography. Again, staying open to chance can open your eyes to discoveries that you would not find due to fear, resistance, or preconceptions.

Other photographers have opened the window of chance by using any one of a variety of toy or disposable consumer cameras designed for the casual hobbyist and not meant for professionals. Toy cameras, such as the Holga or Diana, have the distinct advantage of each one being different than the other. The rendering quality of the lens, the appearance of light leaks and vignetting, are all unique from one camera to another. The charm of cheap cameras has seduced many fine art photographers for decades. Today, one of the great harbingers of chance and unique, fresh types of seeing and framing can come from the use of cameras attached to drones in the sky.

The lesson we might learn from these exercises can be illuminating for artists and photographers, that chance is not always accidental; sometimes it is synchronicity or a convergence of events that take place beyond our conscious knowing, a reflection of a natural order that our rational minds cannot yet fathom. We seek that which we are. Sometimes these chance images teach us about the nature of our own mind.

I have never liked the word *unconscious* to refer to the reservoir of knowing present in the deeper mind. I prefer the words, *depth consciousness,* to highlight the natural wisdom of the unseen and unknown parts of the mind. We make this part of our mind conscious through our active work and our efforts toward awareness—often with a camera. We don't always know if chance occurrences are merely accidents or an intelligent design arrived at through hidden layers of thought, intuition, and unknown impulses from the depth mind that can break through and guide our way. When artists and photographers can stay open to the whispers from within, what seems like magic or accident may be manifestations of a deeper layer of intelligence that lies dormant in the mind, that is quickened and activated by our creative work. In this way, I have come to hold great respect for the delights of chance and accidents in photography and art.

Awake in the World

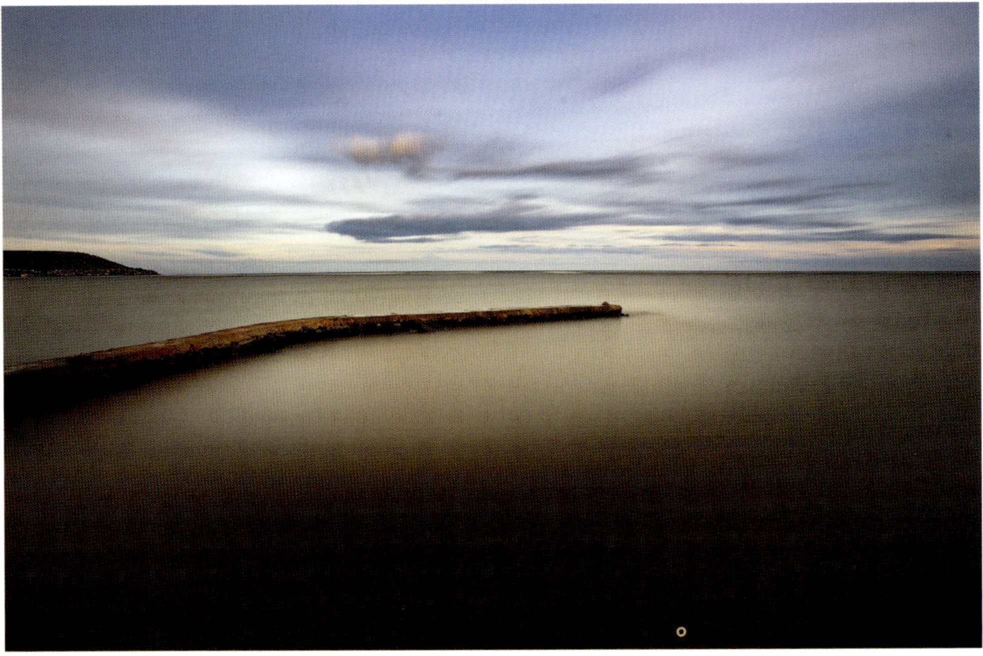

Brown Water, Kawaikui Beach #3, Honolulu, 2018, David Ulrich

An ever-increasing group of photographers and artists—and I count myself among them—believe that the arts are essential to a healthy society. Images can reflect a culture back on itself, offer hope and inspiration, highlight the myriad forms of injustice and inequality, and reflect both the sublime elements of nature as well as the rapid degradation of the environment.

In the eyes of many, within this broken world, using photography only for self-enrichment is not enough. Rather, photographers can concurrently find personal fulfillment and embody social responsibility through an active involvement with their community and surroundings. Instead of the paradigm of the isolated artist seeking personal enlightenment, admiration, and individual accomplishment, we could strive to find a new model for the twenty-first century, that of engaged photography.

Suzi Gablick writes in *The Reenchantment of Art*: "Exalted individualism…is hardly a creative response to the needs of the planet at this time, which demand complex and sensitive forms of interaction and linking.… I believe there is a new, evolving relationship between personal creativity and social responsibility, as old modernist patterns of alienation and confrontation give way to new ones of mutualism and the development of an active and practical dialogue with the environment."

The power of the camera extends in two directions: inward and outward. It teaches us to pay attention and be aware of the intersection between our inner life and outer conditions.

As our vision and skill grow as photographers, our awareness and consciousness expand outward to encompass both self and other. The photographer behind the lens and the society that has shaped them cannot be separated; they are deeply intertwined. The individual dynamics of the artist—their identity, internal terrain, psychological development, and sympathies and antipathies—can fuel one's image-making. The search for awareness helps others on the same path. Likewise, the photographer's genuine and deeply felt perceptions of the world earned by hard experience and through one's unique circumstances can teach, inform, and incite others to look at and even act on some of our collective challenges.

Teaching art, by definition, reaches deep into individuals and opens them to a certain kind of self-knowing—a discovery of their authentic voice or vision—and encourages an expansive engagement with outer life. I find myself often facing the question of which world to explore in the classroom, the inner or outer. A good number of people come to classes mostly to learn the techniques and language of photography. Yet all are touched in some way by each other's creative efforts. I find myself needing to walk a fine line between functioning as a facilitator, bringing them into greater touch with their inner life, and, at the same time, encouraging a careful and rich observation of the world itself. When I forget one side, the inner or the outer, which happens frequently, I feel somehow that something is missing, that I am not offering people what they really need. In those moments, I feel the stirrings of remorse.

Over time, students begin to have an inner measure from which they can identify whether their work rings true, that their observations are made with wholeness, richness, and integrity. Images made with meticulous truthfulness to one's own experience can lead to an opening to the wisdom of the heart. When this measure begins to make itself known, we have the beginnings of art that has the capacity to deeply touch both the maker and the viewer. From time to time, we find this kind of magic in classroom moments when a collective energy descends into the room that opens our feelings in a new way.

Whether you are an Instagram aficionado or are publishing and exhibiting your photographs in traditional venues, consider making images that move beyond merely displaying your skills and seeking likes. Ask the question: what can help? What kind of images will illuminate the kind of world we want for our children and the future?

Delve deeply into your own experience; photograph from who you are. Engage the world richly and honestly; learn to see what is. In your own community and within your own life, there are undoubtedly many pressing issues and intractable conditions that could benefit from your attentive engagement with a camera. There is a rare beauty in disarming candor. Do not shirk from revealing your community and the world to itself: the good, the bad, and the ugly. Understand that your camera is a powerful tool for both expanding awareness and initiating positive social change.

Robert Adams makes the observation in his book, *Art Can Help*: "It is the responsibility of artists to pay attention to the world, pleasant or otherwise, and help us live respectfully in it.

Artists do this by keeping their curiosity and moral sense alive, and by sharing with us their gift for metaphor. Often, this means finding similarities between observable fact and inner experience....

In this way, art encourages us to gratitude and engagement, and is of both personal and civic consequence."

The Cruel Radiance of What Is

"For in the immediate world, everything is to be discerned…with the whole of consciousness, seeking to perceive it as it stands: so that the aspect of a street in sunlight can roar in the heart of itself as a symphony, perhaps as no symphony can: and all of consciousness is shifted from the imagined, the revisive, to the effort to perceive simply the cruel radiance of what is." So writes James Agee on what could be seen as photography's greatest aim and one of its important contributions to our common life. He wrote these words in his Introduction to *Let Us Now Praise Famous Men*, his mutual project with photographer Walker Evans. The text and photographs—in Agee's words, "coequal, mutually independent, and fully collaborative"—document the plight of impoverished sharecroppers in the Dust Bowl during the great depression.

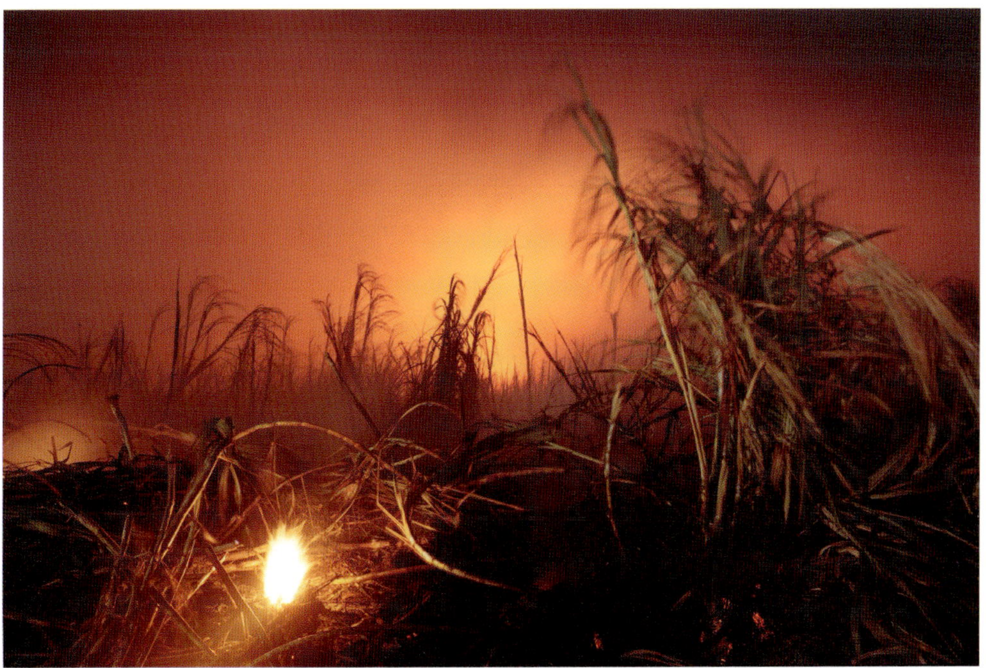

Sugar Cane Burn, Maui, Hawai'i, David Ulrich

Agee continues: "This is why the camera seems to me, next to unassisted and weaponless consciousness, the central instrument of our time; and is why in turn I feel such rage at its misuse: which has spread so nearly universal a corruption of sight that I know of less than a dozen alive whose eyes I can trust even so much as my own."

These are prescient words. Written in the late 1930s, Agee could not have foreseen how photography was to be co-opted by social media and casual, subjectively-addled picture-takers. Yet the power of photography remains as ever potent today as it was a century ago. The camera is an instrument of consciousness. Human evolution is the evolution of consciousness. Thus, the camera can serve and follow what might be the core aim of humanity—collectively and individually—to become conscious instruments of creation, to learn to see what is in all of its glory and pathos. Because, as many have observed, one's way of seeing determines one's path of action.

Agee was likely familiar with James Joyce's *Portrait of the Artist as a Young Man*. Joyce believed that a quality of radiance is found in the experience of seeing the "whatness" of a thing. Apprehended by intuition, the mind attempts to see into the nature of things and into the heart of the human condition. This form of seeing, according to Joyce, arrests the mind into a paradoxical condition that evokes harmony and luminosity as well as pity and terror, emotions which can unite the viewer with a "human sufferer."

How we see, what we choose to pay attention to, creates our lived reality, defines our moral judgments, and drives the way we treat others and the planet. If we could use photography to help us apprehend the radiance at the heart of things as well as the terror of suffering and injustice, the camera might lead us to both consciousness and conscience.

As a society, we have not yet come to realize the creation is whole and that all life is one. We share the same DNA with trees, animals, and every single other person. When human agency turns into violence, exploitation, and greed, we, with our camera, need to bear witness. When acts of touching humanity cross our path, or when we are arrested by the sublime in nature, or when the radiant beauty of ordinary things—a piece of fruit perhaps or a shaft of sunlight—awakens the eye to enchantment, again, we bear witness through the lens. When acute suffering creates a tear in the collective tapestry of life, we bear witness and try to help with respect and empathy, with or without the camera.

Bearing witness to what is takes place in sharp contrast to the ego's insistent desires for admiration and "self" expression. What self are we expressing and why? Looking deeply into things diminishes the false ego—the source of much suffering for self and others—and opens to a penetrative perception that changes the state of the observer and the observed. Our gaze, whether turned to self or others, when accompanied with respect and inquiry into the true nature of things, can be a healing, nourishing, and transforming force.

Let's turn our camera to things that matter.

A picture made of light is a powerful metaphor for the action of a camera. Once something is exposed to the light of consciousness, a transformative action takes place. Seeing something makes a difference. When photographers reveal their deep perceptions, it opens to the transforming influence of awareness for the artist and the viewer.

In the closing lines of Robert Adam's book, *Art Can Help*, he quotes poet Czeslaw Milosz on the quality of hope, which he defines as "trust in the light that shines through earthly forms."

Hope and Despair

Out of despair is born hope. Despair can be existential and shared such as the terror of recognizing our mortality, or it can be personal as when life events shake the very foundation of our happiness. Either way, despair can give way to anger, and then acceptance that leads often toward a rebirth of hope. As artists and image-makers, how can we help people find hope, even though we may express righteous anger and indignation over the conditions of terror and despair for many people in these uncertain times?

The achievements of many photographers over the past century offer an encouraging kind of hope emerging from despairing conditions. Even after fifty years, my respect for Robert Frank's *The Americans* continues to grow from his soberly distressing look at racism, the sad aristocracy of the ruling class, and the noble worthiness of blue collar, everyday folks. Nobility and dignity—the sheer humanity—of working people and diverse Americans are penetratively depicted.

Frank clarifies his work: "Black and white are the colors of photography. To me, they symbolize the alternatives of hope and despair to which mankind is forever subjected."

It is hard not despair about the state of the world, with educational and political institutions crumbling, looming environmental disaster, war and famine, racism and bigotry nearly everywhere we look, nuclear one-upmanship, and loony politicians hell-bent on destroying our great society. We have a tool, a powerful one, to protest these trying times and offer people a vision of hope, of the sanctity of life and experience.

Famed theatrical director Peter Brook writes: "Every form of theatre has something in common with a visit to the doctor. On the way out, one should always feel better than on the way in. I think this derives from the artist's sense of responsibility to the audience."

The *Guardian's* theater critic, Michael Billington, asks Brook, "has he ever been tempted to throw up his hands in horror at a world filled with nuclear threats, environmental disasters and political malfunction from Trump to Brexit?" Brook answers, "We swim against the tide and achieve whatever we can in our chosen field. Fate dictated that mine was that of theatre and, within that, I have a responsibility to be as positive and creative as I can. To give way to despair is the ultimate cop-out."

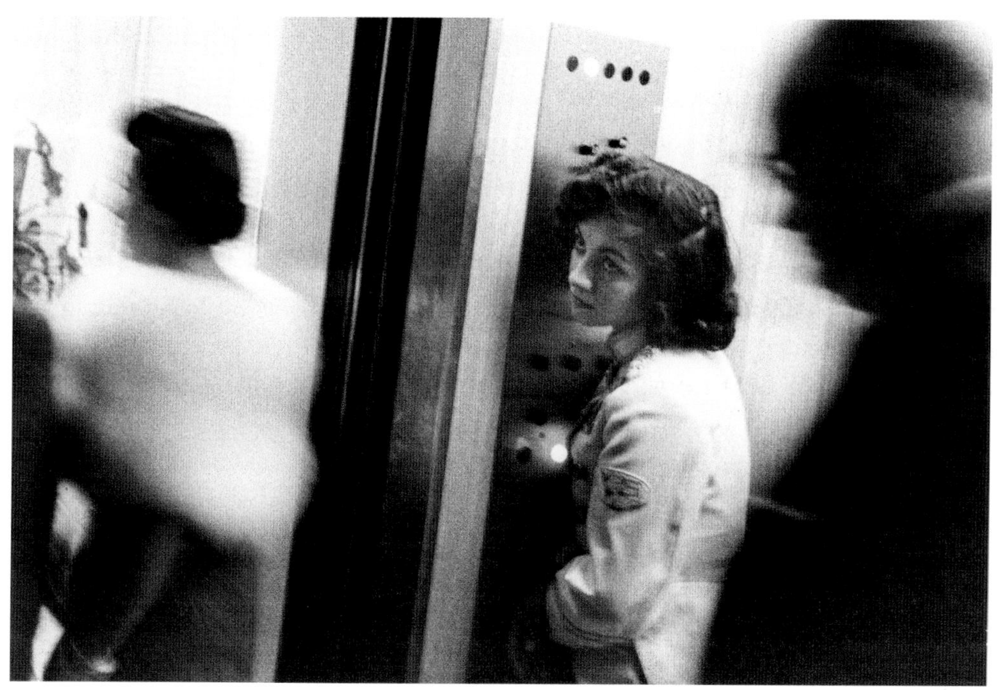

Elevator—Miami Beach, 1955, Robert Frank,
© Andrea Frank Foundation,
from *The Americans*

Artists are among the most honored and most feared in society because of their power to influence the hearts and minds of the people. Through pictures, words, song, and deeds, they speak truth to power. They nod in gracious aesthetic assent to the good and sharply protest what is wrong. Artists highlight the contradictions in society as well as in individuals and look unflinchingly at the radiant terror at the heart of mortal existence. They bring us joy and hope and battle despair by telling it like it is. Artists affirm the opposing dynamics of happiness and suffering. What is the old adage? "Pleasure shared is pleasure doubled; trouble shared is trouble halved."

For instance, many kinds of documentary images can inspire activism and resistance. The civil rights movement and the Black Lives Matter initiative spawned powerful photographs of struggle on behalf of the most basic of human rights: life, liberty, and the pursuit of happiness. The photographs help create new national narratives. Mark Speltz writes in *Time* magazine about real-time news coverage of race relations in America and how images "can influence how events are depicted and remembered for decades to come.… The near ubiquity of cell phones ensures that no poignant moment, clever sign, or altercation goes unrecorded. This also speaks to the many vital roles photos continue to play—they can document, preserve, inspire, attest and provide evidence."

Several, large segments of the contemporary art and photographic communities revel in the cool, ironic post-modern approach that "ridicules hope…and is predictive of nihilism," in art that is "born of cynicism," according to Robert Adams in *Art Can Help*. Parody and irony have their place, but art stands over the centuries as the one arena that celebrates wholeness, embodied richness, and liberty, and can offer grace and hope to many in stunning literary or artistic achievements.

I am enthused by many of today's generation of photographers who refuse to accept despair in the face of overwhelming circumstances. Examples that come to mind are the landscape photographs by Carol Erb, which depict extreme natural conditions due to climate change that she calls a "narrative of reckoning." In her images, she searches for places where one can metaphorically remain safe and protected—that give hope. I am also deeply touched by the body of work of Indonesian photographer Hengki Koentjoro whose photographs of the South Asian environment sustain the spiritual and sublime dimension of the land in Indonesian culture. These photographs awaken awe and subvert contemporary ironies of the landscape as being forever man-altered.

Artists, musicians, photographers, and writers serve society by standing at the vanguard of social change and showing us that a better world is possible. They give voice to our dreams. They broadcast and publicize the dangers of despair, the inequities of society, and the potential of redemption through courage. Maybe that's all it takes—for enough people to want peace, social justice, and a healthy world, for enough people to stand up in unity, and for enough people to take control of their national or global destiny.

Giving voice is giving hope.

"All we are saying is give peace a chance."

Companions on the Way

What role do compatriots and community play in our creative lives? Various forms of linking with others serve our creative aspirations in many ways, including criticism, influence and response, making collective discoveries, and engaging shared passions and pursuits. The artist or photographer is not a solitary being, unaffected by the others and the community of which they are a part. Quite the contrary; abundant evidence exists to help us realize the enormous influence other people might have on our growth as artists and on the shape and direction of our work.

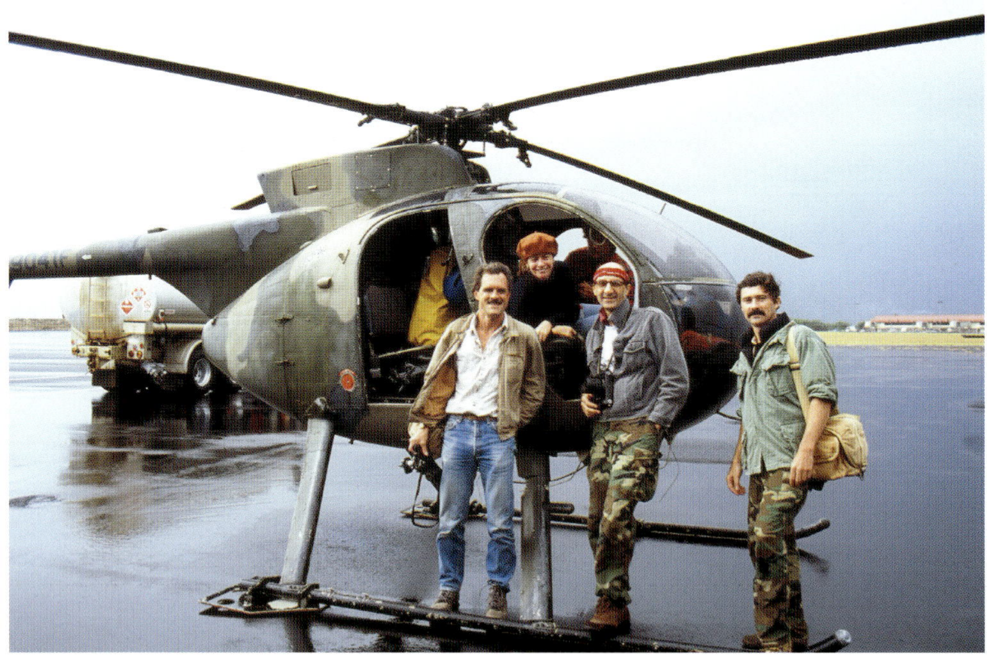

Mobile Photo Unit Crew, Kaho'olawe Book Project, 1993
© Franco Salmoiraghi

Three photographers and the book designer from the Kaho'olawe project, a community collaboration to document the Hawaiian island of Kaho'olawe, sacred to the Hawaiian people and used for ordnance training by the US military for 50 years. From left to right, David Ulrich, Barbara Pope, Franco Salmoiraghi, and Rowland Reeve.

The Abstract Expressionist painters met frequently over drinks and intense dialogue in the legendary Cedar Tavern in New York, sharing their insights and discoveries, arguing over their aims and approaches, and spurring each other to greater heights of expression. Many photographers now learn their medium by going to school—and the shared agreements, disputes, critical dialogue, deadlines, and decidedly honest feedback serve to deepen one's work and make it more relevant to your audience. The dreaded art school critique is a rite of passage that transforms self-centeredness into mutualism and a dynamic linking with your community and audience.

Most photographers have a deep hunger for creative expression and sharing with others. At many times in my life, I have been part of creative communities—in the classroom and beyond—that alternately inspire and challenge, encourage and agitate, and critique and support. For a creative community to be effective, honesty is the first threshold requirement—the agreement for honest feedback beyond the scope of mere like and dislike. The second condition that seems necessary is dialectical tension. People dispute each other, engender larger perspectives through disagreement, and find collective approaches through clashing ideas, all the while in an atmosphere of mutual trust and energetic support.

In *The Powers of Two, How Relationships Drive Creativity*, author Joshua Shenk makes the important point that individuals coming together that "not only support each other, but also startle and vex each other…generate deep rapport and energizing friction" can lead to "daring work that neither could achieve alone….The catalyst is not similarity alone but the joining of profound similarities with profound differences. We need similarities to give us ballast and differences to make us move."

In a creative community, photographers and artists benefit greatly from a kind of collective intelligence: the influence of seeing work made by other serious practitioners, the aggregate insights derived from the history of the medium and from one's own discoveries, and the sparks that fly and lead to flame through vital exchange—however supportive or conflicting—that can engender inspiration and deep insight. We also share energy and incite passion in each other, what psychologist William James calls the "emulous passion." He said in a lecture, "The deepest spring of action in us is the sight of the action of another. The spectacle of effort is what awakens and sustains our own effort."

I believe the principal way we grow and learn as photographers is by working, then frequently sharing our efforts with others, and by offering honesty coupled with kindness in our response to each other's work. Most people are highly subjective in their view of their own work and rarely accurately able to observe their own strengths and weaknesses or the true place of their significant contribution.

Find and cultivate friends and colleagues with whom you can share your work and receive trusted feedback. Or, perhaps take a class. Develop a working relationship with peers whose work is different yet with whom you can share mutual support and critical feedback. Think of criticism as a way of refining your work and as a valuable means of assuring that others connect with your images in a manner consistent with your intent. We need teachers and influences at every stage of development. A good teacher, editor, or curator can help distill meaning and shape your creative expression to new heights. Not everyone reads work in the same way, but trusted viewers can recognize the intangible qualities of excellence, depth, facility with the visual language, and good storytelling. I have learned an inestimable amount about the potentials in my work from those that have experienced eyes and take the time to look at and carefully consider my images or my words.

Collaboration is the art form of the future.

Online communities on social media can make our work visible to a large public. However, the mechanism for response on these sites is usually limited to gathering likes and has not yet evolved enough to provide a forum for genuine critical feedback and in-depth dialogue. In my experience with art and photography, nothing can surpass the richness of face-to-face communication and in-person learning.

Everyone interested in human exchange, and certainly all artists and photographers, would benefit greatly by reading physicist David Bohm's book, *On Dialogue*, which is a thorough exploration on shared discovery through communication. The classroom, meeting hall, or gathering place can become a place of creative ferment in which insights grow from the dialogue itself that transcends the view or pre-defined standpoint of any one individual with the "continual emergence of new content."

Bohm writes, "Thus, in a dialogue, each person does not attempt to make common certain ideas or items of information that are already known to him. Rather, it may be said that the two people are making something in common, i.e., creating something new together."

Collaboration is the art form of the future.

Coherence and Presence

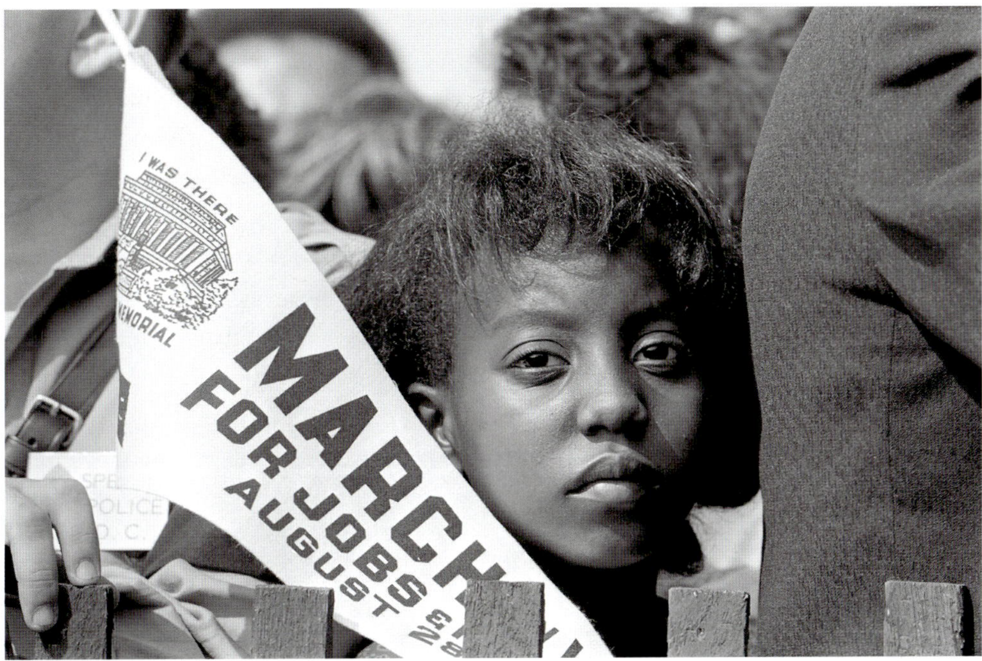

Civil Rights March on Washington, D.C., 8/28/1963, Rowland Scherman. Courtesy: National Archives

Pictures, images, and other symbolic representations speak to the imagination.
The mighty fortress of the human heart silently withstands the assaults by the
rifled cannons of reason, but readily falls before the magic power of mystery.
—Frederick Douglass, 1861

Years ago, one of my smart first-year photography students from The Art Institute of Boston (Now Lesley University College of Art and Design) visited the Boston Museum of Fine Arts for an afternoon. She returned to class visibly moved. She went through much of the museum and visited many of the collections. She proclaimed, "I'm amazed. In all the works I saw, from different times and places, they are all united in the sense that everything seems complete, nothing seems out of place, and the visual elements integrate into one whole." Her final statement floored me. She said, "In their unity, they embody mystery."

"I never thought about this before," she admitted. "All of my teachers in high school stressed technique and highly personal expression—never mentioning the need for visual integration and unity." She went on to say that her art teachers in high school were trained in other subjects and were merely corralled into teaching some of the "minor" enrichment subjects such as art.

I thought, "Wow. Yes." Coherence is key and it silently underlies our teaching in college settings. One of my measures in viewing my own work and that of students and colleagues revolves around the question. Do the visual elements—the frame, moment, shapes and form, color and tonality—cohere into a meaningful whole? Does the work have unity? Life is often messy and unorganized. The task of the artist is to select, refine, and transform life itself into a visual integration that serves to express your intent with clarity and force.

Works of art with coherence and force, as my student suggested, also contain a mystery in which the whole is greater than the sum of its parts. Who can or would try to parse a Beethoven sonata or a Rothko painting? What we call beauty is undoubtedly subjective but most would agree it reflects an inherent, often sublime, order and cannot be grasped strictly by the intellect.

Peter Brook writes of this phenomenon: "On a more intuitive level the painter and sculptor are tirelessly correcting and refining their work so that its coarse outer crust can give way to the true inner feeling. A poet sifts within his thought pattern, giving attention to subtle intimations of sound and rhythm which are somewhere far behind the tumble of words within which his mind is filled. In this way, he creates a phrase that carries with it a new force, and the reader, in turn, can perceive his own feelings being intensified as their energy is transformed by the impressions he receives from the poem."

Sometimes while writing, I come upon the limits of my own intelligence. My mind is intuitive and creative, less attuned to logic and reason. When I conceptualize a thought, it can appear as an image in my mind and it is often a god-awful struggle to articulate the clarity of my insight with verbal reasoning and words. There is a feeling and a rhythm to words. The right word choice, the musicality of the sentence or paragraph, the surprise element of phrases that appear on the edges of consciousness, as if from a deeper region of the mind; these can work together and combine to complete a thought on paper with coherence, elegance, and force. This rare moment of distillation is what I strive for in words or photographs.

The word I use to describe this coherence, elegance, and force is *presence*. Does a work of art have presence? Does it have the livingness of attention? The depth of attention that an artist gives to the subject and to their craft suffuses the work itself. Stephen Shore makes note of the primacy of awareness to photography: "One thing I've always been interested in is what the world looks like when you're in a state of heightened awareness. Those moments which I think everyone has where experience feels more tangible, where experience feels more vivid… and as you walk down the street with that frame of mind, relationships begin to stand out."

To make all my decisions conscious, I started filling the pictures with attention."

Wholeness and Order

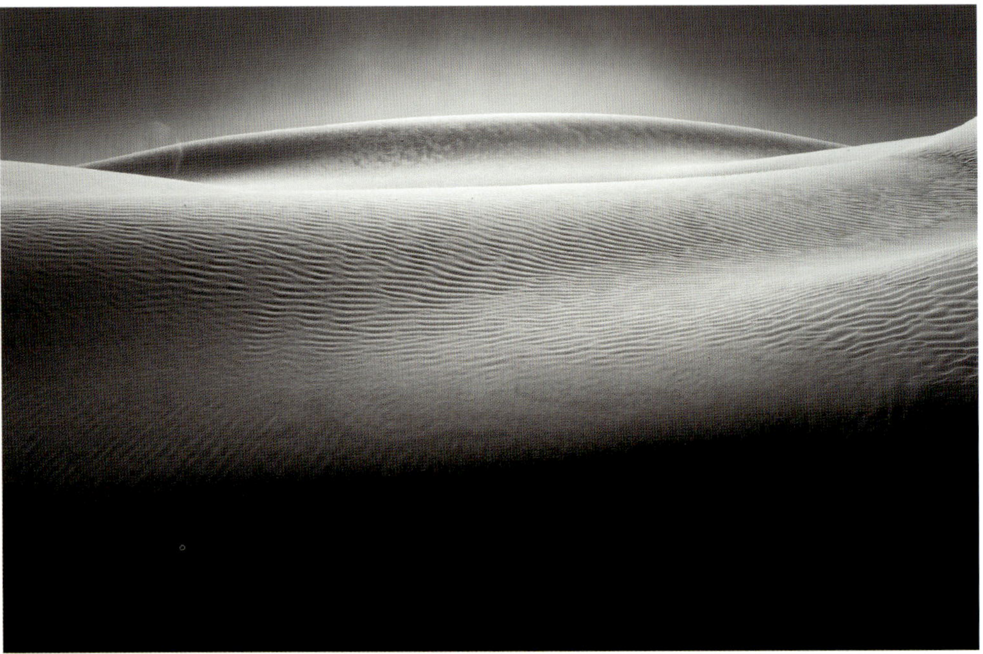

Oceano Dunes #12, California, 2019, David Ulrich

Do photographers create order and meaning in the frame from a chaotic world, or do we give expression to a natural order? Or both? When the eye of the mind and camera reconciles elements in the frame and balances the light and form into a coherent observation, photographers become powerful creators of unity and purpose.

Within the natural order, humans are imbued with the power of creation and indeed it may be one of our most defining characteristics. We bring out or recognize an implicate order every time we struggle with form and content in a way that strives to produce an elegant expression that offsets and gives ballast to the seeming chaotic and random conditions of life. The inner fire of the artist burns brightly and gives light and heat to the world and others. The embers quietly glow within us; our work is the breath, the wind that ignites the flames. Ralph Waldo Emerson writes: "If a man creates not, the pure efflux of the Deity is not his; cinders—smoke—there may be—but not yet flame."

People seem attracted to creativity because it helps complete oneself, giving rise to a unique form of fulfillment offered by personal expression. We learn of our talents and our authentic way of seeing the world, and we encounter what gets in the way of our creativity and natural wisdom.

In assuming the challenges of photography or any art form, we recognize our own fragmentation and lack of wholeness. Both our strengths and our obstacles are thrown into relief in seeking to master the medium. Many conditions may be revealed as we strive toward excellence and fullness with the medium. We might find one or more of these common impediments: inattention, impatience, rigidness, an inability to finish something, laziness and resistance to discipline, insecurities and self-doubt, cynicism, egoism, sentimentality, or its opposite, the dominance of thought divorced from the body and feelings. Photography can be a path toward wholeness that asks us to struggle with our incompleteness and our own particular form of imbalance.

In my own work, one impediment to the flow of creative energy comes from my persistent impatience and trying to force things to completion when they are not yet ready. I need to be constantly vigilant to stay located in the ever-present now and not vaingloriously seek to realize the result prematurely. The process has its own integrity and its own momentum. Images and projects will ripen, with my participation to be sure, but mostly they need to unfold to a state of wholeness and completion organically. Ripeness comes in its own time and sometimes not soon enough for the ego. I personally need to learn to respect the process and allow the work to mature before impatiently trying to display an unformed idea, exhibit an unfinished project, or promote a not fully realized book idea. The struggle with impatience is an important part of my process; battling my demon creates friction and sparks and serves to stoke the flames of sustaining my creativity.

Our demons play a seminal role in seeking wholeness of expression. Anaïs Nin writes perceptively in her diaries: "Great art was born of great terrors, great loneliness, great inhibitions, instabilities, and it always balances them." The search for coherence in images follows the search for completeness and order within oneself. It falls to the artist to not hold back, to live expansively and fully, and to experience deeply the pantheon of life's occasions. Those inward demons that prevent our taking hold of life and impede one's realization of the blissful fullness of experience are the very things that are the engine of creative exploration.

Anaïs Nin explains. "We all lose some of our faith under the oppression of mad leaders, insane history, pathologic cruelties of daily life.…You must not fear, hold back, count or be a miser with your thoughts and feelings. It is also true that creation comes from an overflow, so you have to learn to intake, to imbibe, to nourish yourself and not be afraid of fullness. The fullness is like a tidal wave which then carries you, sweeps you into experience and into writing. Permit yourself to flow and overflow, allow for the rise in temperature, all the expansions and intensifications."

We cannot know what criteria creation used in the evolution of mankind, nor what constitutes the marker or particular state that makes us human. Maybe it was the advent of an expanded consciousness that set us apart from the animals. But we, as photographic creators, do have a useful criterion to aim toward in image making. Has our work with an image reached a state of *coherence*? Do all the elements cohere into a singular, unified expression? Sometimes small, even minute, changes in point of view, cropping, light and tonal balance, color, or relationship between forms can make a large difference in our search for unity and coherence. Why do some images, even of ugly things, appear to be complete, with an often-paradoxical beauty?

I think that our appetite for beauty in photography can be a longing to recognize a natural order to creation. Coherence in an image becomes a shadow, a hint, of a natural completeness and complexity.

Robert Adams believes "the job of the photographer… is not to catalogue indisputable fact but to try to be coherent about intuition and hope. Beauty is a synonym for the coherence and structure underlying life."

Creative Intensity

Something has changed in our collective existence. Speaking of myself, my life has become so ordinary. In our artistic existence in the past, we would stay up all night, drinking and talking about art and love. We didn't drink to drink; we drank for togetherness and dialogue. We had a burning desire to make images, to realize the depths of our being through art. Magic was in the air, synchronicity abounded, and collective energies fueled exciting and soul-nourishing discoveries.

We dreamt of the cafés of Paris and the arts-ridden streets of New York. For a while, we gave our lives to the gods of art and it was an enlivening, exciting time. Our teachers retired with us to coffee houses and pubs after a class, and we learned more from this spontaneous dialogue and sharing than we ever could in the classroom. An intensity

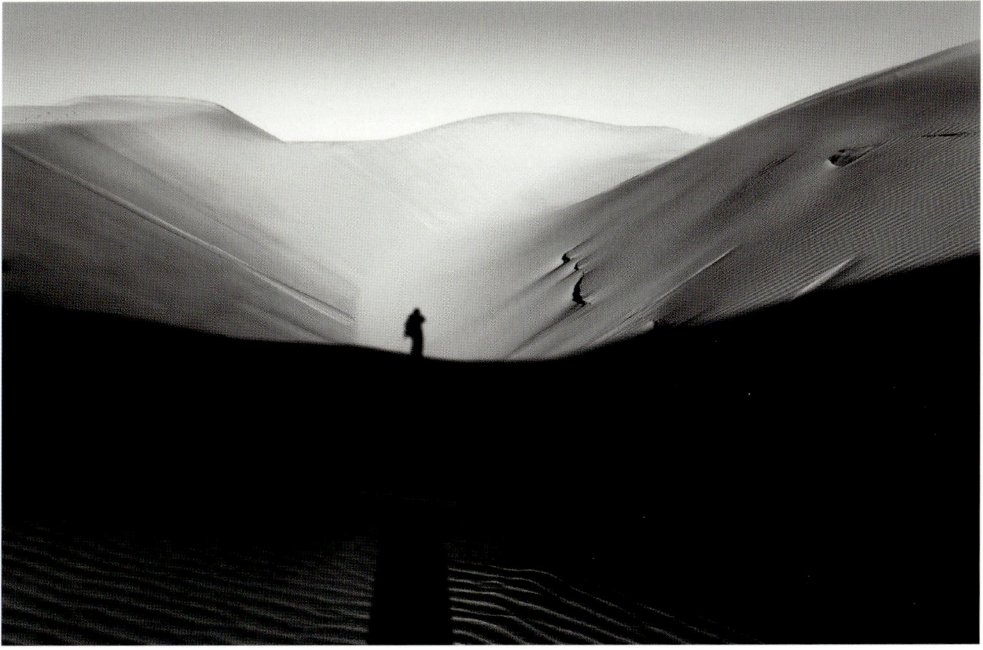

Oceano Dunes, California #133, 2019, David Ulrich

burned throughout our contacts with each other that deeply sparked wild creative explorations that resulted in powerful images and works. Mutual respect prevailed. I do not ever remember being harmed—except affronts to my false pride—through this type of powerful exchange.

What happened? Nowadays, I only meet art students outside the classroom for an occasional coffee. Wildness has gone out of fashion. Students have been harmed and exploited by irresponsible faculty. Dionysian excess is an anachronistic concept viewed with great suspicion as being unhealthy or prone to abuse. Mostly people now attend to their work, their studies, their families, and their economic aspirations. Something has been gained—responsibility, duty, sensitivity—but something has also been lost. Great passion has been traded for good behavior. Why can't we have both, *eros* and *logos*?

Artists and photographers need to burn brightly with creative intensity, but not burn up. We are meant to know, wired to experience, an ecstatic accord with our ideas, materials, and subjects. Psychologist Robert Johnson writes: "Why do we find this transcendent ecstasy such a difficult state to achieve? The advent of Dionysus, the psychological archetype of ecstasy, represented a new stage in human development.… It was the one most missing and least in our control.…We must touch Dionysus, we must bring him back into our lives in a humanized form, or in denying him we will destroy ourselves. This is the burden that is on us now. To keep the fine points of our patriarchal world—its order, form, care, and structure—and bring the Dionysian back in to enliven it without doing a flip-flop and going to pieces. Only in this way can we begin to move toward wholeness and joy."

Great passion has been traded for good behavior.

Photographers and artists are often complicated people. Passion rules. It is a seminal and necessary ingredient in the creative process. Artists ride the wave of their wish, their passion, their deep longing for discovering and expressing something "true" to their soul. The degree of passion that one has for a subject, an idea, or pursuit is a true measure of its worth to you. Great discoveries are never made out of half-heartedness or by being a Sunday afternoon warrior in the arts.

In *The Courage to Create*, psychologist Rollo May, writes: "This leads us to the second element in the creative act—namely the 'intensity' of the encounter. 'Absorption, being caught up in, wholly involved', and so on, are used commonly to describe the state of the artist or scientist when creating or even the child at play. By whatever name one calls it, genuine creativity is characterized by an intensity of awareness, a heightened consciousness.…What the artist feels is *not* anxiety or fear; it is *joy*.…We cannot *will* to have insights. We cannot *will* creativity. But we can *will* to give ourselves to the encounter with intensity of dedication and commitment."

The French word, *jouissance*, has no exact equivalent in English. It means something like pleasure, delight, and ecstasy. French psychoanalyst Jacque Lacan describes *jouissance* as a "superabundant vitality." According to Lacan, it "begins with a tickle and ends with a blaze of petrol." Within our busy lives and multiple commitments, one reliable way we can find this intense joy of creating is through immersive experience. I highly recommend one of several things. Take a vacation or give several days or a week devoted to photography. Take pictures every day. Follow the lead of the dictates of your heart and intuition. Find a way of working that encourages *jouissance*, that brings you joy and pleasure. Do not judge your approach; whatever it might be. Learn the importance of creative momentum through daily, immersive work.

Another tried and true strategy to awaken your creative self is to take a week-long in-residence photography workshop. Many places around the country sponsor these week-long sessions, often in the summer, with a wide range of teachers and approaches: Maine Media Workshops, Santa Fe Workshops, Anderson Ranch in Colorado, and more. Try to find a residence experience where you do not have to go home in the evening. These provide structure, immersion, and excitement as well as companionship and the opportunity for informal exchange with students and teachers well into the evening.

We need both structure and time for free play and the cultivation of surges of vitality. These are dialectic conditions—Dionysian and Apollonian (form and order)—both of which are vital and necessary for the creative process to fully unfold. And we need companions. Photographers do not work in a vacuum; indeed, they are often highly engaged people. Find compatriots with whom you can trust and share your search for immersive creativity. Other people can help kindle your interests, help fan sparks into flames, and validate your experience and expression—in addition to the necessary critical feedback.

Follow your passion. Find your bliss. Seek immersive experience. These can change your life and infuse your work with power, grace, and elegance.

Sea of Images

The world today is swamped with an ocean of images—discrete but connected seas of photographic activity: fine art, documentary, commercial, editorial, illustrative, amateur, and social media. The sheer number of pictures that compete for our attention is overwhelming. What percentage of images are a feast for the eyes and mind, and which represent a diet of immediate gratification without much nutritional value? In the face of this veritable onslaught of daily images, several questions need to be addressed by photographers and society alike. What is the responsibility of photographers to their audience, and what societal norms might evolve to ensure moral, ethical, and responsible usages of images?

Free expression is the cornerstone of a democratic society. With digital technology, photographers have a global platform with breathtaking immediacy for expression of our values, views, beliefs, observations, and ongoing streams of thought. But let's be responsible and not squander our powerful opportunities for exploring issues of importance and fostering a deep humanistic perspective, especially on social media sites where young people congregate. Can we look beyond the excesses of celebrity culture, consumer longing, egoism, living the good life, sexual fantasy, and the need to promote the brand called "me"? There is so much shallowness and distortion in images on news feeds and social media that diminish the very ideal of our cherished free expression. Forces from without, from the political and social system, are already threatening the reality of a free press and the public's right to speak their mind. Let's not allow free speech to erode from within by using it injudiciously for fake news, promoting unrealistic standards of beauty, and ignoring the broad needs for social justice.

Beyond ego display, photography can be a tool for deep self-exploration. The resonances you find through a camera can mirror the shape of your internal terrain and reflect your strengths, obstacles, struggles, and paths of growth, often in metaphoric ways. The mirror of your being, reflecting its processes of growth and evolution, can also deeply help and serve others by affirming their challenges and discoveries. You become a student and a teacher simultaneously in a way that reminds me of poet Theodore Roethke's observation that a teacher is one who "carries on their own education in public."

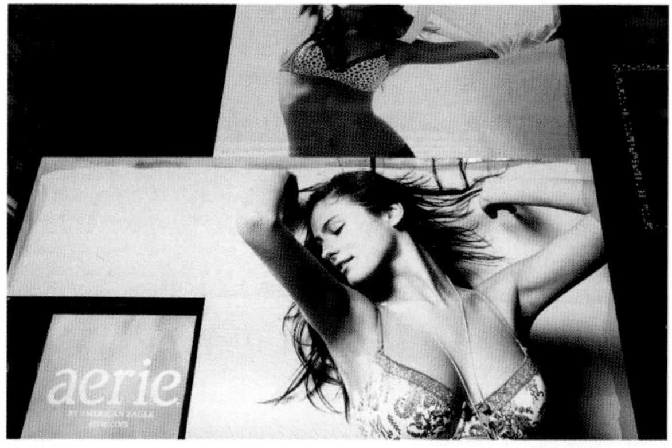
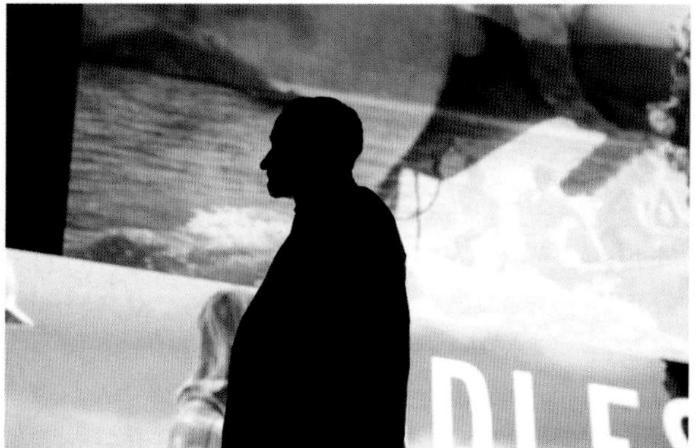

Times Square, New York #14,
diptych from the project
Samsara, David Ulrich

The camera, of course, is also a powerful window to the world. Each of you hold passionate interests and commitments that can be cultivated through photography and reflected back into the world to nourish and influence others. Portraiture, for example, can look inside and help reveal the character of another. It can be a charged act of mutual openness and intimacy—that serves the photographer, subject, and viewer in representing the human condition. Documentary photographs can celebrate what is right with the world, and protest what is deeply wrong. In your own lives and in your own communities, what issues and conditions demand exploration and documentation, that need the light of exposure and critical inquiry—that cannot and should not take place in the dark? Once the public sees something and becomes aware of an ongoing crisis or dilemma, that exposure to light is the first step toward healing and resolution.

We have extremely potent tools with the camera and online platforms to reflect, reveal, and protest social injustice in all of its forms: environmental disaster, bigotry and divisiveness, inequities, and corrupt attitudes and practices. What you soberly and unflinchingly see through the camera can inspire people to reflect on the need for positive social change, to become more socially and environmentally responsible, and to work toward mutually addressing the problems that vex us all.

As a society, we have well-developed laws that protect privacy, copyright, and free expression. However, most legal solutions lag behind the advent of technology and social media and their currency of sharing both ideas and images. New solutions are being developed through such initiatives as Creative Commons that can do both: serve to protect copyright and encourage fair use and sharing in a way that is appropriate for digital platforms based on the expressed wishes of the artist who created a work. In some locations, legal and ethical limits are being placed on digital manipulation of photographs in journalism and in the beauty industry, both of which are sensitive to fake news and false standards. For example, digital retouching and image alteration create unrealistic ideals of body representation for young people. The vision and ethics of the photographer can help create new standards and new ways of serving people with a camera, while avoiding harm.

Always remember that with a camera you are a content producer. Since most of us communicate extensively through images, learning basic visual literacy, just like we learn the grammar and syntax of writing, is rapidly becoming a pressing, societal need. I observe way too much visual illiteracy in many images and feeds that serve to obscure and weaken one's message. In my opinion, basic visual literacy and examination of visual culture should become part of the core curriculum in our educational system, either in the latter years of high school or the early years of college. For those that take pictures who are out of school and never studied the visual language, I highly recommend that you undertake your own education through research, reading, or taking a class. With the ubiquity of visual media today in print, social media, and on websites, when individuals gain some familiarity with the fundamentals of the visual language it will help them communicate more effectively and avoid contributing to the visual pollution of bad design and gauche imagery.

The camera, driven by your vision, can incite wonder and awe in the sublime beauty of a mysterious order in the world. Photographs can awaken hope and cut through the thick crust of jaded nihilism and cynicism, attitudes that are often no more than vigorous defenses against the pain and impotence some feel in response to the calamities of our complex world. We can teach and inspire others to witness the bright spark present in ordinary moments and the noble dignity of the mundane. Imagine countless Instagram feeds that show the beauty and tragedies of this, our only world—and think about how this could change things irrevocably, or even temporarily, for the better.

Photographers are at the vanguard of shaping a new world. Your ethics, sense of responsibility, and conscience can be the guiding lights for how you work with this medium of light. To lay bare the spectrum of consciousness from the mundane to the profound is within photography's grasp, guided by your eye and mind.

The Power of Art

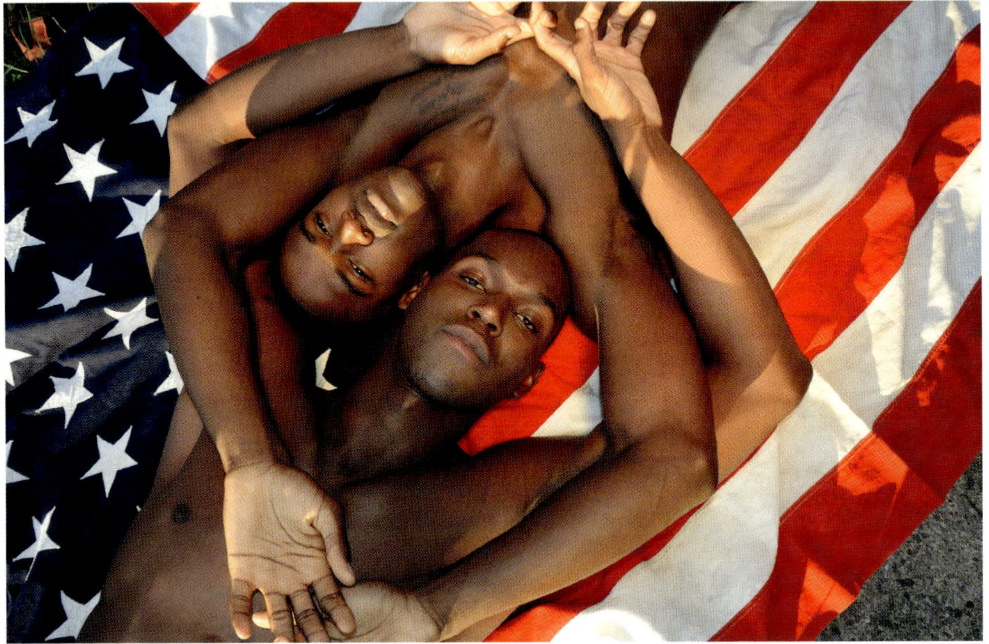

All Black Kings Go To Heaven: Minkah and Scott, Ricky Day

I believe that one of the great awakenings that can come from art and photography is a radical shift from me to we, engendering a greater collective awareness of the common good through a decisive denunciation of the extreme focus on self that has dominated western societies since the Renaissance. For this to happen, we need a large body of art that tells powerful and moving visual stories about individuals and communities that model a new reality. As society evolves, maybe the balance between individual rights and mutual responsibilities leading to collective action can fundamentally shift for future generations.

Photographers—and indeed all artists—hold a measure of public trust and have some responsibility to help redress historic sources of inequality, systemic racism, colonialism, and the capitalist economies that are destroying the planet. We all inhabit this world together and can approach personal, creative expression with integrity, knowledge, and a strong sense of both self and social awareness.

However, large parts of the photographic community—including social media, commercial photography, and institutions devoted to the medium—tell a story of unexamined assumptions and unconscious practices that continue a legacy of oppression, inequality, and exploitation. Here I explore only a few of the problematic practices in photography that I perceive as harmful to society in order to provoke thought and discussion.

Gender discrimination, systemic racism, and the white male-conceived canon of photographic history still exert a powerful sway over makers, curators, and arts administrators. The history of photography text that was standard when I was a student contained an overwhelmingly large number of white male photographers compared to a very small number of women and minority artists. Thankfully, this is in the midst of necessary change in museum programming, publishing, and hiring; although museum board members and many top-level administrative posts still lack diversity. What is encouraging now is the curatorial attention—through exhibitions and publications—given to often-marginalized groups of artists such as Black American, Asian American, LGBTQ, and from countries beyond the Euro-Americentric perspective. These are welcome developments that dramatically expand the scope of photographic representation.

One of the most influential photography magazines, *Aperture,* recently published an issue edited by Sarah Lewis on *Vision and Justice*, exploring art, race, and justice. Lewis is an associate professor of history of art and architecture and African and African-American studies at Harvard University. In the *Aperture* issue, which is recommended reading in many academic photography departments, she selected fifteen images that "chronicle America's journey toward a more inclusive level of citizenship." In choosing the images and essays for the issue, Lewis raises the evocative question, "What does it take to work toward representational justice?"

Recent bodies of work by photographers such as Carrie Mae Weems, Deana Lawson, and Dawoud Bey serve to chronicle the Black experience, and help foster the truth of "inclusive citizenship." Bey recently had a retrospective at the Whitney and SFMOMA, has seen publication of numerous books, and is a Macarthur Fellow as well as a professor at Columbia College. In his photographs—from the Harlem community, from the people in his classrooms, and from a conceptual project of Alabama residents addressing the 1963 Birmingham bombing—the word that continually arises in my mind in viewing his portraits is *transcendent*. His subjects hold such power and dignity; they express the weight of history while simultaneously embodying the spiritual depths of earned individuality and shared humanity. Indeed, in a recent issue of *Aperture,* one of the editors makes note, "With a meticulous subtlety, Bey offers clear-eyed views of America, past and present, buoyed, as always by Black grace."

Our efforts toward representational justice must also address the sexism that pollutes many segments of photography. At a recent photography conference, I was dismayed at the frequent field sessions that involved groups of mostly middle-aged and older men, ogling with long lenses, one or two young, attractive, usually white or Asian, female models. Let's look at advertising, Instagram, and social media where sex sells, thin white women predominate, and blatant narcissism is not only accepted, but embraced. Many of my students are of a typical body type and appearance. The university where I teach once cited a shocking statistic that nearly twenty percent of the young women in the student body had some form of eating disorder. I know there can be many reasons for this, but the highly respected American Medical Association has found a causal relationship between Photoshop and eating disorders in young people. Why is this? I think because they want to emulate the bodies they see around them, on social platforms and in the media, most of which are digitally enhanced.

Photographers can help define a new normal with our choice of diverse models, an embrace of body positivity for all individuals, and restraint with digital editing tools. Instagram photographers can turn their attention to things that matter in the world instead of a constant diet of self-display. And we can embrace the power of representation through a camera to help heal the emotional and psychological damage that advertising and media have done to young men and women trying to "measure up" to false ideals.

The camera can teach us to learn to see what is. Can we find beauty in truth and honesty? The power of photography relates to representing current realities and imagining a new future. In an interview with author Walter Isaacson, Sarah Lewis explains, "If there is any eternal truth about the arts, it is that it forces this reckoning between who we are, who we think we are, and who we actually could be." This reckoning can function as a redemptive experience for individuals and society, reconciling our present state with our potentiality. The arts hold the power of creating new narratives and new histories.

Great art can startle our senses, ignite the mind, take our breath away, causing us to gasp with surprise. It arrests our attention from the quotidian things of life and brings us fully into the timeless present. This "aesthetic force," as Sarah Lewis calls the encounter with great art, leaves us changed, sometimes a little, sometimes a lot. Our consciousness expands and transforms from the encounter.

Most importantly, it can shift our awareness beyond the confines of the self and open us to awe, wonder, and deep respect for life's manifestations. It can release our identification with the ego and untether our attachment from the often fierce allegiance we have to aspects of our identity such as race, gender, appearance, body type, ethnicity, and our multiple roles in life. Personal identity derives, of course, partly from all of these factors but our genuine nature is more synonymous with the essential content of our character and our personal evolution. Works of art can then reflect the entire spectrum of consciousness from the individualized ego to collective awareness and compassion and finally to an experiential recognition of life's unity. This freedom from identification with self—engendered by powerful impressions—helps us realize the spirit of who we are within our mortal frames.

The true purpose of art is to expand our consciousness, enlarge our perspective, and evolve our understanding of the world and others. And, as consciousness transforms through making and viewing art, so do our actions and interactions with life leading to greater empathy, justice, and enlightened decision-making.

Diversity and respect can shape the path toward the future of photography and the evolution of institutions devoted to it such as academia, museums and galleries, publishers, and web platforms. *E pluribus unum*, out of the many, one. If we are to solve some of the intractable problems of the modern age, it will require a collective effort and global consciousness, in which rigid individualism, prejudice, and intolerance simply have no place. The arts and photography can help. Art critic Suzi Gablick writes about the artist as both a seer and healer. "I do think that living in the reality and truth of our situation is one small step towards mastery of it…. It seems as if there is a spiritual and social obligation to participate in this process of healing our world, however one can." Artists and photographers can look soberly at the current conditions of society and natural world. They can then reveal a potent vision of our human potential and the dream of living in harmony with each other and the environment.

Photography and art expand our awareness about both the world and ourselves *simultaneously* and lead us to the realization that the inner and outer worlds are inexorably linked. Images can reveal our contradictions, both societal and individual, and place them in sharp relief. Art can inspire our search for understanding, foster our pursuit of happiness, and incite positive action. Art, literature, and music are shown to have the capacity to increase empathy and expand our awareness of other's circumstance that may be very different than our own. They ignite intercultural understanding through locating us in the place of another. Our imaginative capacities can reflect our personal and societal aspirations, what is possible for us and for humanity, like nothing else can. They can point the way, be harbingers of the future and show us the kind of world that is possible. Through the demands of particular mediums and the creative process, we can grow and evolve as individuals toward greater wholeness and deeper forms of interconnection.

With the power inherent in the camera in our hand, how can we help?

ACKNOWLEDGMENTS

The material for this book has been on the horizon of my mind for decades inspired by my own work as a photographer, the many questions and discoveries of my students, and the critical thought and imagery of numerous contemporary photographers and writers. As artists, we are never alone and I offer my deepest gratitude for those who have and continue to light my way.

Accordingly, the format of this book and its short essays would not exist without the model provided by Natalie Goldberg in her insightful, humorous, and outstanding book, *Writing Down the Bones: Freeing the Writer Within*. In reading her brief, discrete essays for the first time over twenty years ago, I wondered: could this format work for an instructional and inspirational book on photography? Decades later, I now want to extend my warmest thanks to Natalie for her enduring words of wisdom contributing to the realization of this book.

Two individuals have been instrumental in my quest for creative expression through the written word—and to them I extend my warm aloha and deep appreciation. Lisa Hagan, my literary agent, has provided enormous support and expertise in navigating the complex intricacies of publishing. And my partner Laura Dunn, the book's first reader, consistently brings intelligence, grace, and kindness in challenging me toward clear writing, all while finishing her own arduous doctoral dissertation.

I give heartfelt thanks to the photographers and estates whose images grace these essays. Your work lends meaning and depth to what I strive to articulate in words, and I am grateful for your visual clarity as well as your generosity and prompt response to my requests for publishing your work.

Finally, I could not be happier with the collaborative, friendly, and professional team at Rocky Nook, including Managing Director and Publisher Scott Cowlin, Associate Publisher Ted Waitt, Editor Maggie Yates, Project Manager Lisa Brazieal, and Marketing Coordinator Mercedes Murray. You make an author feel like they are coming home and I want to offer one small bit of grateful feedback—you rock!

This book is dedicated to my teachers, students, and you, the reader. I am indebted to all of you. Your encouragement, silent or verbal, and your ongoing creative pursuits helped shape the book you now hold in your hands.

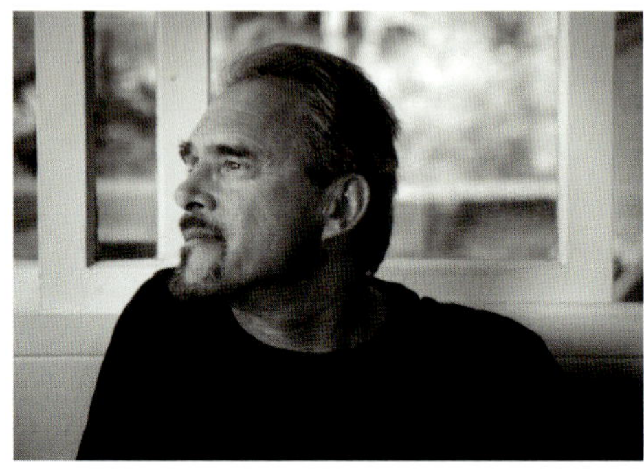

DAVID ULRICH is an active photographer and writer whose work has been published in numerous books and journals including *Aperture, Parabola, Mānoa,* and Sierra Club publications. Ulrich's photographs have been exhibited internationally in over seventy-five one-person and group exhibitions in museums, galleries, and universities and can be found in many public and private collections. He is currently co-director of Pacific New Media Foundation in Honolulu, Hawai'i, and a faculty member at Chaminade University. He previously taught for University of Hawai'i Mānoa and served as Professor and Chair of the Art Department at Cornish College of the Arts in Seattle as well as Associate Professor and Chair of the Photography Department of The Art Institute of Boston (now Lesley University College of Art and Design). He earned a BFA degree from the Museum School of Fine Arts in Boston and an MFA degree from the Rhode Island School of Design. He is a consulting editor for *Parabola* magazine and a frequent contributor.

David Ulrich is the best-selling author of *Zen Camera: Creative Awakening with a Daily Practice in Photography* (Watson Guptill/Penguin Random House 2018), the companion volume for *The Mindful Photographer*. He is also the author of *The Widening Stream: the Seven Stages of Creativity* and coauthor of *Through Our Eyes: A Photographic View of Hong Kong by Its Youth*. His recent book of photographs, *Oceano: An Elegy for the Earth*, was published in 2022 by George F. Thompson Publishing in association with the Center for the Study of Place. Visit his website at: www.creativeguide.com.

INDEX